WASHINGTON COUNTY, TENNESSEE,

SETTLEMENTS OF ESTATES

VOLUME 00

1790 – 1841

WORKS PROGRESS ADMINISTRATION (WPA)

JANAWAY PUBLISHING, INC.
Santa Maria, California
2012

> ## Notice
>
> In many older books, foxing (or discoloration) occurs and, in some instances, print lightens with wear and age. Reprinted books, such as this, often duplicate these flaws, notwithstanding efforts to reduce or eliminate them. The transcript this book was printed from is a carbon copy typed on onion skin paper over 70 years ago. The print quality varied throughout the work---this would seem to be due to the wear on the carbon paper. The pages of this reprint have been digitally enhanced and, where possible, the flaws eliminated in order to provide clarity of content and a pleasant reading experience.

Originally published
Nashville
1939

Reprinted by:

Janaway Publishing, Inc.
732 Kelsey Ct.
Santa Maria, California 93454
(805) 925-1038
www.JanawayGenealogy.com

2009, 2012

ISBN: 978-1-59641-160-9

Made in the United States of America

WASHINGTON COUNTY, TENNESSEE
SETTLEMENTS OF ESTATES, VOLUME 00
1790-1841

Prepared by Mrs. Vera E. Shell, Ms. Margaret E. Broyles, Ms. Nell L. McCrary, and Wm. L. Smith
of the Works Progress Administration, 1939;

Please note: This book has two indexes: the first is the original index followed by a new one prepared at the time of publication in 1939. Note that both have a small errata at their ends.

Unfortunately, these indexes directed the reader to the page number of **THE ORIGINAL COUNTY RECORD BOOK, *SETTLEMENTS OF ESTATES, VOL. 00, 1790 – 1841*, FROM WHICH THE INFORMATION IN THIS BOOK WAS EXTRACTED AND NOT THE PAGE NUMBER OF THIS VOLUME YOU ARE NOW READING.**

Fortunately, the page numbers of the original record have been included within the text of this volume, and are shown in parenthesis throughout the text. For example, on page 7 of this volume, you find the notations "(p-10)" and "(p-11)", which indicates the information following the notations has been transcribed from page 10 or page 11 of the original record. Since this book was transcribed sequentially, locating these original page numbers within the text will not be difficult.

The Publisher

TENNESSEE

RECORDS OF WASHINGTON COUNTY

SETTLEMENTS OF ESTATES, VOL. OO
1790 - 1841

Prepared By
The Historical Records Survey
Transcription Unit
Division of Women's and Professional Projects
Works Progress Administration

Mrs. John Trotwood Moore
State Librarian and Archivist, Sponsor

T. Marshall Jones
State Director

Mrs. Penelope Johnson Allen
State Supervisor

Mrs. Margaret Helms Richardson
District Supervisor

. . . . .

Nashville, Tennessee
The Historical Records Survey
March 29, 1939

The Historical Records Survey

        Luther H. Evans, National Director
        T. Marshall Jones, State Director

Division of Women's and Professional Projects

        Florence S. Kerr, Assistant Administrator
        Elizabeth D. Coppedge, State Director

WORKS PROGRESS ADMINISTRATION

        F. C. Harrington, Administrator
        Harry S. Berry, State Administrator

Prepared By

Mrs. Vera E. Shell
Miss Margaret E. Broyles
Miss Nell D. McCrary
William L. Smith

Indexed By

Mrs. Vera E. Shell

Typed By

William L. Smith

WASHINGTON COUNTY

SETTLEMENTS OF ESTATES VOLUME - OO
1790 - 1841

(p-1) Dr. Joseph Greer as admr. of the estate of Peter Parkison in acct with said Estate Cr. Peter Parkisons estate.

1790			No	Currency	
			£	S	D
May 11th	To Cash rec'd of James Stuart on his note		"	7	-
Nov 10	To Do D D		4	-	-
	To D Do Do my private debt		6	8	-
Feby 24	To D		3	-	-
	To Do of Andrew Caldwell		3	4	-
	To Do of Alexr McGinty		5	-	-
1791	To D of Samuel Tate		3	2	8
	To D in Linnen & money of Hollet		2	2	6
	To D of Leonard Bowers		2	1	-
1792	To Cash of Mr. Stuart ballance of his note		4	1	-
	To Do of Leonard Bowers ballance of his note		1	-	4
Febry 15	To Do of Edward Smith		1	18	-
	To Do of Nathan Davis & David Allison		4	-	-
	To D of Andrew Greer Bakers account		3	15	-
	To Do of George Williams by Humphreys		1	-	-
	To Do of John Tate & J. Ferguson		3	1	10
	To Cash of Moses Reynolds		"	16	-
	To cash of Jacob Smith		1	-	-
	TO Cash of Nathan Davis by Zac Campbell		2	-	-
	To cash of Jacob Tipton 4 0/ of it on acct of cows		4	17	-
Septr 12	To Cash of Col Tipton on Jacobs acct		9	10	3
	To Cash of John Hoskins			8	8
May 15	To Cash of Saml Tipton		3	2	8
	To Cash of Hollet ballance of his note		"	3	-
	To Cash of George William P his Father			7	4
Decr	To Cash of William P Custer		1	7	-
	To Cash of Zac Campbell ½ Skins			8	
	To Cash of Nathan Davis		2	11	4
1793	To Cash of Mrs. Bulbur		4	10	-
1794	To Cash of Nathan Davis		5	6	8
	To Cash of Andw Greer Senr		13	7	8
1796	To Cash of Edward Smith		13	7	8
	To Cash due by myself as admr of Eml. Carters Decd		5	14	-
	Peter Parkison proven amount agt said estate		124	18	7

(p-2)   PETER PARKISONS Estate

			V. Money		
1790			£	S	D
May 12	By Cash to Nathan Davis Dr. Voucher No	1	10	-	

WASHINGTON COUNTY, TENNESSEE

			L	S	D
Sepr 2	By Cash to Landon Carter No. 2		4	10	-
	By Cash to Zac Campbell No. 3			10	6
August 12	By Cash to Jacob Headerick No 4			15	7
1791					
Jany 20	By Cash to Joseph Headerick No. 5		1	10	9
	By Cash to Christian Peters No 6		2		
Feby 18	By Cash to Henry Jones	7	"	5	9
7	By Cash to James Millsop	8	"	6	-
	By Cash to Michael Carriger	9	1	8	6
June 2	By Cash to James Eaden	10	"	6	-
21	By Cash to Wm Swenney	11	"	7	-
Jany 1st	By Cash to the Sheriff 2 years taxes 12		1	12	6
	By Cash to Bass pr Bond	13	1	10	9
April 23d	By Cash to Ezekiel Able	14	1	11	3
October 21st	By Cash to Dempsey Hunter	15	4	-	-
1792					
March 31	By Cash to Godfrey Carriger	16	3	12	7
August 21	By Cash to James Stuart	17	1	16	1
	By Do to Do	18	1	11	6
Febry 22d	By Cash to Francis Baker	19	2	16	3
April 2d	By Cash to Robert Lusk	20	-	2	-
9th	By Cash to Charles Taylor	21	-	6	-
Sepr 12	By Cash Ballance of Tipton proven acct		3	4	6
	By Cash to Tipton season of 2 mares		2	8	-
	By Cash to Tipton for whiskey	22		15	
	By Cash to Tipton for corn		-	8	-
1792					
May 17	By Cash paid to James Sevier	23	2	-	77
Decr	By Cash to Landon Carter	24	1	7	"
April 16	By tax paid	25	"	2	"
	By Cash paid the deed of the bond		£ 41	14	5
					6
	By Cash paid to Old Linsey			4	6
			42	4	11
1794					
March 22	By Cash paid to Simmerly		2	8	-
			44	12	11
	The above is Virginia money equal to		59	10	6½
1796					
May 18	By Cash paid to Edward Smith No 26		5	5	-

(p-3) PETER PARKISONS Estate

	By Sundries pd to the widow No 27	21	15	9
		86	11	3½
1790	By Cash to Blyth for crying vendue	"	10	-
		87	1	3
	By 30 days attend on settling the said estate 6/2	9	-	-
		£ 96	1	3

We the Subscribers appointed by the Courts as Justices for that purpose have made a Settlement with Joseph Greer an Administrator of the estate of Peter Parkison deceased of which settlement the within is the exhibit Given under our hands this 18th May 1796.
James Stuart
William Nelson

ALEXANDER TROTTERS Estate

We the Committee chosen by Court to sttle with the executors of the estate of Alexander Trotter deceased have made said settlement and the ballance due the estate agreeable to the division of the will is ₤123 10 2

Nov. 21st 1797
          John Adams J P
          John Strain J P

LEWIS RENNOES Estate

The whole estate of Lewis Rennoes decd. amounts to	₤ 112	00	-
Virginia Currency	₤ 112	-	-
Contra	33	3	3
due Lewis Rennoes heirs	78	16	9
To the widow	26	5	7
To the daughter	52	11	2
	78	16	9

John Renone his bond against the estate of Lewis Rennoe ₤ 29 1 3
costs of suit 4 2
          ₤ 33 3 3

Errors excepted
    William Nelson J P
    Wm Pursley J. P.

(p-4)   MORDICAI PRICES Estate

	₤	S	D
Mordecai Price Dr. to Chaney Boren administrator	6	16	5½
To Brice Blair recpt for taxation	2	10	2
To James Gordan proven account		17	3
To paid William King	21	18	-
To paid Robert Thornton for tax	1	7	6
to paid John Pitner	2	2	6
To paid Abram Byler order by administrator	1	17	2
To Brice Blairs receipt for taxes	1	4	-
To paid Joseph Anderson fee	6	-	-
To paid Absolom Boren Witness attendance Price agt Jno Sevier		2	5
To paid Thomas Lacky proven acct against the estate Mr. Price Dec'd.		2	6
John Kennedy recipt for two suits attending		2	5
To paid Absolem Boren for money paid by Boren for him		3 18	-
To paid Abraham Byler	3	3	2
To paid Jonathan Tucker	1	1	-
To paid Moyers		7	6
To paid John Brown		3	6
To paid John Love & Abraham Byler	3	3	1½
To paid Turner Smith			6
To paid Reuben Sanders collector of the Still fee	11	2	9
To paid James Sevier costs of suits	1	12	1½
To paid N. Davis for holding inquest on his body before interred	1	4	-
To spoon mold			6
To paid Joseph Denton	5	8	-
To paid James Moore	3	-	-

WASHINGTON COUNTY, TENNESSEE

```
                                                    L   S    D
To the amt of Articles bought by widow at the sale  76  "    6
Archibald Williams recipt                               11
                                                    L 166 12  22
                     Equal to                       $ 555 37 1/3 cents
To his services as administrator                         50
                                                      605 37 1/3
```

(p-5)   MORDECAI PRICES Estate

Chaney Boren Dr to the estate of M. Price
```
     To Cash from James Sevier                 21  6   -
     To Frederick Moyers act                       11   6
     To Cash from John Bail                    1  17   3
     To Cash from Elisha Rodes                     14   9
     To Cash from Ball                             10
                                               24  19   6
     To the amount of articles sold at the sale 180  7   6
                                               L 205  7   0
                     Equal to                  $ 684 41½ cents
```

We the Committee appointed to settle the estate of Mordecai Price Dec'd do certify that the above account as stated is Wright to the best of our Judgment as will appear by papers fild this 5th February 1806
                Thomas Stuart
                William Miller
                Wm Colyer

(p-6)   JOHN NORTHS Estate

Debts paid by the administratior & Administratrix of the estate of John North Decd. (to wit)
```
                                                   L   S   D
Novr.   1793       To paid John Tedlock for salt       12
April   1794       To paid Do for nails  2/             2
                   To paid John Kile    10/            10
May     27/2       paid Abraham Anthony 3/4         3   4
                   paid Clerk for Administration ac-
                   count                 12/        -  12   -
Octor   15         Do to Sheriffs account           2  10   -
                   Do Clerk of Sale                    12
                                                   L 5  1   4
```

STATE OF TENNESSEE }
WASHINGTON COUNTY } This day personally appeared before us Joseph Britten & Jacob Brown esqrs. two of the Justices of the peace for said county George North administrator of the estate of John North Dec'd and made oath that the above account of five pounds one shilling and four pence is a true account of monies paid out of the estate for the purposes above mentioned sworn & subscribed before us this 8th day of August 1804
Joseph Britten Justice of the peace   George North
Jacob Brown Justice of the peace.

STATE OF TENNESSEE }
WASHINGTON COUNTY } We the committee appointed by the Court at August term 1804 do report that we have examined the papers of the administrator of the estate of John North Dec'd and find that said estate sold for one hundred and one pounds nineteen shillings and two pence. That the said ad-

ministrators have paid for debts due from the estate to <u>indeviduals</u> and for funeral expences and also expences on administration and sale of the estate (that is to say)

To John Tedlock	₤ -	14	-
To John Keel	-	10	-
To Abraham Anthony		3	4
To James Sevier clerk of the court	-	12	-
To Sheriffs fees for sale	2	10	0

(p-7)   JOHN NORTHE'S Estate

	L	S	D
To Clerk to attend the sale	"	12	-
	5	1	4
deducted from	101	19	2
	5	1	4
Ballance of remaining	₤ 96	17	10
equal to	$ 322	96	1/3 cents

Examined this 8th day of August 1804

                 Joseph Britten   Committee
                 Jacob Brown   of Court.

SAMUEL MCQUEANS Estate

The undersigned to whome was <u>referd</u> by the Court of Washington County being Justices of the peace do report that Hannah McQuean administratrix of the estate of Samuel McQuean Decd. produced to us Authenticated papers namely--
A receipt in full from Hugh Jenkins for his part of moveable property to amt of ₤ 17 " 10. A Receipt from Richard Earles in full for seventeen pounds ten shillings being for his part--

    A receipt in full from George Walter for the sum of seventeen pounds ten shillings for his part amounting in all to fifty two pounds ten shillings the receipt aforesaid accompanying this report. all which is Submitted August 17th 1796.

                 Charles McCray J. P.
                 Saml Wood J. P.

(p-8)   DAVID JOBES Estate

Amount of Vendue Money	D	Cents
Abigail Job 1 bay and sorrel mare 1 Gray mare 1 sorrel horse colt 1 bay Colt	46	-
Abegail Job to 4 cows & 2 <u>clves</u> 1 bed	8	50
Do 13 head of sheep	3	50
Do to all the household & kitchen furniture 1 Gun	20	50
Do To 24 head of hoggs	6	-
Do To 1 Gray mare	40	-
Do to 1 speckled heifer and calf	9	-
Do To 2 pair plough geers	2	-
Do to 3 ploughs	1	-
Do to 5 axes and 1 drawing knife	2	50
Do to 6 hoes		50
Do to 3 negroes Ben Steve an Vine	1100	-
Do to 4 bee stands	2	-
Jessee Humphreys to 4 sheep first choice	6	-
Do 4 Sheep 2d choice	4	

	D	Cents
Do 3 Sheep 3d choice	3	
Joseph Young to 1 white assed steer	10	95
Do 1 Black and white ditto	8	--
George Sheffield 1 Brown Cow	10	--
Joseph Young 1 Red and white Steer	6	75
Moses Humphreys to 1 muley heifer	7	
Do 1 red and white heifer	6	
Abraham Job to 2 white & red & 1 black yearlings	7	6
Do 1 Gray mare	70	6
Stephen Tipton to 20 cwt cotton	6	25
Abigail Job to 40 cwt Cotton	10	30
Jesse Humphreys to 20 lb cotton	6	66
Do 20 lb Cotton	6	57
Jehue Humphreys 1 negro boy named Bob	395	--
Solomon Herdred to 2 negroes George & Win	370	75
Archibald Williams 1 negro girl named fan	460	--
	$1936	35 cents

(p-9)   DAVID JOBS Estate

	D	Cents
Moses Humphreys 1 broad ax	1	
Abigail Job 2 negroes named Ned and Lueke	320	--
Do 1 Grind Stone		35
M Humphreys 1 ewe and lamb	1	--
Abigail Job to sundries	7	51
M. Humphreys 976 ¾ lb bar Iron	30	
Abel Job 25 lb Cotton	5	
Jonathan Tipton 25 lb cotton	5	50
	$370	36
	1936	35
	2306	71
To ballance on Hendreys note	60	--
To Do on Saml & Abraham Tipton	147	40
	2514	11
To fees on vendue officially	23	25
	2490	86
Amount paid to the Legattes etc.	1439	9
	1051	77
To Charles Whitson fifty store goods & 50 cash	100	
	1151	77
paid five legatees (vos) Moses Humphrys Abraham Job Geo Sheffield Phebee Job Joseph Davis	34	10
Ballance due	1117	67

To £ 350 No. Carolina currency on John Wood (Desperate)
A list of what Abigal Job admx of David Job Decd has paid

To Jemimas Davis	270	--
To Phebe Job	227	51
To Joel Coper	236	58
To George Sheffield	266	
To John Kennedy for services	10	
To James Sevier for services	2	40
To Saml Blyth services	2	--
To Solomon Hendrix Subscription M. House	10	--
To Abraham Job	120	39

SETTLEMENTS OF ESTATES, VOLUME 00, 1790-1841

```
To M. Humphreys                                    285 --
To Joseph Crouch for services                        3 94
To Philip Denham for schooling                       5 27
                                                  1439  9
```

```
                    Bricem Garner  |
                    Jessee Payne   | Commissioners
                    Jos Young      |
```

(p-10)   JOHN MAUKS Estate

STATE OF TENNESSEE |
WASHINGTON COUNTY | We Jessee Payne Alexander McLin and Jonathan Collem Justices of the peace being appointed as Commissioners by order of Court to settle with Adam Gann administrator of the estate of John Mauk Decd we the said Commissioners being met and the said Gann laying the sale of said estate before us & other accounts which sales appears to amount to one hundred and seventy six dollars and eighty eight cents $176 88
                    Substraction   129 61
                                                    47 27

debts against the estate of John Maulk by vouchers rendered by Adam Gann administrator. His own proven account   57 50
    paid to John Kennedy   10 --
    paid David Yearley   5 --
    paid Joseph Brown   10 75
    paid to Michael Brown cryer of the sale   2 50
    paid Abraham Fellows for clerk of sale   2 --
    paid James Sevier for granting administration   75
    paid Thomas Prather   10 36
    Seven gallons & a half of brandy furnished for
    sd sale   3 75
    to feeding a horse 12 days   1 50
    allowance made by the commissioers to Adam Gann
    administrator for settling the said estate date 25 50
                                                  $129 61

On settlement as above stated there appears to be a ballance in the hands of said administrator of said estate the sum of forty seven dollars and twenty seven cents-- $47 27 cents
this 16th day of April 1812

                    Jessee Payne
                    Alexr McLin
                    Jona Collom

(p-11)   WILLIAM WARDS Estate

                                                   D Cents
Joseph Browns acct for land tax 1808   1 16
James Aiken for transcript of record   1 50
John Littles receipt   25
Mary Dean provend account   2 50
Isaac Lincoln Do Do   20 50
Danl Stovers recpt from Lincoln for brandy for
sale   2 16

WASHINGTON COUNTY, TENNESSEE

	D	Cents
Nathl Taylors proven acct	5	--
John Norwood recpt	1	50
Hameltons recpt	17	--
Kennedys receipt	5	--
Chas Rennoes recipt	2	--
Jos Moorisons recpt	17	22
Duffields receipt	2	50
Mary Fords receipt	2	25
Saml Blaches recpt	6	40
Isaac Floyds proven account	5	74½
John Adams recpt		37½
Danl Stover for puplishing a grant	1	75
James Seviers recipt	2	50
Daniel Stover salt for use of stock		50
James Seviers account	8	62½
Daniel Stover for services to the estate	30	--
	116	43½
Amount of sales	767	57¾
due the legatees	651	14

        Jacob Hoss Justice of the peace
        Joseph Young Justice of the peace
        Nathan Shipley Justice of the peace

(p-12)   WILLIAM WOOD Estate

STATE OF TENNESSEE }
WASHINGTON COUNTY } In persuance of an order of the County Court to us directed we met at Joseph Youngs in order to settle with Jeremiah Campbell administrator of William Wood Dec'd and he the said Jeramiah Campbell hath produced to us a recipt signed Hannah Wood that she has received all rights and other things she was entitled to receive of the aforesaid administrator wherein he was concerned-- witness our hands & seals this 16th day of November 1811

        Jos Young (Seal)
        Justice of the peace
        Jacob Hunter (Seal)
        Justice of the peace
        H Y King (Seal)
        Justice of the peace

ANN MILLERS Estate

Settled February 18th 1796 with the administrator of the estate of Ann Miller Decd agreeable to an order of Court appointing us William Pursley & John Strain for the above purposes--
    Accounts against the estate

	£	S	D
William Kelseys account		7	10
William Montgomery		50	
Robert McLin 28 dollars	8	8	
The notes not lifted due the estate			
David Richards note		7	2
Margaret Lusk Do	1	7	5
John Carney Do		16	6
Ann Hunter Do	2	8	4

```
     Recd in Cash                                    20 16  6
The whole amount paid out of the Cash to Robert Maclin
                                                     26 18  9
     For his berrying expences and other charges
     allowed by them by Court                         8  8  -
```

(p-13)   ANN MILLERS Estate

    Likewise one note of thirty three dollars and thirty three cents upon James Reed $33 33 cents

We do certify that the within is a true account of our settlement with Robert Maclin administrator of the estate of Ann Miller Decd besides an account of James Carmicel brought in time the other settlement

                        John Strain
                        William Pursley

                HENRY POWELS Estate

17th January 1816 we William Bayles John Stephenson & John Strain being a commission of court appointed to settle with the administrators of the estate of Henry Powel Decd find as follows
    Proven accounts against the estate and other authenticated vouchers--

		D	Cents	Mills
1	John Doane proven account	2	56	
2	George Pursells Do	3	58	3
	John Helms Do	9	16	6
3	George Smith Do	1	12	5
	James Patterson Do	1	14	-
	Isaic Thrasher Do	"	66	6
	Martha Smith Do	1	19	
	William Shields Do	-	-	-
	David Stuart Do	1	33	6
	John Korts Do	16	33	3
	Jonathan Barcroff			
	Alexander Stuart		75	
	Isbell Carmicles Judgment	4	-	-
	John McAlister Probate	7	56	8
	Sarah Nelson Do	6		
	Archabald Frame	3	33	3
	Henry Hartman	4	50	
	William P. Chester	6	8	2

(p-14)   HENRY POWELS Estate

	D	Cents	Mills
John Ralston Do	6	-	-
James Jones	2	71	-
Joseph Martin Do	1	58	-
Joseph Tucker Do	6	43	-
William Crawford Do	2	33	
Thomas Brabson Do	34	-	-
Elias Bowman Do	7	44	-
Joseph Duncan Do	1	50	-
John Stephenson Do	5	98	-
Lucke Carrol probate	4	62	5
Alexand Irwin Do	3	25	-

	D	C	M
Daniel Bails Do	1	-	-
Wm Miller Decd.	3	40	-
Elijah Matheny in behalf of Saml Davis Decd.	50	-	-
Nathan Nelson	8	75	
James Nelson	14	61	-
Joseph Cook	2	25	-
Hugh McAdams	7	-	-
Henry Marsh paid in behalf of the estate clerks fees	2	80	-
Ditto by Ditto to Taylor attorney	5	-	-
Reciept for taxes for 1813	1	58	5
Recpt for ditto " 1812	1	56	2
Clerks fees for copy of Inventory		70	
M. Whitehead for clling the sale	4	-	-
for running out land	3	50	-
Thomas Ball for finishing leathe	4	-	-
David Deadericks proven account	20	5	-
Pointer Chaltons Do	7	-	-
	272	48	4

We the within mentioned commissioners of court having settled with the administrator of the estate of Henry Powel Dec'd by vouchers to us presented do find paid by said administrators the sum of two hundred and seventy two dollars & forty eight cents and four mills and we find paid unto the estate the sum of on account of the (p-15) HENRY POWELS Estate money received into the estate of Henry Powel Decd by due bills vendue money and otherwise as found by us William Bayles John Stephenson and John Strain commissioners appointed by Court to settle with administrators of said estate

		D	Cents	Mills
1	Isaac DePew paid to the estate	1		
2	Isaac Bales	1		
3	James Kibler	1	66	6
4	Mattock Harrold	1	-	-
5	Benjamen Johnston		25	
6	Careck Campbell	2	-	-
7	Benjamin Sands	2	-	-
8	Thomas Blakely	42	-	-
9	Bartholomew Odeneal	1	-	-
10	Joseph Hartman		25	
11	William Shields	10	-	-
12	Joseph Glass	6	-	-
13	James Willcocks	6	-	-
14	Samuel Bayles	3	-	-
15	Archibald Carmicl	22	8	-
16	Adam Fraker	6	-	-
17	Levi Matherly	4	-	-
18	William Shanks	1	66	6
19	Nathal Smith	2	25	-
20	Joseph Duncan	-	50	-
21	Harr Mills	-	46	-
22	Samuel Stanfield	-	50	-
		73	4	2
Amount of vendue left		480	74	-
Cullen Cotton priece of one horse		70	-	-
To one Judgment against Thomas Blair		11	66	6
To one note on John Rector		4	-	-

639 44 8

(p-16)   HENRY POWELS Estate

We the within mentioned commissioners of court having settled with the administrators of the estate of Henry Powel Dec'd by vouchers to us presented we find paid into the hands of said administrators the sum of six hundred and thirty eight dollars & twenty four cents and eight mills as by the within calculation doth appear out of which they have paid two hundred and twenty two dollars and forty eight cents and four mills leaving a balance of three hundred sixty five dollars and seventy six cents & four mills in the hands of the widow exclusive of that part of the estate that remains unsold which is also in her hands out of which is allowed to be paid to the administrators (to wit) Henry Marsh and the administrators of the estate of William Miller Dec'd the sum of twenty five dollars each after which deduction there will remain a ballance of three hundred and fifteen dollars and seventy five cents and four mills-- Given under our hands this seventeenth day of January 1817

        John Strain
        John Stephenson
        Wm Bayles
        Commissioners

SAMUEL HAIRS Estate

STATE OF TENNESSEE To the worshipfull Court of pleas &c of Washington County at april term appointed Jacob Brown Wm P. Chester & Henry King esqrs. to settle with Wm Bayles admin of the estate of Samuel Haire & in persuance of said order we the above named commissioners have this day provided make settlement and the said Samuel Hairs wages in the army (where he died) is $10 75 being the whole amount of his estate & rec'd by said administrator and this the said Wm Bayles admr has disbursed the following sum as pr vouchers

To John Blair	6 5	-
To clerk of Court for letters of administration	" 80	-
To copy of recod	1 60	-
For seal & certificate to power of attorney	80	-
To one days attendance to the business of said estate	1	- -
Amount disbursed	10 25	-
The ballance of the estate	60 50	

Given der our hand & seal this 15th day of April A. D., 1823.
        Jacob Brown (Seal)
        William P. Chester (Seal)
        H Y. King (Seal)

(p-17)   JOHN MERCERS Estate

We Jessee Payne Jonathan Collom & John Stephenson being appointed by court to settle with the administrators of the estate of John Mercer Dec'd and having met on the 12th of February 1818 and called on them for the papers relative to said estate do find as follows

Property sold at vendue	$246 54½ cents
Collected on a note from Thomas Brabson	82 30
Out of which a deduction is to be made for	328 84½

twenty pounds for an allowance made her by the commissioners for maintainace of her and family   66 66 2/3

	262 18
Debts paid out of the estate	
To Jessee Payne Sen	34 15
To Wm M Fink on probate	3 -
To Henry Earnest & Co	5 5
To Jacob Overholser	2 92
To William Iles on a note	2 5
To making coffin	10 -
To John Stouts on a note	10 65
To Clerks fees on administration	2 72
To William Patton probate	3 37½
Alexander Mathes probate	5 50
To William Mitchell note	3
To John McGhee probate	1 -
To John Gray note	9 92
Debt and cost to Spencer E. Gibson	28 50
Debt and Cost to John Blair	6 25
To Arnold Green probate	17 50
To John G. Eason	11 42
To James Sevier for order for commissioners	50
To James Gray on note	12 98
To D. G. Vance on probate	2 75
To Wm Mitchell note	1 25
To James McAlister probate	3 66
To William McCoy	4 50
To Wm & D Mitchell	12 58
	195 22

(p-18) **JOHN MERCERS Estate**

paid Joseph Duncan for arrears of rent	18 -
Debts paid out of the estate & vouchers produced to us	220 22
Allowance to Eliza Mercer for services don in settling the estate	10 -
To Daniel Yeager for his Services	20 -
	243 22
Paid Jesse Payne Junr	7 --
	250 22
Leaving a balla of the estate in the hands of the administrators of	11 96 cents

      Jessee Payne
      Jona Collom &
      John Stephenson
      Commissioners

JOSIAH FRANKLINS Estate

			Paid for the Estate
Voucher	1	John McAlister	195 32½
Do	2	Adam McKee	12 47½
Do	3	George Harris	3 92
Do	4	Samuel Bayles Senr	1 66¾
Do	5	Jacob Brown of Abrm	3 54
Do	6	Robert Million	2 41 2/3
Do	7	Henry Salts	12 -
Do	8	Conrad Brown	9 91

Do 9	Widows allowance	45	--
Do 10	Expences at sale	6	50
		292	75 1/3
Voucher	Against McAlisters note and costs	385	32½
	George C Harris	5	23¼
	Isaac Miller	2	66¼
	Micholas Pring	1	
	Michale Cowan	1	20
	Amt of Sale	951	49
		1345	91¼
		292	75 1/3
		1054	16½

JOSIAH FRANKLINS Estate

April 24th 1818. We the committee appointed to examin the accounts and settle with the administrator of the estate of Josiah Franklin Dec'd certify that the estate is now worth Ten hundred and fifty four dollars 16½ cents $1054.16½ cents filed at July Sessions 1818.

         D. G. Vance
         Wm Colyar
         Wm Bayles   Committee

ARCHABALD CARMICLES Estate

We the undersigned Commissioners appointed by order of the court of pleas and quarter sessions of Washington County to settle with the administrators of Archibald Carmicle Decd By the vouchers presented by said administrator do find they have recd the following assetts (Viz)

		D	Cents
From Thomas Payne		1456	--
Absolem Kyle		600	--
First vendue sale on 18th & 19th May 1819		7586	69¼
John Tedlock		100	--
John Carmicle		713	50
John McAlister		8937	45
Devidend in Bank		15	48
Thomas Lacky		7	
Joseph Duncan		13	--
John Ryland book account		32	50
Absolem Kyle a negro		600	--
Uriah Hunt		12	60
Daniel Carmicle		35	--
Second vendue Sale 7th April 1820		903	--
Third vendue Sale 9th Dec. 1820		38	62½
Slum Cox and Danl		250	--
		21300	84¼

And that they have paid out the <u>followen</u> sums (Viz)

To John Stephenson 2 notes	866	25
Archabald Frame 2 notes	663	--

(p-20)   ARCHABALD CARMICLE Estate

William Tyler	745	50
William Massingail	2268	25

Joseph Duncan 4 notes	276	15
Jonathan Barcrofft	633	87½
Joshua Royston	858	--
Henry Martin	52	75
Thomas Blakely	208	25
Robert Stuart	203	75
Davis Bragg	563	--
Samuel Blair	335	--
John Kennedy	605	25
Adam Gann	605	25
Abraham Williams	1262	75
Jacob Kibler	139	--
Andrew Duncan	21	12½
Charles Bacon	962	9
Leady Blakely	15	50
John Blakely	12	--
John Ryan	32	50
Loss of Intrest	73	--
Absolem Kyle	2864	62½
Note in bank & interest	6192	--
Traveling expences	42	50
Amount of contingent expenses	25	68¼
Jane Carmicle ballance of Pats time	10	--
	20537	4¾
Hire of Jonathan	7	8
Postage paid	3	94½
Muskengam bank note on hand	5	
Kennedy attorney	25	--
Robert Church on acct of Judgment	150	--
James V Anderson		60
James Sevier	8	40
John A McKinney	20	--

(p-21)   ARCHABALD CARMICLE Estate

Allowed the administrators for their trouble	300	--
amount expended	$21059	7¼
Amount of assetts	21300	84½
	241	77½

We do hereby certify the above ballance to remain in the hands of the administrators this day and the final Settlement to be closed on the first Monday of our next County Court-- Given under our hands and seals this 2nd November 1822

     Sam Greer (Seal)
     D. G. Vance (Seal)

To amt. of ballance in the hands of said administrators on the 2nd day of Novr 1822	$241	77½
By cash paid John Kennedy for his fees	5	--
By Do paid John A McKenney for Do	12	50
By Do paid S. D. Mitchell	1	60
To allowance for additional trouble	200	--
To amt of expenditures & additional trouble	219	10
Bal due 13th January 1823	22	67½

     Saml Greer (Seal)
     J. Peace
     D. G. Vance (Seal) J. Peace

SETTLEMENTS OF ESTATES, VOLUME 00, 1790-1841

(p-22)   WILLIAM TYLERS estate

A list of vouchers produced by William Wilson one of the executors of William Tyler Decd for settlement with the courts committee

No.				
No.	1	William Bayles recpt	11	20
No	2	William Bayles Do	86	80
	3	William Bayles Do	25	--
	4	William Bayles Do	63	33
	5	William Bayles Do	1840	58
	6	William Mitchell note	28	6
	7	John Greenway & Co proven account	1	25
	8	William McCoy proven Do	25	25
	9	Frederick Sergant Do Do	7	50
	10	John Blairs receipt	15	--
	11	Dan D Andrews Do	274	46
	12	Dan D. Andrews Do	134	--
	13	Dan D. Andrews Do	10	--
	14	William Bayles Do	47	87½
	15	William Bayles Do	17	70
	16	James S. Johnston Do	19	48¾
	17	William Bayles Jr Receipt	248	72
	18	Dan D. Andrews receipt	320	57
	19	John McAlisters proven account	134	42
	20	John Nelson recpt for taxes	11	28¾
			3322	49

We the committee appointed by Court to settle with Joseph Crouch and William Wilson executors of the estate of William Tyler decd do hereby certify that the above schedule to be a true acct of the vouchers produced by William Wilson one of the executors

           John Link
           William Mitchell
           John Patton
           Nathan Shipley

(p-23)   WILLIAM TYLER Estate

A list of vouchers produced by Joseph Crouch one of the executors of William Tyler Decd for settlement with the courts committee--

No	1	Adam McKees receipt	1	20
	2	Thomas Brown recpt for calling the sale	2	--
	3	Batey Phillips on Ingles proven account	2	--
	4	Daniel Stouts proven acct	3	37½
	5	Paid for postage		18¾
	6	William Slemmons proven acct	2	71½
	7	John Stouts note	39	10
	8	Vilet Bayles proven account	7	44
	9	Charles M Lovell reciept	5	--
	10	Jacob Howard reciept	1	50
	11	Acct for whiskey at the sale	2	50
	12	Paid for recording will	1	80
	13	Joel Williams proven account	1	--
	14	John Nelson proven account	4	75
	15	William Bricker proven acct	4	44
	16	Jonathan Collom proven account	14	50
	17	Alexander Colyer proven account	5	--
	18	Jonathan Collom proven account	9	--

19	John Kennedys receipt		10 --
20	John Bricker receipt		2 --
21	Robert McLin receipt		60
22	William Nelsons receipt		600 --
23	William Nelsons recept		201 70
24	William Nelson receipt		350 --
25	Dan D. Andrews receipt		151 25
26	Dan D. Andrews receipt		50 --
27	William Bayles Guardien receipt		40 --
28	William Bayles Do receipt		10 --
29	Dan D. Andrews receipt		10 --
30	William Nelson receipt		110 --
			$1643 5¼

We the Committee appointed by Court to settle with Joseph Crouch

(p-24)   WILLIAM TYLER Estate

and William Wilson executors of the estate of William Tyler deceased. do hereby certify that the above schedule to be a true acct of the vouchers produced by Joseph Crouch one of the executors--

                 John Link
                 William Mitchell
                 John Patton

THOMAS FORDS Estate

STATE OF TENNESSEE
WASHINGTON COUNTY   Persuant to an order of court made August term 1815 when Henry King Jacob Ellis and Moses Humphreys Esqrs was appointed a committee to settle with Jonathan Coreathers and Isbell Ford administrator & administratrix of the estate of Thomas Ford. decd. The amount of the good and chattles of Thomas Ford Deceased is $ 157 50 cents

Clerks fees	2 50
George House note	11 66¼
Mathew Aiken note	11 26
Jonathan Coreathers account	18 25
Horatio Ford Jur account	32 14
John McCracken his account	8 69½
Jonathan Youngs account	2 50

The allowance to the widow for her maintainence fee 115 --

A true statement from the records given and our hands this 8th day of August 1815.

                 Hy King
                 Jacob Ellis
                 Moses Humphreys
                 Commissioners

(p-25)   HUGH MCADAMS Estate

We the commissioners appointed by court to settle with Isabella McAdams alias Isabella Hale administratrix of Hugh McAdams Decd do find her chargeable to the Estate of said McAdams by amount of sale of the personal estate
                                                    $592 59½
    For debts owing the estate collected   65 50
                                                    $658   09½

Ats that she has paid of said estate	
To Uriah Hunt by ballance of a note	20 50
Alexr M Nelson proven account	13 50
Levi Taylor Do	1 --
John McAlister Do	19 80
Charles Howel Do	2 29
John Patton Do	1 25
John Doane Do	2 79
Enoch Keen Do	15 --
Peter Gardner Do	12 50
David Deaderick Do	9 5½
Hugh Martin Do	1
Leeroy Taylor Do	2 17
Thomas Hunt Do	4
Mathew Aiken Do	10 --
Elisha Cahil Do	5 50
Jonathan Bacon Do	1 75
Thomas Brown for crying sale	2 --
Charles Bacon proven account	2 50
George Purcell Do	4 97
Adam McKee Do	1 75
John Stephenson Do	5 25
Paid David Deaderick	75 --
Paid James Sevier for letters administration	2 50
John Stephenson p account	2 --
Whiskey expended at Sale	5 --
Allowance by us made for sales & collection fee	50 --
	273 49½

Given under our hands
this 22nd day of July 1819

Nathan Shipley
Archl Glascocke
Jno Stephenson

(p-26)   ALEXANDER MOORES Estate

A statement of claims **againt** the estate of Alexander Moore Decd.

Note to Thomas Gillispie dated 3d Novr. 1814 with intst from the date for $912 58 cents pd May 15th 1816	994 56
A Moores order in favour of James Penny dated Augt. 27th 1810 for $70 paid May 15th 1816	94 15
John Kennedy, fee $200 pd May 7, 1816	200 --
A Moores note to WK Vance for $91 dated 20th Augt. 1810 payable in 6 months pd 20th December 1815	117 39
P M Millers fee $100 pd May 7 1816	100 --
Samuel Blackburn Judgt agt A Moore in County Court of Blount	126 62
John Snapp assignee of P Snapp Judgt in Madison County Mississippi Territory for which I was Garnisheed in Green County Court for	117 43½
John A McKinneys fee pd May 8th 1816	100 --
A Moores note to G. T. Gillispie	50 --
Paid Mrs. Moore	10 --
Paid to Ira Greene Acct Agt A Moore	9 --
Allowance to George T. Gillispie for services as administrator	19 91½
	$2000 7

George T. Gillispie Recd of the estate $2020 7
    Ballance remaining in the hands of G. T. Gillispie   20 0

April Sessions 1817

We the Committee appointed by Court to settle the estate of Alexander Moore Decd. with George T. Gillispie the administrator do find that said Gillispie has received of said estate the amount of two thousand and twenty dollars and seven cents. And has paid acct the sum of two thousand dollars and seven cents including the sum allowed him for Services as administrator leaving a balance in his hands of said estate the sum of twenty dollars as the anexed schedule represents-- Given under our hands this 26th day of April 1817

            Nathan Shipley

(p-27)   JOHN MCGINNIS Estate

Report of committe appointed to settle with William Bayles Adminstr and Elizabeth McGinnis administratrix of John McGinnis Decd do find that they received and paid out the Sums as hereafter stated (Viz)

Received from Sample Orres	$40 --		
John Chester	250 --		
Jessee Hampton	25 --		
Samuel Bayles Jr.	9 --	324	
Samuel G. Chester	7 25		
John S Hundley	1 --		
Jacob Starnes	1 25		
James Harvey	96		
Edward L. Martin	3 50		
Saml Bayles Jur	3 37½		
Thomas Russell	3 --	20 33½	
William Felts	6 --		
Amount of Sale	375 1½	381 1½	
Sample Orres account	1 50		
William Bayles bill	50	2 -- 0	
	727 35		

Paid out & allowed

No			
1	William Bayles debt	2 --	
2	Joseph McGinnis debt	7 27	
3	Tax for 1818	53	
4	Abraham Brown	6 70	
4	Ditto on account	3 --	
5	William Truit	1 81¼	21 31¼
6	Jacob Brown	3 21	
7	Do an account	1 84	
8	James Parker	19 26	
9	Samuel Bayles	16 13	
10	William Brown	11 14	
11	David G Vance	32 12¼	
12	William Wheler	8 50	92 50¼
13	Turner Smith 2 notes	31 50	

(p-28)   JOHN MCGINNES Estate

14	Geo C. Harris for G. Hinkle	32 18
15	Spencer Henry	17 58
16	Nimrod Willet	4 50

" 17	David Deaderick	2 54	88 30
18	John Slyger	25 62½	
19	Conrod Brown	1 50	
20	Ephriam Murrey	2 --	
21	A & W McKee	37 88	
22	John Kennedy	10 10¼	77 10¾
23	Henry McCraken	10 2¾	
24	Richard Smith	13 91¼	
25	Benjamin Austin	5 50	
26	Robert Moore	1 --	
27	John McCraken	2 --	
28	Doctor D Nelson	14 50	
29	John Patton esqr	11 87½	58 81½
30	Jacob Million by John	70 6¼	
31	Harris and Guinn	18 90½	
32	Jacb Howard	1 50	
33	Widows maintainance	110 --	
	Isaac N Brown	2 --	
34	Judgt Wm B Carter	76 13½	
35	Order Hen McCray	7 --	
A	Allowance for money	2 --	
	For Services	18 40	306 "¼
		$644 4	
		737 35	
		$83 31	

On examination of the accounts and making necessary allowances for services to William Bayles & Elizabeth McGinnis administrator & Administratrix of John McGinnes Decd we find that a ballance is now in their hands of eighty three dollars & thirty one cents Given under our hands October 31st 1822.

John Patton Justice of peace
Thos C Patton Justice of peace

(p-29) RICHARD ROBERTS Estate

A list of funeral expenses of Richard Roberts deceased.

No 1	Robert McAdams cent for a coffin	7 --
	Cr by five bushel corn	2 50
2	Debt in bank	150 --
3	Doctor Nelsons bill	28 25
4	Doctor Chesters bill	19 25
5	Rachel Owens	61 --
6	John Doan	2 75
7	Harris & Guinn	25 --
8	William Mitchell	16 57
9	William Mitchell & Co	67 36½
10	Mitchels due bill	65 19½
11	Mitchell & Co principal interest	47 40½
12	Intrest	11 38
12	Geo Hendley not to Mitchell for estate of R. Roberts	5 20
13	Daniel Findley	5 40½
14	Isaac Hendley	12 --
15	William Nelson	18 20
16	William Patton	11 82
17	William Tyler	48 84

No	18	John McAlister	190 83
	19	John Crusoe	5 --
	20	William McGee	2 --
	21	Rachel Owens	40 --
	22	Joseph Crouch	8 75
	23	Adam Ingle	7 66½
	24	Rachel Owens	26 66 2/3
	25	Do Do	26 66 2/3
	26	Jacob Howard	1 --
	27	James Sevier	5 20
	28	Mathew Aiken	31 12½
	29	Rachel Owens	26 66 2/3
	30	John Nelson	19 72
	31	John Bricker	3 50

(p-30) RICHARD ROBERTS Estate

	32	Jacob Varner	75
	33	William Mitchell	5 20
	34	Jonathan Lislee	1 --
	35	Ceasor Linn	12 --
	36	Jonathan Leslie	1 --
	37	Thomas C Patton	1 --
	38	John Nelson	13 --
		John McCraken for crying of the sale	2 --
			1035 82
		Cr. by two dollars & fifty in number 1st	2 50
			$1033 32

Allowance to George Hendley for his services
as administrator of the estate of Rihd Roberts
Decd.   35 --
John Doak Decd a/c for attention to Roberts
family   6 --
                                                        $1074 32

We the Committee appointed by the Court to settle with George Hendly administrator of the estate of Richard Roberts Decd find the amount of his vouchers to be as above $1074 32
The amount of sales & hire of negroes filed 1205 94¼
18th July 1823

      Jno Collom
      Jacob Brown
      Wm Mitchell

(p-31)   JOHN HAMMERS Estate

STATE OF TENNESSEE
  Where as the worshipfull court of pleas and quarter Sessions of Washington County at the April term 1823 ordered and appointed James W. Young Jacob Ellis Henry King Wm P. Chester & Saml Greer esqrs or any three of them to be a committee to settle with Samuel Bogart & James White executors of the estate of John Hammer Decd.
  In persuance of said order we the said James W. Young Jacob Ellis & Henry King attended at the house of the said Henry King in said County on Saturday the twenty fourth day of May A D 1823 and then & there made the following settlement with the aforesaid executors-- And we the said Commissioners find that the amount of the sale of the of John Hammer Dec'd is
                 728 67¼

SETTLEMENTS OF ESTATES, VOLUME 00, 1790-1841

Including a black mare sold at the sale which was bequeathed to Margaret
Hammer widow of the said John Hammer amounting to   58 37½
        and there remains $670 29¼

The amount of a note and <u>intrest</u> not return with the   289 90
amount of sale but the executors now settle the same $960 19¾ cents
And the executors have disbursed the following Sums of money to sundry person as pr vouchers &c.

To Daniel Bowman	$4 --	
To John G. Eason	2 50	
To Nathaniel Davis for direct tax	2 40	8
To Frederick DaVault for smith work	1 50	
To John Ingle	33 1/3	
To Henry King for services at sale of property	3 --	
To Samuel Bogart	2 --	
To James Sevier	2 40	
To John Miller Decd	6 --	
To Joseph Kener for Services at sale	4 --	
To John Miller Decd	1 33½	
To Jonathan Hammer an heir	2 --	
To Jacob Hammer Do	2 --	
To Joseph Hammer Do	2 --	
To John Hammer Do	2 --	
To Isaac Hammer Do	2 --	
To Kinchen Kelley Do	1 --	

(p-32)   JOHN HAMMERS Estate

To John G. Eason for Kinchen Kelley	21 --	
To Kinchen Kelley	10 --	
To Kinchen Kelley	60 --	
To Kinchen Kelley	49 0-	
To Kinchen Kelley	20 --	
To Kinchen Kelley	50 --	
To Kinchen Kelley	50 --	
To James Range	50 --	
To James Range	3 --	
To James Range	48 10	
To James Range	50 --	
To James Range	50 --	521 57¼
To Samuel Bogart an heir	257 1	
To Kinchen Kelley	20 --	
To Samuel Bogart as an executor and other services	20 --	
To James White an executor for services	30 --	327 1
The amount disbursed	$848 58¼	

When the aforesaid executors came to examine the desk
of the said John Hammer Decd they found   3 92
and received at the sale   1 --
                                         4 92

         Amount of sale   960 19¾
         whole amount   965 11¾
         Amount disbursed   848 58¼
Ballance remaining in the hands of the executors is   116 52½

We the under signed commissioners do certify that the above Statement
is correct and true agreeable to the vouchers produced to us Given under

our hands the day and date above written

          James W Young
          Justice of the peace
          Jacob Ellis
          Hy King
          Commissioners

(p-33)   JOHN SWONGER Estate

STATE OF TENNESSEE

 Whereas the worshipfull Court of pleas & Quarter sessions of Washington County at January term 1823 ordered and appointed Jacob Hunter & Henry King two of the acting Justices of the peace for said County of Washington to be a committee with Esther Young executrix & James W. Young exr of Joseph Young Decd administrator of John Swonger Decd. as for as relates to the estate of the said John Swonger-- In persuance thereof we the sd Jacob Hunter and Henry King attended at the house of the aforesaid Esther Young where Joseph Young Dec'd formerly lived on Saturday the 22d day of March A. D. 1823 and then & there made the following settlement with the aforesaid Esther Young & James W Young executrix & executor of Joseph Young Decd. Administrator of John Swonger Decd--

 That is <u>agreable</u> to the sale paper the whole amount of the goods and chattles of John Swonger is $475 93½

An Joseph Young administrator of said John Swonger Decd have disbursed to different persons the following amounts as pr vouchers--

John Swonger note to the said Admr amt in principal & <u>intrest</u>	38 91
John Swongers account to Ditto	61 5
Chaney Borens receipt	38 15 1/3
Samuel Lusks receipt	85 --
Jacob Ellis receipt	29 40
David G Vance receipt	2 50
Samuel B Loves receipt	36 4
James Aikens receipt	39 13½
Jonathan Young receipt	29 84
Jonathan Carrethers receipt	42 82
James W Youngs receipt	14 31
Abraham Jobs receipt	14 62
Jonathan Lesleys receipt	6 --
James Barnes receipt	8 84
McClellan Greer & Co receipt	12 70
Joseph McClarey constable his recpt Judgt Jno McAlister	19 86
Darling Jones account	1 29½
David G Vance recpt for costs	87½

(p-34)   JOHN SWONGERS Estate

Isaac D Cox his proven account	3 25
John Burres account & due bill	1 25
The amount of costs in Civil suits	7 --
The amount of the disbursment of the estate of John Swonger Decd is	$492 85 1/3
And the amount of the estate of the said John Swonger	$475 93½

And we find that Joseph Young the administrator

         has paid $16 92 more than he had
of said estate. There were a number of papers containing proven accounts
filed with Joseph Young the aforesaid administrator amounting to $189 9 cents
which there was no money to pay-- a true Statement from the papers & documents handed to us witnes our hands and seals the day and date above written
                              Jacob Hunter (Seal)
                              Justice of the peace
                              Hy King (Seal)
                              Justice of the peace

ABRAHAM TIPTONS Estate

STATE OF TENNESSEE
    Whereas the worshipfull court of pleas and quarter sessions of Washington County at October 1822 Ordered and appointed James W Young and Henry King two of the acting Justices of the peace for said County of Washington to be a committee to settle with James I Tipton Administrator of Abraham Tipton Decd In persuance thereof we the said James W Young & Henry King attend at the house of Thomas King in said County of Washington on Saturday the Seventh day of December A D 1822 and then & there made the following settlement with James J Tipton the aforesaid administrator The whole amount of the sale of the goods and Chattles of Abraham Tipton Decd amounts to
                                                            $281 57½
The whole amount of the books of said Tipton that
can be collected is $134 54 1/3
                                                            $416 11
James J Tipton to one Stud horse sold by virtue of
several execution obtained against Abraham Tipton in
lifetime & before adms was granted $250 --
              Amount   666 11
And the said administrater has disbursed the following
accounts as per vouchers--
    To Thomas King   83 3½
    To Benjamen Duncan   3 81¼

(p-35)   ABRAHAM TIPTONS Estate

To Nathaniel Davis collector direct tax   20 --
To Wm Grayham for costs rec'd in his office   3 87½
To Adam Burrie   22 50
To Saml Hunt Shff in part of a Judgt McCracken agt
A Tipton   5 --
To Doctor Frances A McCorcle   8 87½
To Saml Hunt Sheff for taxes for the years 1819 & 1820   8 81
To Saml Hunt Sheff for a Judgt Wm Lindsey agt A Tipton
& Costs   6 17½
To George W Carter   155 83
To David Grant   10 60
To Carter Taylor & Carter   14 48
To James Robinson   26 --
To Caldwell Brown   1 37½
To James Robinson   19 78
To James Robinson   15 --
To Abraham Job   41 28
To John Frances Jr.   6 50
To James Robinson   41 55¾
To Jacob Brown   11 12½
To James P Taylor for advice & other services   17 50

To David Pugh	2 --	
To Thomas Arrington	2 --	
To Jacob Range	10 46½	$537 57½
To Leeroy Taylor	4 75	
To Doctor Isaac Taylor	4 50	
To Joseph Young	11 7½	
To John Kennedy	2 64¼	
To John Tipton	11 25	
To John Howard printer for admr	1 50	
To John L. Williams	4 18¾	
To Elijah Smith season for one mare	5 --	
To Jonathan Corrathers	15 --	
To Thomas Price	3 45	
To Jonathan Hammer	5 12½	
To John Hoss on account	3 --	

(p-36)   ABRAHAM TIPTONS Estate

To John Hoss on a c/o hand of Abraham Tipton	12 6¼
To Samuel Wright	5 --
To James Price	21 25
To Samuel W. H. Peoples	3 --
To John Range	2 37½
To Jacob Brown esqr	5 --
To Jonathan Young	3 --
To Dolphin Price	2 --
To Jonathan Lesley several executions & costs amt to	53 --
To George Humphreys Constable cash	4 50
To Thirty days attending to business as an administrator a 1. 50 cents pr day	45 --
To other expences	5 --
	232 66¾
	537 57½
The amt of what the administrator has disbursed	$770 24¼
Amount of the whole estate of A Tipton	666 11
And there is due to the administrator Jas J. Tipton	104 13¼

Given under our hands & seals the day & date above written
      Hy King (Seal)
      James W Young
      Commissioners

JERIMIAH DUNGANS Estate

STATE OF TENNESSEE
  Whereas the worshipfull Court of pleas & quarter sessions of Washington County at the July term 1823 appointed and ordered James W Young and Henry King two of the acting Justices of the peace for said County of Washington to be a committee to settle with John Love & John Houston administrators of Jeremiah Dungan Decd. In persuance there of we the said James W Young & Henry King attended at the house of John Houston in said County on Thursday the ninth day of October A D 1823 and then and there made the following settlement with John Love & John Houston the aforesaid administrators and we find the goods and chattles sold by the said administrators at public sale in the year 1813 amounted to $2103 73¾

(p-37)   JEREMIAH DUNGANS Estate

	$2103 73¾	
And the amount of the estate of Mary Dungan Decd to be	2025 12½	
Amounts	$4128 86¼	

And the administrators have disbursed the following sums to different persons as per vouchers &c.

To Joseph Bowman for making Jera Dungans coffin	$8 --	
To Richard Kelley	12 --	
To Nathan Shipley	30 --	
To Seth Thompson	10 --	
To Jeremiah D Gibson	30 --	
To James Pearce	301 --	
To Jeremiah D Gibson	60 --	
To Henry King (Clerk at sale	6 --	
To Moses Humphreys	12 --	
To Thomas Gibson	8 86	
To George Humphreys	2 --	
To James Sevier Clerk of the County Court	2 50	
To Andrew Taylor	7 21	
To Abraham Hendry	13 50	
To Jonathan Caruthers	10 --	
To Zebulon Smith	2 13	
To Zebulon Smith	1 33 1/3	
To Zebulon Smith	18 --	
To Zebulon Smith	14 --	
To Zebulon Smith	26 22½	
To James Pearce	3 75	
To James Pearce	10 --	
To Zebulon Smith	90 65	679 15
The amount of what John Houston bought at sale	330 96	
The amount of the property that John Love bought at sale	74 31½	
The amount of property sold on fifth day of sale for which there was no notes given to Mary Dungan	3 74½	
To Zebulon Smith	4 56	
To Jeremiah D Gibson	2 --	

(p-38)   JEREMIAH DUNGANS Estate

To Seth Thompson per voucher	2 --
To Charles Rennoe per Ditto	15 --
To Thomas Gibson	4 --
To James Harvey	3 --
To George William Clerk of Carter Cty Court	1 --
To Nathan Shipley for deviding Dungans land	10 --
To Seth Thompson	134 --
To Seth Thompson	6 --
To Seth Thompson	35 --
To Seth Thompson	2 --
To Seth Thompson	2 --
To Seth Thompson	5 --
To Seth Thompson	12 --
To Jeremiah D Gibson	20 --
To Thomas Gibson	65 --
To Thomas Gibson	10 --
Thomas Gibson	20 --
To Thomas Gibson	2 66½

To Thomas Gibson	4 --	
To Thomas Gibson	5 --	
To Zebulon Smith	15 --	
To Zebulon Smith	38 --	
To Zebulon Smith	100 --	
Zebulon Smith (note for)	333 --	
To James Pearce	20 --	
To Mary Dungan to cash by John Love	53 40	
To John Loves expence as admr	24 25	
John Love on buisness as admr 93 at 1 dollar per day	93 --	
To Andrew Taylor per order in full for his services	2 66	
To Mary Dangan	5 --	
To Jeremiah D Gibson (note for	87 89	
To Jeremiah D Gibson (note for	40 --	
To Mary Dungans (note for	52 26½	
To Zebulon Smith note for	38 98	$1766 45¼

(p-39) JEREMIAH DUNGANS Estate

To Orpha Gibson her note for	19 25
To Orpha Gibson her note for	7 1
To Mary Dungan her note for	84 57
To James Pearce his note for	2 27
To Seth Thompson	12 --
To Samuel Hunt shff for tax the year 1818	2 92½
To Saml Hunt Shff tax for the year 1819	1 --
To Saml Hunt Shff for the heirs of Jery Dungan	1 6
To Saml Hunt Shff tax for year 1820	2 95
To James Pearce for the use of Wm Bayles per order	1 --
To George Smith for making Mrs. Dungans coffin	8 --
To Henry King esqrs for taking depositions	3 96
To Seth Thompson upon Ellenor Coopers acct	3 66
To John Hoss his note for	2 25
To Wm Carter for taking depositions Dungans heirs vs J. Gibson	4 37½
To Saml Hunt Shff on the exo Jero D Gibson agt Mary Dungans & others	216 92
To Peter Parsons clerk of the Court of errors & appeals of the first Circuit of the State of Tennessee in a suit where in John Love & John Houston admr of Jera Dungan Decd were plff & Jeremiah D Gibson & others Defts	135 42½
To John Blair attorney at law his fees is a suit in equity where in John Love & John Houston were plaintiff & Jeremiah D Gibson and others defendants	12 50
To John Houston adm of Jeremiah Dungan Decd for his services as admr 116 days at $1 per day	116 --
To John Houston proven acct against Mary Dungan Decd	40 83
To John Houston for cutting 25 acres of grain at 50 cents pr acre	26 75
To Joseph Brown Sheff for taxes for the years 1811 & 1812	22 72

```
To Thomas Stevens constable for summoning witness      .50
To James Pearce his note                             22 50
To John Kennedy his fees in the suit against
Jery D Gibson                                        55 --    801 25½
```

The Services & expences of John Houston & John Love administrators of Jera Dungan Decd of a law suit with Jera D Gibson and drew off by the commissioners at settlement to be deducted from the amount of the estate

(p-40)   JEREMIAH DUNGANS Estate

```
John Loves expences as administrator                       24 25
John Love 93 days on business as admn at $1 per day        93 --
Henry King esqr for taking depositions in said suit         3 96
Wm Carter for ditto in Carter County                        4 37½
Saml Hunt Shff on an execution Jerey D Gibson vs Mary
Dungan & others                                           216 92
P Parsons Clerk Court errors & appeals Costs              135 42½
John Blair attorney at law his fees in said suit           12 50
John Houston admr for services 116 day at $1 per day      116 --
John Kennedys fees & other advice about said suit          55 --
John Houstons to the said committee 5 days                  5 --
Mary Browns bill for expences when deviding the
Jonesboro land                                              6 --
Henry Kings services 4 day                                  3 --
To the clerk of the Court of pleas &c                       1 10
                                                         $676 53
```

```
And it appears that John Houston has disbursed to several persons the sum
of                                                       $435 25
And Received of money due the said estate                 434 21
                Remains due Houston                      $   1  4
And paid out of his own money the sum of                  290 14
Which is to come out of the estate
And the amount of the estate is                        $4128 86¾
The costs of the law Suit fe                             676 53
                                                       $3452 33¾
The amount that John Houston has paid his cash           290 14
                                                       $3162 19¾
                Each person share                       632 43 4/5
```

A true Settlement agreeable to the vouchers and other documents presented to us certified the day and date first above written.

                                James W Young
                                Hy King
                                Commissioners

(p-41)   WILLIAM MILLERS Estate

                                                          D   C
John Miller admr of the estate of William Miller Decd stands chargable with
the amount of   385 53¾
Book accounts that can be collected included in the above
sum and produced vouchers to the amount of   362 4
                Due the estate   23 49¾

And allowing John Miller $20 for his services rendered in settling his part of the above estate included in the above sum of $362 4

Find John Miller adm Indebted to the estate the sum of 23 49¾
And has notes in his hands not collected some of them doubtfull to the amount of $152 ¼

Memorandum of notes Thomas Mitchell   5 --
                     John Kurts   4 41½
                     Andw Carson   15 92
                     Jessee Payne esqr   10 99
                     Wm Mitchell   1 75
                     Wm Shields   5 60
                     Moses Carson   3 83
                     Jessee Payne Jr   5 4
                     Saml Blair   2 80½
                     Allen Gillispie   4 --
                     John Kerwood   28 86
                     Robert Morrison   9 1
                     Pointen Charleton   6 56¼
                     James Mathes   4 81
                     John Charleton   3 79
                     Andw Carson   5 7
                     Wm Glass   19 25
                     Wm Smith   15 --
                                          $152 ¼

We John Strain John Link & David Wilson esqr being a committee appointed by Court to settle with the administrators of the estate of Wm Miller Decd after examining the papers find them as above stated Given under our hands and seals 30th of December 1823

      John Strain (Seal)
      Jno Link (Seal)
      David Willson (Seal)

(p-42)   WILLIAM MILLERS Estate

Thomas Brabson admr of the estate of William Decd. Stands charged with the amount of $1500 47
And produced vouchers to the amount of   1665 37
And allowing Thos Brabson $20 for his Services rendered in settling his part of the above estate leaving a ballance in favour of Brabson to the amount of $184 90 cents
Including his services in this amount.

 We John Strain John Link & David Wilson esqrs being a committee appointed by Court to settle with the administrators of William Miller Decd after examening the papers find them as above stated given under our hands and seals 30th of December 1823

      John Strain (Seal)
      Jno Link (Seal)
      David Wilson (Seal)

      JOSIAH FRANKLINS Estate

STATE OF TENNESSEE
WASHINGTON COUNTY We the undersigned appointed by order of the Court of pleas of said County a Committee to settle with Jacob Brown esqr Guardian of the minor heirs of Josiah Franklin Decd pointed to make said settlement and have found a ballance of Interest in the hands of said Guardean of forty

three dollars & forty eight cents up to this date which interest has accrued on the principal in his hands belonging to said heirs, Given under our hands and seals this 23d January 1823

          Nathan Shipley (Seal)
          John Stephenson (Seal)
          Saml Greer (Seal)

(p-43)   ROBERT S BLANCHARD Estate

 We the undersigned being a committee appointed by the Court of pleas and Quarter sessions for Washington County to settle with John McEfee admr of Robert S Blanchard Decd do find the amount of the sale of the property of said Blanchard to be $797 11 cents
And that said McEfee has expended & paid to sundry persons
as per receipt and charges   467 48
To Allowances to said admr for attendances of said Blanchard when sick Burying expences attendance on sales and
loss of time and expences in attending law Suits $110 --
                  $577 48

And do find the ballance in the hands of said administrator at   219 63
Given under our hands and seals this 18th July 1823.
        Sam Geer (Seal) Ju peace
        John Patton (Seal) Justice of peace

        HANNAH FORD Estate

WASHINGTON COUNTY TENNESSEE
 On a settlement with William Jackson Guardian of Hannah Ford we the under signed appointed Commissioners by Court to settle with him find that he is chargeable at this time with the sum of three hundred and fifty eight dollars and ten cents witness our hands this 11th day ofOctober 1824.
            $358 10 cents
       Henry Hoss
       John Gott
       Archabald Glasscocke

(p-44)   MARTIN FEAZEL Estate

Agreeable to an order of Court of Washington County to us directed we the Court appointed to settle with John Bricker & William Patton administrators of the estate of Martin Feazel Decd have provided to examin the following voucher (viz)
     Feb No 1 notes $390 67¼
        2   65 39¼
        3   11 --
        4   24 3¾
  Allowance to administrator in No 3 19 50
     The amount of the sale $490 73½
Cr by loss of $2.8 in two notes of corn & iron one on
Samuel Ball & the other on Joshua Hendley being exposed 2 8
to public sale   488 65½

 We find the accounts to be as here in stated in witness whereof we have here unto set our hands and seals this 24th Jany 1823.

WASHINGTON COUNTY, TENNESSEE

            Jonathan Collom (Seal)
            Wm Mitchell (Seal)
            Justice of the peace
            Jacob Brown (Seal)
            Justice of the peace

JOHN FORDS Estate

We the committee to settle with Nathan Shipley administrator of the estate of John Ford Decd find that the amount of sale is $323 20
    Note of John Kennedy   900 --
Novr 28th 1823   Sale of four negroes due in twelve months
                                      2016 --
                                    $3239 20

We the committee find that the administrator is chargeable with above amount
    David Deaderick receipt   5 50
    Greer & Kennedy   15 39½
    John G. Eason   3 56¼
    Samuel Hunt for tax   4 55
    Samuel Hunt for tax   6 2
    Account rendered by Nathan for expenses of Sale   8 25

(p-45)   JOHN FORD Estate

Samuel Hunt Shff receipt for tax   14 39
                                                  $57 66¼

Jan 1824
    We the Committee appointed to settle with Nathan Shipley administrator of the estate of John Ford Decd do find that there is in the hands of the said administrator after Striking the ballance three thousand one hundred and eighty one dollars and Sixty six cents.
                                   John Patton
                                     Jacob Brown
                                     James W Young

KILLION ERNHEART Estate

No		
1	John Holebee prov account	" 62½
2	Jacob Brown waggon maker	25
3	Nicholes Lineberger	1 50
4	Thomas Finch	3 75
5	John Bacon	3 37½
6	Killion Ernhart note to Daniel Clinger	48 --
7	Daniel Clinger account for a raised bank note	20 --
8	Registers receipt for two deeds in Green County	2 --
9	James Fullers recpt as clerk of the sale	2 --
10	Elijah Brown recpt for cryer of the sale	1 75
11	Clerks recpt for copy of Inventory	60
12	Oliver B Ross receipt winding short &c.	3 --
13	Elijah Brown Recpt for collection fees	1 75
14	Clerks fees for letters of administration & record	1 40
15		$90 --

We Jacob Hunter Ths C Patton & Jacob Brown Justices of the peace for the

County of Washington being a committee appointed by Court to settle with
Conrad Kiker admr of the estate of Killion Ernheart Decd do find that by
vouchers produced to us that he hath paid debts due the said Decd & other
expenditures to the amount of ninety dollars & the inventory produced to
us from Court of the amount of the estate to be four hundred and two dollars
& two cents amt of the Inventory $402 2
    Debts paid by admin   90 --
                                                     $312 2

Given under our hand this 16th
of October A D 1824
                           Jacob Hunter
                           Thos C. Patton } Justeces
                           Jacob Brown

(p-46)   EDMOND BEANS Estate

We the undersigned appointed commissioners by the Court of Washington County to settle with Jacob Ellis executor of the estate of Wm Ellis Decd who
was administrator of the estate of Edmond Beane Decd find on examination
that the estate of Edmond Beane sold for and with which sum he the said
Jacob Ellis stands chargeable is $755 47½
and has produced vouchers of demand agt the estate
which has been paid of   218 65¼
Leaving a ballance against him of $536 82¼
Out of which we are of Opinion that he is entitled for
his Services 6 pr cent   45 32
leaving a ballance of   491 50
Given under our hands this 11th day of December 1824
                         Henry Hoss
                         Nathan Shipley
                         John Gott

JOHN MCNEALS Estate

Joshua Greens proven account	12 50
James Seviers recpt	1 40
Do Do	50
John Wilkles Judgt against J McNeal	25 50
Henry McCrackens recpt for Costs	1 --
David Mitchell proven accounts	4 75
Note to John Blair	2 50
David Deadericks receipt for	3 --
John Stouts Judgment	27 17
Mechalir Copps Judgment	32 7½
John McNeals note to A Gann with interest	10 75
	$121 82

We the committee appointed to settle with the administratrix of the
estate of John McNeal Decd do certify that the foregoing is a true list
of all the receipts & vouchers produced to us
                         Jacob Hunter
                         Jacob Brown
                         Wm Colyar

(p-47) WILLIAM TYLERS Estate

Money receipt by Wm Bayles Guardean for the minor children of Wm Tyler Decd
Money recd January 24th 1823 & before Interest 1st April
1823 $2091 61
February 19th that part of the <u>dividen</u> They are to
have   49 9
March 8th of Wm Wilson   47 87½
Interest on the 1st item to the 1st April 1823   96 56½
Interest on the 2d item to same time   33
Interest on 3d item Do   17½
The debts for rent due June 22 1822 $113 8¾   42½
Hire of negroe woman Jenney 20 days   1.61   8½
            Principal $2307 1¼
            Interest   97 58
   1   Principal & Interest   2404 59¾
No/Receipt of Dan D Andrews dated July 16th 1822   13 50
   2   Receipt of Thomas C Patton dated Dec 22, 1821   1 --
   3   Receipt of Dan D Andrews dated Feby 1823   97 50
   4   Receipt of Thomas Long dated February 13th 1823   9 92
   5   Receipt of John Blair dated March 10th 1825   5 --
   6   Receipt of Henry Long dated October 24th 1822   8 50
   7   Receipt of Reuben Bayles dated Decr 24 1822   2 --
       To Guardian services up to the present date   18 5
We the undersigned commissioners appointed April $272 92
Septr 1823 find that the amount that William Bayles Guardean for the minor
heirs of Wm Tyler Decd recd of the executors of said Wm Tyler principal
& interest to the first day of this instant is $2404 59¾
and we likewise find that Wm Bayles the aforesaid Guardean has
disbursed according to vouchers produced to as the sum of
                                                                    $272 92
And there remains in the hands of the Guardean $2131 67¾
Given under our hands & seals this 15th day of April A D 1823
                                      Hy King
                                      William P Chester
                                      Jacob Brown

(p-48) PHILIP HUFFINE Estate

We Jacob Hunter James W Young & William Bayles being a committee appointed
to settle with Thomas Earley administrator of the estate of Philip Huffine
Decd report as follows as appears by the paper to us produced --
1st   That the sale of the goods &c $368 73¼
To paid in debts To John Early & Joseph Kerlin   3 11
       To A & W McKee   14 16
       Samuel Early   2 --
       Jacob Hartsell   15 37½
       Henry Gyre   2 18¼
       Thomas Irelands note   14 66
       Jacob Brown note   4 --
       Sam Maxwell   6 25
       Dad Deaderick   3 86
       Jacob Hartsell   15 50
       John H. Hicks order   8 --
       Thomas Earley a/c   20 --
       John Simpson   5 75

```
    Sam Miller                                            "   .50
    John G Rubles a/c                                     3  --
John C Harris                                            10  76½
John McAlisters note                                     23  45½
Charles Davis a/c                                         3  --
Jacob Hornbergers a/c                                     3  --
Josiah Parker a/c                                         1  12½
Joseph Hunter a/c                                            87½
Jacob Hartsell a/c                                        6  56
On the papers produced we find this the estate of       168  32¼
```
said Phillip Huffine Decd amounted to three hundred &
sixty eight dollars seventy three & one fourth cents   368 73¼
And the said admenr Thomas Early has paid out in debts &
charges one hundred & sixty eight dollars thirty two
and one fourth cents $168 32¼
Leaving a ballance in the hands of the said administrator
of two hundred dollars forty one cents $200 41
Given under our hands & seal this 24th day of April 1824
filed April 14th 1824

                          Jacob Hunter (Seal)
                          James W Young (Seal)
                          Wm Bayles (Seal)

(p-49)   WILLIAM ELLIS Estate

    We the undersigned being appointed Commissioners by the County Court
of Washington County to make settlement with Jacob Ellis executor of the
estate of William Ellis Decd find that the amount of the estate sold of
said William Ellis was $2532 13¼
Recd debts due the estate over & above expences invoiced 224 83½
out of which he is entitled for 2 years 1 months $2756 96¾
services as made his duly by the will   200 --
For debts paid for which he has produced vouchers   540 29½
Services as Executor 5 pr cent on $2556 96   127 80
                                                        $868 9½
                                                        $1888 87¼
Due by the estate of Wm Ellis to the estate of Edmon
Bean   197 80
    Leaving a ballance against him $1691 7¼
Also we find the execution is chargeable with the sum
that the widow of Edmond Beane is accountable for to the
estate for a waggon and two horses $265 --
                    in all $1956 7¼
Given under our hands this 11th day of December 1824
                          Henry Hoss
                          Nathan Shipley
                          John Gott

                    WILLIAM TYLERS Estate

    The following settlement made by the committee at the January Court of
pleas &c 1825 with William Bayles Guardean of Malinda Tyler Wm Tyler Phebe
Tyler Minerva Tyler & Betsey Tyler minor children of William Tyler Decd do
find that said Guardean by the report of the Committee at the april Court
1823 had in his hands on 1st April 1823 $2131 67¾

Interest thereon till January 1824	95 92½
May 31st 1823 Mitchells & Colloms note	243 72
7 months interest	8 53
June 1st 1823 Jenneys hire	30 --
Interest thereon 7 months	1 5
Augt 13th 1823 debts due for rent	88 58½

(p-50)   WILLIAM TYLERS Estate

Interest till 1st January 1824	1 99
Augt 4th 1823 Bank dividend	49 9
Interest thereon 4 months 27 day	1 88½
1st January 1824 Amount	$2652 45¼
William Bayles paid in tax	2 21
paid Elijah Brown	1 --
Febr 1823 Two days advertising & settling rent given at $2 per day	4 --
1st Decr 1823 advertising and settling rent	4 --
Octr. 1823 Three days trying to detain my wards in this county	6 --
paid Elijah Brown for crying sale	1 --
	$2634 24¼

leaving twenty six hundred & thirty four dollars twenty four in the hands of said Guardian on the 1st day of January 1824

Interest on that sum one year	158 4
Feb 4th 1824 Bank Dividend	49 9
Interest there on till 1st January 1825	2 6½
debts due for rent June 1st 1824	72 3
interest thereon till 1st Jany 1825	2 52
Hire of negroe Jenney due 7 June 1824	37 --
Interest due thereon till 1st January 1825	1 32
Hire of Jenney to John Cromwell in 1824	6 --
	$3162 86¼
1824 June 14th hiring negroe Jenney	2 --
In August writing notes & taking depositions	4 --
11th Sept 1824 writing notes &c	2 --
Writing notices on 12th Decr 1824	4 --
Advertising & selling grain &c 1st decr 1824	4 --
Attending to get a note to secure rent	2 --
paid M Deaderick & son goods for Jenney	1 21
paid S Greer esqr for six depositions	3 96
paid 37½ cents for a letter from agent	37½
paid clerk for a copy of other settlement	60
Omitted in proper filing a bill against executors & interogatorees	4 --
	28 14½

(p-51)   WILLIAM TYLERS Estate

	$3162 86¼
	28 14½
There appears to be in	$3134 72¾

the hands of William Bayles on the 1st day of January 1825 thirty one hundred and thirty four dollars and seventy two and three fourths cent-- Witness our hands and seals this 12th day of January 1825.

                      Nathan Shipley (Seal)

Thos C Patton (Seal)
James W Young (Seal)
Committee

ADAM WATTEBERGER Estate

We the undersigned Commissioners appointed to settle with Christian Zetty & Frederick Fenceler executors for Adam Watteberger Decd. who was the executor for Robert Fawbush Decd do find that there are due from said Wattenberger executors to the heirs of sd Fawbush (to wit) the daughter one hundred and thirteen dollars and eighty cents the other legatte the widow has been paid by Watteberger in his lifetime as appears by receipt produced 11th July 1826

Signed
James McAlister
Reuben Rodgers

HANNAH FORD (alias) HARRISON Estate

We John Patton & Nathan Shipley a committee appointed by Court at October Sessions 1825 to settle, with William Jackson Guardean of Hannah Harrison formerly Hannah Ford, do find that the said William Jackson stands Chargeable to the said Hannah Harrison formerly Hannah Ford the sum of three hundred & seventy six dollars and seventy six cents--- Given under our hands the 11th day of October 1825

John Patton
Nathan Shipley

(p-52) ## HENRY BOWERS Estate

STATE OF TENNESSEE
WASHINGTON COUNTY We the undersigned being appointed by the County Court of Washington County to make settlement with John Bowers & Nancy Bowers Executors of the estate of Henry Bowers Decd find that they stand chargeable with the following sums

Amt of sale April 30th 1818	$406 21¾
One note on Daniel Bowman	55 --
One note on John McEfee	150 --
One note on Lawrence Snapp	40 --
A debt on Charles Bacon	1 --
A debt on Baxter Be'ane	17 50
	$669 71¼

Out of which he is entitled to a credit for the following sums

Court charges	3 --
Robert Burk cryer	2 --
Whiskey for sale	1 50
Debts due Bowman Exr	2 33
William P Chester for med attendance	16 8
One note due Henry Hoss	4 38
One note due James Depew	300 --
An account due Michael Krous	1 21½
Due John McAlister	17 8
paid Daniel Bowman for coffin	3 --
Samuel Crawfords account	5 93

```
        paid on Bowers note to Jac Bowman              46 --
                                                    $402 51½
Out of which the executors are entitled for         $267 20¼
their services six per cent on $669 71               40 18
leaving a ballance against the executors of         $227  2¼
```
Given under our hands & seals this 8th of day of
April 1825

         Henry Hoss J P (Seal)
         Jacob Ellis J P (Seal)

(p-53)   JOHN HUNTS Estate

STATE OF TENNESSEE
WASHINGTON COUNTY We the undersigned being appointed a committee of Court to make settlement with George Crouch admr & Elizabeth Hunt Admrx of the estate of John Hunt Decd do find on examination that they stand chargeable with the following sums.

```
    Amount of sale                              $704 87
    One note on John McAlister                   100 --
                                    Amt          804 87
```
out of which they are entitled to the following credits as pr vouchers
```
    Doctor David Nelsons bill                     22 --
    John McAlister a/c                            14 87½
    Smith Hunts a/c                                6 --
    Direct tax for 1815                            6 88¾
           for 1816                                3 44
    John McCracken Cryer                           2 --
    Attorney Peter Parsons                         2 50
    Jacob Miller for whiskey                       3 --
    Daniel Bowman for coffin                       4 25
        Tax for 1815                               1 26
                1816                               1 67
                1817                               1 66
                1818                               1 88
                1819                               1 67
            leaving a ballance of               $731 77¼
```
out of which the administrators are entitled to 6 pr cent on $804 87 equal to   48 28
   leaving a ballance against them of $683 49¼

Given under our hands and seals this 27th day of May 1825
       Henry Hoss
       Nathan Shipley
       Jacob Ellis

(p-54)   WILLIAM TYLER Estate

January sessions 1826 We Jacob Brown Daniel Berkley & Thos C Patton Justices of the peace appointed a committee by Court to settle with William Bayles Guardean of Milinda Tyler Wm Tyler Phebe Tyler Minerva Tyler and Betsey Tyler the minor children of William Tyler Decd do find that said Wm Bayles had in his hands at the last settlement thirty one hundred & thirty four dollars
```
seventy two & three fourth cents               $3134 72¾
        Interest there on t1 1st January 1826    188  8   $3322 80¾
About 15th March 1825 75 pr cent bank stock     1227 27
and bank dividend                                 49  9
```

Interest on these two sums	60 57	1336 93
5th October 1825 bank dividand	17 49	
Interest 1st January 1826	18	
Money due for rent on 1st June 1825	80 34	
For the hire of Jenney 1st Decr 1825	18 50	
Interest on these sums	2 90½	119 41½

Making in all four thousand seven hundred & seventy
nine dollars fifteen and one fourth cents $4779 15¼
And we find that said Bayles has paid the following sums
and performed the following services (voz)

No			
	1	John Cromwell	1 92
	2	Abraham Williams	1 --
	3	Nathaniel Kelsey	10 --
	4	Joseph Smith	1 50
	5	Robert McCraken	2 --
	6	D D Andrew & Nancy Andrew	390 --
	7	James Sevier	1 20

Sept Court 1823 two days Sept & March in 1824 &
1825 three days each making 14 days at $2 pr day   28 --
                                                    $435 62

March 1825 writing notices and taking deposition   2 --
October 11th 1825 attending to get the bill of injunct-
ion for Dan D & N Andrew   2 --
Carrying said bill to Dandridge 4 days   8 --
Advertising and attending sale Decr 1st 1825   4 --
Writing and making this settlement   2
                                              Amt $453 62

(p-55)   Amt &c $4325 53¼

And we find that after deducting the monies paid out by said Wm Bayles in
expences & disbursments services &c said Bayles has yet under his controle
four thousand three hundred and twenty five dollars fifty three and one
fourth cents-- to the 1st of this month-- witness our hands and seals this
13th day of January 1826

                                     Jacob Brown
Sworn to the above   Daniel Berkley
according to law   Thos C Patton
                                     Committee

JAMES ROBERTS Estate

STATE OF TENNESSEE }
WASHINGTON COUNTY   }   We John Patton Saml Greer & Daniel Berkley three
Justices of the peace for said County being a committee appointed to settle
with Thomas O Roberts administrator of the estate of James Roberts Decd we
find that the said T O Roberts has received of the estate $507 43
Paid out

4 notes to Gammon & Crawford	158 91	
John Rylands receipt	55 40	
John Rylands receipt	97 19¾	
Samuel Crawfords receipt	9 39	
Elijah Brown receipt	15 70	
	$336 59¾	
	$170 83¼	

We find in the hands of Thomas O Roberts a Ballance of $170 83¼ Given under
our hands this 8th day of July 1826.

WASHINGTON COUNTY, TENNESSEE

                Daniel Berkley
                John Patton
                Saml Greer

July Sessions 1826
    Examined and Approved by the Court
                Nathan Shipley Chairman

(p-56)   JAMES PARKERS Estate

Voucher

No	Description	Amount
1	Solomon Brown note	22 87½
2	Rent paid the estate of Benja Harris Decd	30 --
3	R Rodgers receipt	30 83
4	William Dosser Constable receipt	2 62½
5	Samuel Watson receipt	22 --
6	Samuel Brown receipt	2 --
7	Paid John Bacon pr Parkers note	31 50
8	John Holibee proved account	8 17
9	Ben Austins Judgment	3 18¾
10	Thomas Finches proved account	22 15
11	Thomas Finches Judgment in County Court	62 55¾
12	Mathew Aiken Judgment in County Court	62 55¼
13	Henry McCray Judgment in County Court	62 --
14	Paid Thomas Finches note	20 --
15	John Walters proved account	1 --
16	Samuel Bayles Judgment	35 55
17	Thomas Finches note	8 4
18	Thomas Finches note	50 --
19	David G Vance proved account	3 50
20	Samuel Brown Judgment	10 --
21	Sarah Parkers receipt	50 --
22	Saml Greer receipt for money James Parker owed in bank	56 5
23	Saml Watson receipt for part of Judgment	73 21
24	James Seviers receipt for Costs	4 20
25	Receipt for Judgment against administrator	43 46
26	John Kennedy receipt for fees vs Thomas Finck	5 --
27	Labon B Pool proved account paid Henry McCray	9 --
28	Administrators account for postage	50
29	Administrators allowance	25 --
30	John C Harris medical accpts against JamesParker	2 87½
		$759 79¼

STATE OF TENNESSEE
WASHINGTON COUNTY   July 12th 1826
    We the Committee appointed by Court at April sessions last to settle with John C Harris administrator of the

(p-57)   JAMES PARKERS Estate

Estate of James Parker Decd find from the records of said Court that sd administrator stands charged as such in the amount of $795 21¾
    We find in the above amount that the administrator is charged in his Inventory returned to Court the amount of the following notes which said

```
are returned the drawers there of could not be found--
    One on Philip T Norris                              5 --
    Do   Do for                                        27 50
    two others on Micajah McDennee & David Teamil       -  -
    one for                                            15 --
    The other amounting to                             16 --
                    deduct                             63 50
                                                     $731 71¼
```

And find on examination of his vouchers produced by him that he has paid
out the sum of $734 79¾
and we allow him for his services as administrator this
sum   25 --
                                                        $759 79¾

        Jacob Brown Justice of the peace
        Jacob Hartsell Justice of the peace
        Jacob Hunter Justice of the peace

(p-58)   JOHN HUNTS Estate

WASHINGTON COUNTY }
STATE OF TENNESSEE } We the under signed being appointed a Committee
of Court to make settlement with Benjamin Shipley Guardean of Sally Hunt
& Maria Hunt minor heirs of John Hunt Decd do find on examination that he
stands Charged with the following services
```
                    Principal rec'd of Admr        $496 --
                    Interest to this time            41 50
                                                   $537 50
```
Out of which he the Guardean aforesaid is entitled to the following credits
```
For amt paid Thomas Beard for schooling             12 --
Ditto pd Henry Hoss for Do                           5 19
Amt pd Saml Blackburn for Do                         1 --
For supporting the aforesaid minors during the term
they were schooling                                 50 --
For trouble and expence incurred by said Shipley as
Guardean                                            10 --
                                                   $78 19
leaving a ballance against him of                 $459 31
```
Given under our hands and seals this 7th day of December 1826

       Henry Hoss
       Jacob Ellis
       Richard Carr

(p-59)   JAMES FARMERS Estate

WASHINGTON COUNTY }
STATE OF TENNESSEE } We the undersigned being appointed by the Court of
said County to make settlement with Joseph Bowman a admr of the estate of
James Farmer a man of color do find that he stands chargeable with the
following sums
```
    Amt of the sale                                $163 68
    Amt due by Joseph Bowman to the estate is        19 16
            amounting in all                       $182 84
```
Out of which he is entitled to a credit for the following sums as pr vouchers
    Amt of Bowmans A/c $78 27

```
    Tax for 1822                                        $5 48
    Kinchen Kelleys a/c                                 13 --
    John Malonee a/c                                    81¼
    Atto Blair fee                                       2 50
    Court charges                                          80
                                                       100 86¼
Leaving a ballance of                                   81 97¼
Out of which he is entitled to receive 6 percent
on $182 84 for services as administrator making         10 97
    Ballance in his hands                              $71 --
Given under our hands and seals this 11th day of April 1825
                          Henry Hoss  J P  (Seal)
                          Jacob Ellis J P  (Seal)
```

(p-60½)   JOHN MILLER Estate

WASHINGTON COUNTY }
STATE OF TENNESSEE }   We the undersigned being appointed a Committe of Court to make settlement with Henry Hoss & James White admrs of the estate of John Miller Decd do find that they stand Chargeable with the following sums

```
    To amt of a sale Feb 1st & 2d 1822                 $1546  2½
    Cash recvd that was on hand                           49 38
    Amt of a sale Sepr 21st 1822                          59 86¾
                                                      $1655 27¼
```
Also the following notes due the estate which they have collected
```
    One note on Jacob Miller Jr                           40 30
    Do Collected by Kennedy from Joseph Cooper           129 75
    John Simmerman                                        15 22
    Samuel Miller                                         18 --
    Henry Miller                                          90 --
    John Miller                                           40 --
    John Malonee                                           6 78    342  5
    John Duncan                                            2 --
```
Also the following notes due the estate payable in specie which they have collected   One note on John Crawford   85 57
```
    One do Joseph Bowman                                 182 86
    One Do on Mathew Aiken                               445  7    713 50
    making a sum total of                              $2710 82¼
```
In addition to which seven of the heirs acknowledge the
receipt of $707 0 during the lifetime of the entestate 707 0

                    making the entire value $3417 82¼

Out of which the administrators have produced vouchrs to shew that they are entitled to the following sums for expenses of administration &c.
```
    Cash pd Thomas Brown Cryer                           $5 --
    Do to James Range for whiskey                         2 12½
    Tax for 1822                                          8 99½
                    Amt ap                              $16 12
```

(p-61)   JOHN MILLERS Estate

```
                    Total amt of                      $3417 82¼
                    Amt expences ap                      16 12
Saml Hunt Sheriff for summoning Commissioners & Jury      9 40
```
Allowance made by Court to Commissioners & Jury appoint-

ed to lay off widows dower & <u>devide</u> real estate	$39 --
Paid James Sevier clerks fee	4 --
Henry Hoss 5 days attendance as surveyor by order of Court and making a return of plots	12 50
Attorney Blair fee for attending the administration business	5 --
Isaac Hammer for schooling	4 --
	$90 2
leaving a ballance of	$3327 80¼

Out of which the administrators are entitled for their
Services 6 pr cent on $2710 82½   162 --
                               $3165 80¼

We also find that the administrators have paid to the heirs
of said estate as follows

To Jacob Miller	241 26¾
To Samuel Miller	242 1
To Solomon Miller	242 89
To George Walters	242 92
To Nicholas Reasoner	239 78
To John Hammer	241 86
To Joseph Miller	242 55
To John Miller	242 65
To Henry Miller	242 59
To Abraham Miller	242 90
To Adam Sell	239 38
To Joseph Bowman Guardean of Cath Miller	242 80
To Widow Catharine Miller	242 34
	$3145 93¼
leaving a ballance due the legatees o/c	19 86½

Given under our hands & seals this 24th Decr 1825.
                     Saml Greer (Seal)
                     Justice of the peace
                     John Patton (Seal)
                     Justice of the peace

(p-62)   JOHN LITTLES Estate

STATE OF TENNESSEE
WASHINGTON COUNTY   We the undersigned being appointed a Committee of Court to make Settlement with Richard Carr administrator and Elizabeth Wheeler administratrix of the estate of John Little Decd formerly of our County do find that the said administrators stands Chargeable with the following sums--

To amt of sale made Nov 20th 1812	$1519 7½
Notes due said estate	267 66
Amt	$1786 73½

Out of which sum the administrators are allowed for the following charges as pr vouchers

Henry King Clerk of sale	2 --
John McCracken Cryer	2 --
Isaac Taylor for Medical attendance	2 --
Joseph Bowman for coffin	6 --
Tax for 1812	2 3½
John Kennedy attorney	10 --
Also a proven a/c due by Decd to Jona Caruthers for	1 --
	$25 3½

```
        leaving a ballance of                              $1761 70
```

And the Committee are of opinion that the administrators
are entitled to five percent on the amt of said estate
for his services making the sum of   88 83
```
                    leaving the neat value                 $1672 87
```
The administrators has produced a receipt in full from one
of the heirs George Little.
Also a receipt for $187 89 cents from Vincent Boren an
other of the heirs   187 89

The committee having no evidence before them when the notes due to said estate became due and not being satisfied (p-63) JOHN LITTLES Estate whether or not the administrators would be chargeable with Interest on any part of said estate would respectfully refer that question to the court for their decision if they think the administrators not chargeable with any interest. the foregoing statement exhibits a Just view of the situation of the estate as the vouchers shew-- Given under our hands & seals this 11th day of January 1827

                            Henry Hoss (Seal)
                            John Gott (Seal)
                            John Malonee (Seal)

ANDREW CARSON Estate

Pursuant to an Order of the County Court of Washington to us directed to settle with the administrators of Andrew Carson Decd we the undersigned met at the house of David Wilson esqr in the County aforesaid on the 17th May 1827 and after examening the <u>vendew</u> bill and papers to us exhibited we find William L Humphreys administrator charged with the sum of four hundred and ninety five dollars eighty four and three fourth cents $495 84¾
And William L Humphreys administrator produced vouchers to us in the following manner (viz)

No			
1	Thomas Brabson proven account	$15	9½
2	Thomas Brown receipt	4	--
3	David Deaderick Do	25	--
4	Samuel Duncan Do	3	--
5	John Nelson Do	5	68½
6	John Ryland Do	10	--
7	Samuel Caruthers proven account	4	50
8	Samuel Greer receipt	1	--
9	Jessee Glass proven account	3	50
10	Daniel Berkley Do	4	40
11	John Ryland receipt	4	62
12	Wiland Barger proven account	4	12

(p-64)   ANDREW CARSONS Estate

13	Ballance of a note to Edward Ress	1	50
14	George Pursel Proven account	2	77
15	James P Taylor note	12	50
16	John Rylands receipt	3	50
17	James Holms note	9	72
18	E L Mathes receipt	5	--
29	Jno Doane three receipts	7	99½
22	Daniel Bickley account for 5 yd of muslin	5	--

23	A note on Rebecca Charleton	51 75
24	Moses W Carson account admitted by the heirs	12 66½
25	Two Judgments one vs Joseph Melbourn for M Stephenson use one in favour of M. Stephenson & Co vs Absolem Carson and both stayed by Andrew Carson and James Holms and paid by the administrator	159 48
26	Lemuel Carsons note	25 28
27	Moses Carson recpt by consent of parties	13 10
28	George Barger proven account	22 63 1/3
29	To one note paid Samuel Duncan	32 --
30	To 1 note to Brabson & Miller admrs of Wm Miller Decd	21 97
31	To 1 Do Do Do	7 46
32	Wm P Chesters proven account	13
33	John Rylands recipt for money paid on an execution of D A Deaderick agt said Carson Decd	11 20
34	Daniel Berkley	2 44
		$515 9 1/3

from which it appears that the representatives of Andrew Carson Decd. have paid out $20. 4 more than they have received assets--
Given under our hands & seals

        John Stephenson (Seal)
        John Link (Seal)

(p-65)   JOHN COWENS Estate

STATE OF TENNESSEE
WASHINGTON COUNTY We the undersigned being appointed a Committee of Court to make settlement with Richard Carr & Jacob Ellis as executors of the Estate of John Cowan Decd formerly of our County do find that they stand Chargeable with the following.

To amt sales at the sale of said estate	$972 79½

And that they are entitled to a credit for the following sums as pr vouchers, Robert Bark Cryer at said

sale	3 --
Henry King Clerk	2 --
Daniel Bowman for a coffin	6 --
Henry Hoss for surveying & deed	1 --
Aron Finck attorney	1 --
Charles W Dunworth a/c	2 50
Adam Fox a/c	1 11
George Humphreys (costs)	1 51
Jeremiah Gillum	1 25
Jacob Ellis a/c	5 50
Jacob Howard a/c	1 50
John Sherfey for a coffin for the widow of John Cowen Decd	5 50
Tax for 1824	2 64½
Bureal clothes	8 45
	42 84
Out of which the sum the executors are entitled to	$929 84
5 per cent for their services making	46 49
leaving a ballance in their hands of	$883 35

WASHINGTON COUNTY, TENNESSEE

Given under our hands & Seals this 22d day of June 1827
                                                          Henry Hoss (seal)
Approved by Court July Term 1827   John Gott

(p-66)   MASHECK HALE Estate

Schedule of the settlement made by John Gott & Nathan Shipley appointed in the County Court of Washington County to settle with Zachariah Hale administrator of the estate of Mesheck Hale deceased stands as follows
Vouchers produced by the administrators

A note given to William Pearce	$33 8
To Horner Brook	18 63
Samuel Hunt receipt for taxes	2 56
Mathew Stephenson Clerk	1 90
Joseph Thompson proven account	3 --
John Bowman proven account	1 2
David Nelsons doctor bill	2 --
Samuel Kennedys proven account	2 68¾
John Fry proven account	1 75
Nicholes Keefhaver proven account	1 --
Coffin and funeral expenses	14 25
William Odeneal for calling sale	1 --
John G. Eason proven account	87
Gammon & Crawford proven account	4 73¾
John Ryland Sheriffs recpt for costs	50 97
Gammon & Crawford proven account	7 81¾
	$147 27¼

We find that Zachariah Hale administrator of the estate of Mesheck Decd
stands chargeable to the said estate the sum of $643 59¼
and that he has produced vouchers against the said estate to the amt of $147 27¼
leaving a ballance in favour of the Estate $469 32
Given under our hands the 7th day of July 1827
                                    Nathan Shipley
                                    John Gott
allowed for services by the ninety six dollars July term 1827. William P. Chester Co.

(p-67)   NICHOLAS HALE Estate

STATE OF TENNESSEE
WASHINGTON COUNTY   We the Committee being appointed by Court April sessions 1827 to settle with Richard Hale administrator of the estate of Nicholas Hale Decd find the amount of the sale to be fifty six dollars and eighteen and one fourth cents-- We find the estate indebted fifty two dollars-- We find receipts for nineteen dollars paid by the administrator-- we certify this to be a true settlement
                                    Terry White
                                    John Gott

Clerks fees	1 56½
Amt of sale	56 18¼
Out of which sum the Committee consider that the Administrator is entitled to	20 --
	36 81¼
Sum of receipts	19 --

```
                Ballance in his hands                              17 81¼
Given under our hands this
9th day of July 1827                    Terry White
                                        John Gott
```

(p-68)   CATHERINE YOUNG Estate

STATE OF TENNESSEE }
WASHINGTON COUNTY } We the undersigned being appointed a Committee of
Court to make settlement with Joseph Miller administrator of the estate of
Catherine Young Decd do find that he stands Chargeable with the following
Sums (Viz) To amt of money recd of Joseph Bowman Guardean of Catherine
Young Decd (Viz)

```
        One note on Joshu Boren & John Hoss         $173 --
        One note on Jacob Miller                      72 --
        Also a legacy du Catherine Young Decd in the hands
         of Joseph Bowman                            127 67
                                Amt                  372 67
```
Out of which the administrator has paid the following
sums as pr vouchers
```
        Doctor David Nelson for medical attendance    3 --
        John A Welds for burying clothes             11 12½
        Joseph Bowman for a coffin                    4 --
        Court charges                                 2 17½
        Aron Finch attorney                           5 --
                                                     25 30
        leaving a ballance of                      $347 37
```
Out of which the administrator is entitled to 6 pr cent
```
for services amounting to                            22 36
                Making the neat ballance            325  1
```

This amt divided by 12 the number of heirs would make the sum $27 .8 cents
due to each.
Given under our hands & seals this 22d day of August 1827.
```
                                        Henry Hoss   (Seal)
                                        Jacob Ellis  (Seal)
                                        Richard Carr (Seal)
```

(p-69)   WILLIAM COLYAR ESTATE

STATE OF TENNESSEE }
WASHINGTON COUNTY } Whereas we John Stephenson & Daniel Berkley acting
Justices of the peace for the above County being a committee appointed to
settle with Alexander Colyar one of the administrators of the estate of
William Colyar Decd. And find that Alexander Colyar & William Colyar administrators of said estate has received of sd estate $856 13¼
appears from the vendue list and we find that Alexander Colyer has made the
following payments as by receipts appears--
```
        John G Eason                                 $62  8
        James S Johnstons receipt                    200 --
        David Deaderick receipt                       10 23¾
        Samuel Jacson receipt                         20 --
        Ballance of note to John Colyar              128  5
        Joseph Crouch receipt                          8 50
        Adam & Wm McKee 2 receipts                    61 10
```

WASHINGTON COUNTY, TENNESSEE

```
    John Brickers receipt                        429 --
    John Nelsons receipt for taxes                25 --
                                                 943 96¾
    October 26th, 1827
                                John Stephenson
                                Daniel Berkley J of the peace
```

He also produced the following papers that there is an acct exhibited that he Alexander Colyar is charged with $380.25 cts of the estate and the following certificate under written. I do hereby certify that the above is all that Alexander Colyar is accountable for of the estate of William Colyar Decd. this 11th February 1825
                                Signed Wm Colyar
And further that the ballence of the estate I have & will manage on my own responsibility each legatee refunding their proportionable part if any and further that Alexander Colyar is no further considered in the management of said estate
                                Signed Wm Colyar

(p-70)   JOHN GRIMSLEYS Estate

We the undersigned having been appointed Commissioners to settle with Magdaline Grimsley Administratrix of the estate of John Grimsley Decd have met this day at the house of Magdaline and having examined the papers & from the vouchers to us shewn we do find the following (Voz)

```
The amt of the personal estate from the vendue list    $331 15½
Out of which she has paid the following sums to wit
    A proven account to Terry White                    $5  1
    Do John Dogan                                          50
    Do Jessee Jones                                     8  5¾
    Do Richard White                                    4 15¼
    Do M & J Stephenson                                16 30
    Do Gabriel Morgan                                   2 37
    Do Wm Hall                                          1 50
    Do John English                                    10 58½
    Do Benjamin Rector                                  6 25
    Do Daniel Horton                                    1 25
    Do Nathan English                                   2 --
    Do John Brown                                       2 40
    Recpts Jonathan Jislen                              1 12½
    William Crawford                                    7 --
    John Ryland on Judgment                            24 50
    Saml Hunt tax for 1823 & 1824                       2 50
    Do  Do  Do for 1825 & 1826                          2 50
Notes paid to George Henderson                         10 62½
    To John Carder                                      7 --
Paid Samuel Carder an apprentice for his freedom in horse
ece                                                   100 --
Paid for burying expenses                              12 --
Paid to Amason Harold on note                          23 20
                                                      250 82½
```

Given under our hands & seals this 9th day of Nov. 1827
                        Archibald Glasscock (Seal)
                        John Stephenson   (Seal)
                        Terry White   (Seal)

SETTLEMENTS OF ESTATES, VOLUME 00, 1790-1841

(p-71)   JOHN HUNTS Estate

We the Committee appointed by the Court to settle with Benjamin Shipley Guardean of Samuel Hunt heir of John Hunt Decd do find that the said Benjamin Shipley is entitled to receive from the person or persons having charge of the estate of the said John Hunt Decd the sum of twenty eight dollars and thirty three cents by vouchers produced to us by the said Benjamin Shipley for books and schooling furnished the said Samuel Hunt heir of the said John Hunt Decd Given under our hands & seal this 14th day of January 1828
                        Richard Carr (Seal)
                        Nathan Shipley (Seal)
                        Jacob Ellis (Seal)

                    WILLIAM TYLERS Estate

January Sessions 1828
     We Jacob Brown Thomas C Patton and William Gillaland Justices of the peace appointed a Committee by Court to settle with William Bayles Guardean of Matilda Tyler Wm Tyler Phebe Tyler Minerva Tyler & Betsey Tyler minor children of Wm Tyler Decd, do find that said William Bayles had in his hands at the last settlement four thousand three hundred and twenty five dollars fifty three & three fourths cents $4325 53¾
     Interest on this sum two years   519 6
     Hire of Jenney & due for grain on 1st June 1826   95 12
     Interest on this till 1st January 1828   9 4
     Three dividends $12 each   36 --
     Ten months interest on the whole   1 50
     Making four thousand nine hundred & eighty six
       dollars thirty four and one fourth cents 4986 34¼
And we allow said Bayles the following sums services &c Viz
     Atto Fench Vs Chester and Blair $10 --
     Atto Powel in Virginia vs Wood   50 --
     Atto Blair vs Wilson Crouch & Nelson &c 150 --
                Amt carried over $210 --

(p-72)   WILLIAM TYLERS Estate

                Amt brought over $210 --
William Bayles for attending from Jellico to Jonesborough three times 28 days each time at $5 day   420 --
                                               $630 --

And after deducting which there yet remains under the controle of said William Bayles four thousand three hundred & fifty six dollars & thirty four and one fourth cents to the first of this month. $4356 34¼
Witness our hands and seals this 16th day of January 1828
                        Jacob Brown (Seal)
                        Thos C Patton (Seal)
                        Wm Gillaland (Seal)
                        Committee
Examined and approved by Court January
Term 1828
     William P Chester Chairman

WASHINGTON COUNTY, TENNESSEE

JOSIAH FRANKLIN Estate

April 17th 1828 Settled with Col Jacob Brown administrator and Guardean of Josiah Franklins estate total amt due the estate debt and Interest

$1086 41

To amt of a/c rendered & interest   150 93¾
                                           935 47¼

We the Commissioners appointed by the Court to settle with the above administrator and Guardean of Josiah Franklin Decd find that Col Jacob Brown is indebted to said estate nine hundred and thirty five dollars and forty seven cents as witness our hands & seals this 17th day of April 1828.

        William P Chester (Seal)
        Thomas C Patton (Seal)
        Wm Gillaland (Seal)

(p-73)   WILLIAM YOUNGS Estate

STATE OF TENNESSEE }
WASHINGTON COUNTY } We the undersigned being appointed a committee of Court to make settlement with James W Young as <u>Guerdean</u> of William Young his Brother do find that he has paid out the following sums on account of said William Young.

This sum paid costs of a Suit Mary Young agt Joseph Young & James Young as executors & Guardeans for Wm Young	$22 49
This sum paid John Parker for attendance	6 --
John Kennedy recpt for fees in said suit	25 --
William Youngs property on a/c expenses for deviding estate	7 50
Tax 1814	1 60¾
Do for 1815 direct tax	14 28½
Do for 1816	7 14¼
Do for 1815	1 49
Do for 1813	1 52½
Do for 1812	1 21
Tax for 1819	2 65
Tax for 1823	6 77½
Tax for 1820	3 70½
Tax for 1821	5 82
Tax for 1814 (direct tax)	5 92½
Tax for 1816 and 1817	6 50
Tax for 1826	6 77¼
Tax for 1822	6 73¼
Tax for 1818	3 73
William Youngs proportion of a Coffin	1 25
Alexander McBride Cryer	1 --
James R Isbell for medical attendance	6 --
James Sevier <u>receipt</u> for Court Charges	2 2½
Amt paid by J W Young to secure the title to the lands of Wm Young	113 --
William Youngs receipt	42 50
Joseph Godbeys receipt	21 50
William Wards receipt in full	13 --
John Davis recpt last will Mary Young Decd	7 --

(p-74)   WILLIAM YOUNGS Estate

    James Aekins receipt $6 16
    John McAlisters receipt   8 75
    Store bill paid   1 56
                                                       $360 15½

Which amt appears from the vouchers produced to us to be the sum that James W Young as Guardean of William Young has paid for his use for which he is intitled to credit--
Given under our hands & seals this 15th day of January 1828.
                                    Henry Hoss (Seal)
                                    Jacob Hartsell (Seal)
                                    Richard Carr (Seal)

Cr William Young by one horse $60 --
    By thirty two dollars & fifty cents property that
    was sold at his mothers sale at her decease   32 50
                                                       $92 50

Amt received by James W Young after reducting the credit out.

It will a ballance to James W Young of $267 65½

January Sessions 1828 allowence made by court   150 --

                        Henry Hoss   (Seal)
                        Jacob Hartsell (Seal)
                        Richard Carr (Seal)

(p-75)   HENRY POWELS Estate

STATE OF TENNESSEE
WASHINGTON COUNTY   Pursuant to an order of the County Court to us directed. We the undersigned met at the House of Henry Marsh Sr in the founty aforesaid for the purpose of settling with him as Guardean for the minor heirs of Henry Powell Decd and having called on said guardean for his papers he has produced the following (Viz)

    A Coppy of the last will and Testament of Henry Powell Decd from which it appears that the minor daughters were each to have when they came of age one good Bed and furniture a horse and saddle & three head of cattle to be paid them by the widdow in whoes hands the whole of the personal estate was left and that the sons were to have their legaces in land. He also produced the following receipts. June 17th 1826. Recd of Henry Marsh Guardean of Joanna Powell Daughter of Henry Powell now the wife of George Bayles the following articles to wit, One Horse one side saddle one Beauro one good Bed and furniture and three head of Cattle it being the full of a Legacy left her by her father which receit we both acknowledge
                        George   His   Bayles
                                x
                              Mark
                              Her
                    Joanna   x   Bayles
                        Mark

June 17th 1826. Recd of Henry Marsh Guardeen of Mary Powel daughter of Henry Powell Decd, now the wife of Hurtle W Atkinson the following articles to wit, One Horse one side saddle one Beauro one good bed and furniture and three head of cattle it being in full of a Legacy left her by her father which receit we both acknowledge--

        Hurtle W Atkinson
          his
        Mary x Atkinson
          Mark

And there being no witness to the foregoing receipts the

(p-76)   HENRY POWELS Estate

said Guardian brought forward Wm Campbell who declares he took a part of the property mentioned in the foregoing receipts to Greeneville Tennessee and saw Henry Marsh deliver to the persons mentioned in the foregoing recpts., and heard them acknowledge that was the Ballance of the property coming to them from the Estate of their father and saw them Execute their Receipts and all parties appeared well satisfied-- October 25th 1827 Then received of Henry Marsh my Guardian all my Interest in my fathers Estate both real and personal that has fallen in to his hands as Guardian
            Henry Powell

John Stephenson
And also a receipt of Jas Sevier for a copy the order of Settlement for fifty cents--
  Given under our hands and seals 7th January 1828
         Jno Link (Seal)
         John Stephenson (Seal)
         John Strain (Seal)

Jany Sessions 1828 approved by Court
        William P Chester

(p-77)   ELIHU EMBREE Estate

WASHINGTON COUNTY
STATE OF TENNESSEE   We the undersigned being appointed a committee of Court to make settlement with Elijah Embree executor of the estate of Elihu Embree Decd do find that he Justly stands chargable with the following

  To cash Recd for debts due said estate $178 54
  Proceeds sales of property   412 75
                591 29

And that he is entitled to a credit for the following sums as pr vouchers
  By amt of Elihu Embrees a/c with Messers E & E
  Embree at Pactoles pr Ledger 6 folio 301   535 59
  By bal on a/c with E & E Embree & Johnston at Jones-
  borough per ledger fo 98   160 8
  By bal on a/c with E & E Embree Jonesboro store Book
  B fo 1   1476 70
  By this sum paid Mr McKee   9 81
  By amt sundry notes and accounts due by $2182 18
  Decd as pr vouchers exhibited as follows
  Acct of E Tetris Hartsell   40 --
  Doctor Gibson   64 88
  Doc Delaney   12 --
  A. C. Clifton   1 50
  D Deaderick   60 --
  John B Estes   24 25
  Walter Hale   23 50

Mrs E Stephenson	$20	--
Doctor David Nelson	58	--
Jesse M Thompson	1	50
John McCorcle	23	25
R Gray	65	--
Thomas Barnes	2	66
Recpts-- Recpt-- Esther Egemon recpt	96	50
Cox and Harris	457	56

(p-78)   ELIHU EMBREES Estate

Notes	To F D Wearer	153	42
	John Clock	156	88
	John Gott	49	--
	John Peters	140	5
		$1449	95

To amt paid by Elijah Embree for tuetion & clothing		
the heirs of Elihu Embree Decd as pr account	817	46
Cr by amt brought over	2182	18
	4449	59
From 14th Decr 1820 to Jan 1st 1828 Bal due	3858	29
Amt remaining on acct in favour of the Executors	3858	29

Given under our hands & seals this 12th day of January 1828
                               Nathan Shipley   J P (Seal)
                               Henry Hoss   J P (Seal)
                               Saml Greer   J P (Seal)

   In the foregoing account no charge was exhibited to us for boarding the minor heirs of the Decd by the executor
                               Nathan Shipley   J P (Seal)
                               Henry Hoss   J P (Seal)
                               Saml Greer   J P (Seal)

January Session 1828
    Approved by Court

                               Daniel Berkley Cha potem

(p-79)   SAMUEL TEMPLIN Estate

August Sessions 1813
    We the Committee appointed by Court to settle with the administrators of the estate of Samuel Templin Decd do hereby certify that we find by the amount of sales of said Estate Bonds Notes and other accounts amounting to two thousand and forty four dollars & thirty seven cents and that the vouchers filed by said administrators amounts to one thousand three hundred and twenty one dollars sixty five cents and that there is the sum of 977 dollars and 88 cents secured by said administrators for the use of said estate as the annexed schedule sheweth and that we make the following allowance to be paid out of the aforesaid estate To Priscella Cox formerly Priscilla Templin the sum of 389 dollars for her services as administratrix and for support & Schooling the children of said Templin Decd also to the said Priscella Cox the sum of 77 dollars and seventy one cents for expenditures to the use of said estate--
    To John McAlister for services performed as administrator the sum of 34 dollars--

To James Deakins for Services performed as administrator the sum of 34 dollars-- All of which is respectfully submitted
Given under our hands this 4th day of May 1813.
Nathan Shipley
Jacob Brown
Wm Bayles

We the Said Committee also find that the said Priscella Cox late Templin has taken from the personal property of said estate and applies to her private use the sum of six hundred and thirty four dollars and sixty six cents out of which the Committee has allowed her for her own support and that of her children for the 5 years ending on the first of May 1813 the sum of three hundred and eighty nine dollars leaving a sum still in her hands of two hundred and forty five dollars & sixty six cents for which she is accountable to the said heirs-- The sum then on hand is seven hundred and thirty two dollars and 22 cents-- But the said Samuel in his lifetime became indebted to his father now living in the State of Maryland who holds his bond for about four hundred dollars bearing interest from the date

(p-80)   SAMUEL TEMPLINS Estate

which the old man has informed the late Mrs Templin now Cox that he intends to leave as a legacy to the children of the said Samuel but as his mind may change and as the bond is still in his hands the Committee are of Opinion that a fund should be set apart expressly for the purpose of Cancelling that bond if it should alternately be presented for payment-- if that should be proper the sum then left unappopriated would be about three hundred and thirty two dollars which the Committee thinks ought to be placed in the hands of those who may be Guardeans of said Children for their use & benefit with the interest accruing there on this Committee further represents that the rents arising out of the real property belonging to said estate amounts to one hundred and forty dollars pr anm-- being the terms on which it is now rented for the ensuing five years & they believe it ought to rent for that sum untill the children become of lawfull age by which time the funds in the hands of the Guardean would be at least two Thousand eight or nine hundred dollars including what the Court may allow for said Mrs Cox right of dower and the support of the sd children, the care & management of the said real property is also of considerable importance and ought to be regarded as such The said Committee therefore submits the property of the Court requiring from those offering as Guardeans of said Children good freehold security clear and free from incumberance to the amount of four thousand dollars binding them and their heirs for the true account and faithfull performance of that trust.

Given under hands this 4th day of August 1813
Nathan Shipley
Wm Bayles
Jacob Brown

(p-81).   MATILDA & ELIZA J HAIRS Estate

STATE OF TENNESSEE }   October Sessions
WASHINGTON COUNTY }   1828

I received as Guardean of Matilda & Eliza Jane Hair forty six acrs of land which he sold for two hundred and fifty dollars recd also twenty six dollars from David Russell executor of the estate of David

Russell Rec'd of David Russell administrator of Benjamin Russell Dec'd Thirty eight dollars and twenty three cents and also eighteen dollars and ninety cents makeing in the whole three hundred and thirty three dollars & thirteen cents which sd Guardean has in his hands ready to account for at any time when called on this Guardean further states that his said Wards are his own children and that he has said children in his care and is raising and schooling of them, sworn in Open Court at October sessions 1828 & ordered by Court to be recorded

        Isaac Hair

HANNAH E MCCARDELS Estate

Daniel Salts Guardean for Hannah E McCardell Reports that he has in hands fifty dollars of the property of his Ward for which he is responsible and can pay over as his ward requires it he further reports that said ward lives with him and he supports her with such necessaries as she needs
13th October 1828

        Daniel Salts
        Guardean

Sworn to in open Court at October Session 1828 & ordered by Court to be recorded--

AMAND JANE RUSSELL Estate

James Russell Guardian of Amanda Jane Russell Reports as follows in relation to his Guardeanship. Recevd as Guardean October 8th 1827 on a note of hand on Doctor Daniel Kenney five $5 00 November 14th 1827 of Isaac Hair $5 00 he further reports that according to the will of William Russell the rent of a certain tract of land left to his Ward and the hire of a negroe girl should be applied to said wards support and that Jane Allison the Grand mother of said ward supports her in consideration of said rent & hire he also reports he received as rent of a certain other part of a tract of land fifteen bushels of Oats at 20 cents &

(p-82)   AMANDA JANE RUSSELLS Estate

five bushells of wheat at 50 cents after deducting expenses of repairing the place rented. all which is respectfully submited & sworn to in open Court October Sessions
1828 & ordered by   James Russell
the Court to be recorded

DICEY HUNT Estate

Amount of property Rec'd of the estate of Uriah Hunt Decd that Jessee Hunt recd as Guardean of Dicey Hunt May 3d 1827 on Gray mare one yearling Colt one cow and calf a& red heifer 1 spinning wheel 153 bushels of corn 16th January 1828 one bushel of rye 3 doz wheat-- October 1825 1 Bureau $22 75 April 9th 1827/in Eason Store Novr 9 1827 $60 Do in Gammons Store $60 for an Order on Elijah Embree $5.0 to Benjamin Rector $5 -- October 8th to 1 bed
at $8 --
$8-0 pr order to John Eason Store   8 --
All the rent grain of Wm Hunt Decd plantation up $110 75
to the present date July 14th 1828. 1 bed & furniture 1 yearling colt--

Recepts of Dicey Hunt other wise Dicey Squibb   May 3d 1827
Recept Do 3d May 1827 Recpt Do May 3d 1827 Recpt Do 16 Jany 1828 Recpt Do
October 13th 1828 Receipt Do May 3d 1827 $22 75 Recpt Do $7 13 October 13
1828 Recpt Do $60 Novr 9th 1827 Recpt Do $5 December 23d 1826 Recpt Do $8
October 8th 1826 Recpt Do $8 June 2d 1827 Recpt Do July 14th 1820 Recpt May
3d 1827 Recpt May 3d 1827 Recpt from Clerk $1 75
$112 50

We the Committee appointed to settle with Jessee Hunt Guardean for
Dicey Hunt do find that the above account as charged is settled by the above
receipts and that Jessee Hunt has over paid $1 75 cents 14th October 1828
Daniel Barkley
William P Chester

(p-83)   ADAM WATTENBERGER Estate

STATE OF TENNESSEE }
WASHINGTON COUNTY } Persuant to an order of the Court of pleas & quarter
Sessions of said County dated July Sessions 1828 and to us the undersigned
directed to settle with the executors of the estate of Adam Wattenberger
Decd we met in Leesburgh at the house of Frederick Davault on the 16th August 1828 and after calling on the executors for their papers Concerning the
estate the produced the amount of a sale bill in the words & figures following Marked (A) Amount of the sale of personal property of Adam Wattenberger
Decd returned by the executors of said estate--

Cash in hand $3 85¼
notes on hand   247 99
To Fencelers note   16¾
                            $252 1

STATE OF TENNESSEE }
WASHINGTON COUNTY } I James Sevier Clerk of the Court of pleas &c for
said County do hereby certify the foregoing to be the amount of the sale of
the personal property of Adam Wattenberger Decd as appears from the Inventory in file in my office Given under my hand at office this 25th July 1828
James Sevier Clerk
By Saml Greer D C

Frederick Fencelers Part produced to us the following vouchers in words and
figures following
    No 1   A Judgment against the estate & Wm and Adam Werttenberger
Decd Security for four dollars twelve & a half cents Cost to Hiram Glass
$4 12½
    No 2   4th August 1825 Recd of Frederick Finceler one dollar and
eighty cents for expences of recording will & other expences of Adam Wattenberger   1 80
James Sevier clk
    No 3   Recd of Frederick Fenceler one dollar on account of Adam Wattenberger for going with said Fenceler on business of said Wattenberger 16th
Augt 1828   1 00
    No 4   Recwd of Frederick Finceler executor of Adam Wattenberger
Decd four dollars thirty two & a half cents in full of all debts & costs
that Hiram Glass recovered against Wm Wattenberger & Adam Wattenberger Decd
Security   4 32½
                                                                       11 24½
18th October 1824 Recd by me 19th August 1825 Wm Dosser Constl--

No 5   July 29th 1825 Recd of Frederick Fenceler one dollar the Amt of my
bill for crying Adam Wattenberger Decd sale Jno/Guinn $1 --
No 6   Recd of Frederick Fenceler executor of Adam Wattenberger Decd the
amount   (p-84)   ADAM WATTENBERGERS Estate of taxes due on Wattenberger
estate for the year 1826 three dollars thirty two & three fourth cents
John Bricker D S $3 32¾
No 7   Recd of Frederick Finuler eight dollars twenty one cents the
amount of tax due from the estate of Adam Wattenberger Decd for the years
1824 & 1825   8 21
No 8   August 15th 1826 Frederick Finuler executor of Adam Wattenberger
Decd and the estate of Wattenberger is due two dollars and sixty cents
                                                         2 60
STATE OF TENNESSEE
WASHINGTON COUNTY   Personally appeared before me Jno Link one of the
Justices of said County Saml Overholster & made oath that the above account
of two dollars & sixty cents is Justly due given under my hand & seal the
day & date above written
                        Saml Overholster (Seal)
Test
John Link Justice of the peace
No 9   Ten days after date I promise to pay Joseph McLin two dollars for
value recd. of him this 7th August 1827   2 --
Saml his McKehen (seal)
      x
    Mark
No 10   Recd of Frederick Fenuler administrator of the estate of Adam
Wattenberger Decd six dollar & thirteen cents in full of a small account &
ballance of a note paid by him for his son Peter August 4th 1828
                                                         6 13
                        Samuel Maclin
No 11   Jonesborough 13th 1826 Frederick Finuler bought for the widow Wattenberger of John A Wilds & Co 6 lb Coffee @ 2/   2 --
No 12   Mr Frederick Fenceler please to pay unto D & Ebenezer Berkley
seven dollars the amount of making Coffin for Adam Wattenberger by yourself
and oblidge yours &c Leeroy Campbell   7 --
                                                         $43 51½
No 13   Recd of Frederick Fenevler executor of Adam Wattenberger Decd
twelve & a half cents 4th March 1827 Recd by me Frederick Davault
                                                         .12½
No 14   Recd of Frederick Fenicler twenty nine dollars & thirty one cents
the amount of costs of an execution together with the principle fees in the
suit Frederick Fenceler & Christian Zetty against Wm P Chester & others
16th March 1827-- John Bricker DS   29 31
No 15   Frederick Finceler settled to George Pursell one side of
bridle leather for Adam Wattenberger Sixteen shillings. George Purcell
                                                         2 66 2/3
         Frederick Fenulers amount $75 61¼

(p-85)   ADAM WATTENBERGERS Estate

No 1   Christian Zettey, executor vouchers--
   Recd of Christian Zetty & Frederick Fenuler executors of Adam Watten-
berger Decd seventy nine cents in full of an account that David Deaderick
had against him Sept 11th 1826 & costs fifty cents   79
Wm Dosser Constl.   50
No 2   Mr Frederick Finuler -- Sir please to let the barer hereof Joseph
McLin have three dollars & fifty cents on my account & this shall be your

recpt for the same & in so doing you will oblidge yrs $3 50
                                    R W Strain
No 3   Adam Wattenberger in account with S G Chester
ballance.   1 18¾
STATE OF TENNESSEE }
WASHINGTON COUNTY } This day came S. G. Chester and made oath that the
above account is Just to the best of his knowledge. Decr 24th 1825.
                                    John Patton--
No 4   Recd of Christian Zetty Senr executor of Adam Wattenberger
estate one twenty dollar saddle agreeable to the will this 9th July
1828--   Test   her   20 --
Sol Wattenberger   Sarah x Wattenberger
Charles Browning   mark
                                                    $25 97¾
No 5   Recd of Christian Zetty & Frederick Finuler executors of Adam Wattenberger Decd seventy two dollars & fifty cents for suit in equity against John Aikens suit in County & circuit vs Wm P Chester & others suit in County Court vs Wm P Chester & various small matters with relation to the estate this sum advanced to me by John Kennedy to whome it was refered by said Zetty & myself October 20th 1827 Jas P Taylor   72 50
No 6   July 30th 1825 Recd of Christian Zetty Senr one dollar & fifty cents for writing performed on account of the estate of A Wattenberger Dedd   Received by me Augustus Grahl   1 50
No 7   Recd of Christian Zetty four dollars & thirty seven cents in full of debt & costs O B Ross recovered against Zetty & Finvler executors of A Wattenberger Decd before Saml Greer esqr Octr 20th 1827 Jno Ryland
Shff   4 37
No 8   Recd 4th Aug 1828 of Christian Zetty executor of Adam Wattenberger Decd two dollars & fifty cents in full of my fees of an appeal in the County Court of Washington Wattenberger executors vs Joseph Hinkle 2 50
                                    John Kennedy
No 9   Recd 1st March 1828 of Christian Zetty executor of Adam Wattenberger

(p-86)   ADAM WATTENBERGERS Estate

Decd twelve dollars & fifty cents for Jessee Paynes answer and attending to the suit in equity in the circuit Court of Washington County wherein Thos McGinnis wife & others are plffs & said Payne & Wattenberger executors are Defts   Jno Kennedy $12 50
No 10   Recd of Frederick Finuler & Christian Zettey twenty eight dollars seventy eight cents being the amount of a Judgment Samuel Stormer received before Wm P Chester against Frederick Finuler with interest & costs
                                                    28 78
Test Jno Blair   Jno Stormer
No 11   Wm P Chester proven account before Jessee Payne Wm P Chester
                                                    14 8 1/3
                                                    $162 21
No 12   Recd of Christian Zetty seventy five cents for a search and a copy of Robert Fawbush estate and for search of a will of said Fawbush 7th July 1826   75
E G Sevier D C
No 13   Joseph McLin proven account   3 19¾
No 14   Solomon Wattenbergers receipt for schooling   8 --
No 15   Recd of Christian Zetty excr of Adam Wattenbergers estate ten dollars for Ironing the running geers of a waggon November 5th 1827 Wm Smith Jur   10 --

No 16   Recd of Christian Zetty seventy four pounds of Iron at six & a fourth cents per pound being the ballance due me from Wattenbergers estate for schooling Sepr 2d 1826   Allen H Mathis   4 62½
No 17   Wm Crookshanks proven account   33 1/3
No 18   Recd of Frederick Finuler & Christian Zetty admrs of A Wattenberger Decd sixty two & a half cents for recording an Inventory January 5th 1828   Jas Sevier Clk by Saml Greer D C
                                                                      62½
No 19   Michael Crouse proven account   2 32
No 20   James Gray & James Cowans receipt   197 66
No 21   Recd of Christian Zetty & Frederick Finuler executors of A Wattenberger Decd thirteen dollars for a house plank part that I furnished on the plantation of P Wattenberger for the use of a tenant Recd July 28th 1828 by me   13 --
Test Jno Link   Jacob Whistler
No 22   Recd of Christian Zetty one dollar as executor of Adam Wattenberger as fees of office July 25 1828   1 --
                     Jas Sevier Clk
                     By Saml Greer D C

(p-87)   ADAM WATTENBARGERS Estate

No 23   Recd of Christian Zetty Senr execur of A Wattenberger Decd a twenty dollar saddle agreeable to the will,   20 --
Elizabeth x Wattenberger
Test Solomon Wattenberger   423 22
Charles Browning
No 24   Recd of Christian Zetty executor of A Wattenberger Decd three dollars fifty six the amount of the tax due from the estate of A Wattenberger Decd for the year 1827   Jno Bricker D S   3 56
No 25   Samuel B Cunningham proven account   4 50
No 26   April 22d 1828 Recd of Zetty & F Finuler executors of A Wattenberger Decd four dollars cash in part of my demand against them for tuition   Wm McPheters   4 --
No 27   Mathew Stephenson & John Stephenson proven
account   23 37
No 28   Notes paid to M & Jno Stephenson Peter Wattenberger note 4th Sepr 1827 principal & interest   28 --
No 29   David Mitchell Do   20 47
No 30   David Mitchell ballance Do   3 4
No 31   John Ryland note Do   7 88
No 32   M & Jno Stephenson Do   15 16
No 33   John Doane Do notes on the above   6 55
No 34   Jacob Wattenberger ballance of a note 25th
         Octbr 1827   45 71
No 35   Martha Cunningham note 14th Jany 1828   62 48
No 36   Henry Slyger note of twenty five dollars in
         silver at six per cent & interest discount
         paid 1st Decbr 1827   32 13
No 37   One day after date we or either of us promises to pay Joseph Hinkle Guardean of Polly Faubush the sum of   105 61½
one hundred and thirteen dollars & eighty cents for value recd 11th July 1826 interest to ninth of April 1827 tell paid
                     Christian Zetty
                     Frederick Finuler
No 38   Christean Zetty bought of M & Jno Stephenson August 20th 1828 59 lb of bacon for widow Elizabeth Wattenberger & family at 6d   4 32½

Recd of Christian Zetty excetr of A Wattenber in full 4 32½
M & Jno Stephenson   790 51¾

(p-88)   ADAM WATTENBERGERS Estate

         Amt Brot over   790 51¾
No 39   Recd of Christian Zetty executor of A Wattenberger Decd the sum
of four dollars & fifty cents for the use of the widow Elizabeth Wattenber-
ger August 21st 1828   her   4 50
                  Elizabeth x Wattenberger
Test Solomon Wattenberger   mark
No 40   Recd of Christean Zetty & F Finuler executors of the Estate of A
Wattenberger Decd seven dollars & fifty seven cents for repairs done on the
plantation of the said Wattenbarger 20th Sepr 1828 Recd by me Solomon
Wattenberger   7 57
Test Christian Zetty Jr
Adam Wattenberger
No 41   Recd of Christean Zetty admr of A Wattenberger Decd two dollars
& fifty cents my fee for money settlement with Commissioners of the County
Court & advance & Sepr 9th 1828   2 50
                  Jas P Taylor
No 42   1828 Sepr 11th Recd of C Zetty & F Finuler executors of A Watten-
berger twenty five dollars my fee for defending the suit in equity of Thos
McGinnis against them as admrs aforesaid for which I gave them a former
recpt & which is said to be lost   25 --
                  Jno Blair
No 43 $70 Recd of Christean Zetty & F Finuler executors of A Wattenber-
ger Decd seventy dollars the full amount for building a barn on the planta-
tion of the heirs of the above named Wattenberger Decd 29th Sepr 1828
                                                          70 --
Danl Simmerman
Test Christian Zetty Jr
No 44 $100 Recd of Christian Zetty & F Fenuler executors of A Wattenber-
ger Decd one hundred dollars of the extra part of my portion according to
the will 2d October 1828   100 --
                  Solomon Wattenberger $1000 8¾
Test Christean Zetty Jr
Saml Holms

STATE OF TENNESSEE |
Washington County | We the undersigned Commissioners have examined the
papers produced to us by the executors of Adam Wattenberger Decd.

(p-89)   ADAM WATTENBERGERS Estate

and find them charged with the Inventory two hundred and fifty two dollars
and one cent and find that Frederick Fenceler one of the executors produced
to us vouchers to the amount of seventy five dollars sixty one & one fourth
cent and Christian Zetty produced to us vouchers for money that he has paid
out to the amount of one thousand dollars eight & three fourth cents and
find that they have paid out eight hundred and twenty three dollars sixty
nine cents more than we find them charged with. Given under our hands &
seals 13th October 1828 filed October 1828
                                  John Link (Seal)
                                  Wm Wilson (Seal)

DAVID MITCHELLS Estate

Washington County Tennessee

We the Committee appointed by the Court to settle with the executor of David Mitchell Decd do certify that we proceeded on the settlement of said estate on the 16th October 1828 and find the said executor of estate chargeable with the sum of three hundred and sixty six dollars & sixty three cents & one halff cents which sum of property it appears come into his hands (to wit) three hundred & eighty nine dollars & fifty eight cents.

1	Samuel B Cunningham Recpt proven	$30 --
2	Thomas Taylor proven account on recpt	6 --
3	John Mitchell proven account	22 50
4	Daniel Commin probate	15 --
5	Polly Mitchell recpt for	70 --
6	David Mitchell note	27 25
7	William P Chester proven account on recpt	11 54
8	William Dosser proven account	2 50
9	William P Chesters due bill	3 60
10	David Mitchell note to Wm Colyar	2 66½
11	Elijah Embree Recpt	51 12½
12	Thos J Brown probate	51 25
13	William Vance probate	2 75
14	David Mitchels note to Archl McGlaughlin	36 --
15	James Sevier recpt	1 87½
16	Thomas Browns proven account	32 --
		$366 5½

(p-90) DAVID MITCHELLS Estate

Amt Brot over $366 5½

We the Committee appointed to settle with the executor find him Chargeable with the sum of twenty three dollars & sixty three & one half cents and no more which is submitted to Court--- Given under our hands & filed at October 1828

        Wm Colyar (Seal)
        Jacob Hartsell (Seal)
        Jacob Hunter (Seal)

SARAH HUNT SAMUEL HUNT & MARIA HUNT Estate

STATE OF TENNESSEE }
WASHINGTON COUNTY } George Crouch states that he has recd as Guardian of Sarah Hunt Samuel Hunt & Maria Hunt four hundred & fifty nine dollars thirty one cents the said George Crouch states he has that much in his hands at the time and which he has ready pay over at any time he may be requested this 12 day of January 1829 $459 31

Sworn to in open Court Jany sessions 1829 filed & ordered to be recorded
        George Crouch Guardean

MARY FAWBUSH Estate

STATE OF TENNESSEE }
WASHINGTON COUNTY } January Sessions 1829. Joseph Hinkle Guardean of Mary Fawbush he states that one note came into his hands on Christian Zetty & Frederick Finuler amounting to one hundred & thirteen dollars & eighty

cents dated the 11th day of July 1826 calculating the interest up to this time amounts to $129 95 in the whole that came into my hands of said estate a Guardean of Mary Fawbush Seventy nine dollars & ninety five cents I have paid & laid out and expended for her use leaving a ballance in her favour of fifty dollars which I have and am ready to account for at any time when called on this 14th day of January 1829

              Joseph Hinkle Guardean

January Sessions 1829
Sworn to in open Court -- filed & ordered to be recorded.

(p-91)   WILLIAM TYLERS Estate

At October term 1828 I reported that there was nine hundred & eighty six dollars & forty two cents in my hands as Guardean of Wm Tyler a minor heir of Wm Tyler Decd. $986 42

Interest on that amount up to this date is	14 79
My account for services rendered & money expended	1001 21
To one day when appointed Guardean at July term 1828	1 --
To one day to make report October term 1828	1 --
To one day to make Settlement January term 1829	1 --
To fifty cents paid clerk for Guardean bond	50
	3 50

At January sessions 1829 there is in my hands belonging to said heir nine hundred and ninety seven dollars and seventy one cents. January 12th sworn to in open Court filed and ordered to be recorded

               1001 21
                3 50
               997 71

         E L Mathes Guardean

         JOHN BAYLES Estate

STATE OF TENNESSEE
WASHINGTON COUNTY   Pursuant to an order of Court of said County dated January sessions 1829 and to us the undersigned directed to settle with Rees Bayles serving executor of the estate of John Bayles Decd. we met in Jonesboro 14th of January 1829 and after examening all papers we find the

executor charged with	$417 76
and produced vouchers to the amount of	502 78¾
	417 76
	85 2¾
commission for executor	25 33
	$110 35¾

And find that the executor has paid out eighty five dollars & two & three fourths cents more than we find him charged with. Given under our hand fourteenth of January 1829 to which at Commission twenty five dollars & thirty three cents makes in all one hundred & ten dollars thirty five & three fourth cents--
filed July Sessions 1829 & ordered to
be recorded   Jno Link
                  Daniel Berkley
                  Hes Bayles
                  Committee

SETTLEMENTS OF ESTATES, VOLUME 00, 1790-1841

(p-92) WILLIAM TYLERS HEIRS Estate

William Bayles who has here to fore been the Guardean of Milenda Tyler Wm
Tyler Phebee Tyler Minerva Tyler and Betsey Tyler five of the minor children
of William Tyler Decd do find that said William Bayles had in his hands on
the 14th of October last four thousand four hundred & thirty eight dollars
ninety four & three fourth cents. $4438 94¾
and said Bayles on the said 14th Oct 1828 paid Ebenezer
L Mathes nine hundred & eighty six dollars & forty two
cents   986 42
And that said Bayles is entitled to eleven days in traveling and making said settlement at two dollars pr day &
sixty two and a half cents paid the clerk in all amounting to   22 62½
                                                         $1009 4½

which with the sum paid Mathis make one thousand and
nine dollars & four and a half cents leaving a ballance
in the hands of said Bayles of three thousand four hundred & twenty nine dollars ninety & one fourth cents   3429 90¼
Interest on this till 14th Instant   51 44¾
Making the sum of three thousand four hundred & eighty one
dollars and thirty five cents $3481 35
William Bayles allowed for twelve days attending to make
this settlement & going home at $2 per day & sixty two and
a half cents to pay the clerk for recording this   24 --
settlement   62½
                                                         $3456 72½

Which sums when deducted from the foregoing leaves in
the hands or under the Controle of said Wm Bayles three
thousand four hundred and fifty six dollars & seventy two
& a half cents for Milinda Tyler Phebee Tyler Minerva &
Betsey Tyler the four minor children of William Tyler Decd.
                                    Wm Bayles
January 12th 1829   Sworn to in open Court filed & ordered to be recorded.

(p-93)   CYRUS BROYLES Estate

STATE OF TENNESSEE   )
WASHINGTON COUNTY   )   Pursuant to an order of County Court dated October
Sessions 1828 and to us the undersigned diredted to settle with Adam Broyles
administrator of Cyrus Broyles Decd. and after calling on the administrator
for his papers he produced to us a copy of the sale bill & Inventory in the
words & figures following
     Return of Inventory amount $407 84
     Amount of notes returned good to be   149 70
     Two notes out of the above amounting to $99 70   557 54
     That was returned as good that cannot be collected 99 70
Debts returned desperate to be $457 84
On Wm Vaught for $600 00
On Joshua Blackburn   11 25
On Thomas D Broyles   24 50
On Thomas D Broyles   8 00
                    (643 75   desperate   643 75
And produced to us vouchers in words & figures following
No 1 one day after date I promise to pay Adam Broyles seventy
five dollars in current money for value recd. witness my   75 --

WASHINGTON COUNTY, TENNESSEE

```
hand seal February 28th 1826            his
                                 Cyrus ⊥ Broyles  (Seal)
                                        mark
Test James T Broyles
```

No 2   One day after date I promise to pay Adam Broyles
seventeen dollars & fifty eight & a half cents for value $17 58½
recd. witness my hand and seal March 6th 1824
                                      his
Test Daniel Stout   Cyrus x Broyles
                                      mark

No 3   Adam Broyles proven account against the estate   90 4
No 4   William Pattons proven account Do   8 87½
No 5   Recd of Adam Broyles twelve dollars in full for
making a coffin for Cyrus Broyles Decd I say recd by me   12 --
december 13th 1826   Jessee McGinnis $203 50
Test Jacob Kepple
No 6   James T Broyles proven account   5 25
No 7   James P Taylors recpt   6 --
No 8   Recd of Adam Broyles admr of the estate of Cyrus
Broyles Decd two dollars in full for my services as clerk   2 --
at the sale of the estate of sd Broyles Decd. by me 5th
January 1829
                              David Shields

(p-94)   CYRUS BROYLES Estate

No 9   Recd of Adam Broyles admr of Cyrus Broyles Decd
three dollars for drawing Inventory and crying sale two
days Received by me   3 --
this 6th January 1829   Wm Wilson
No 10   John Stouts proven account   7 33 1/3
No 11   Attached to the Copy of the Inventory for whiskey
& Brandy for sale   8 37½
No 12   Recd of Adam Broyles admr of Cyrus Broyles Decd
one dollar & twenty five cents for services rendered as
one of the Committee in settling the estate of Cyrus Broyles
Decd 6th Jany 1829   Jno Link   1 25
No 13   Recd of Adam Broyles admr of Cyrus Broyles Decd one
dollar for services rendered as one of the Committee in
settling the estate the estate of Cyrus Broyles Decd 6th
Jany 1829   Wm Gillaland   1 --
No 14   Recd of Adam Broyles admr of Cyrus Broyles Decd
one dollar for services rendered as one of the Committee in
Settling the estate of Cyrus Broyles Decd Wm Wilson   1 --
No 15   12th Jany 1829 Recd of Adam Broyles admr of Cyrus Broyles
decd the sum of two dollars & forty cents for cost on said   2 40
administration   James Sevier Clk $240 11

    We the undersigned Committee being appointed by Court to settle with
Adam Broyles admr of Cyrus Broyles Decd find him charged by the Inventory
                                                             $407 84
with the sum of notes returned to the amount   149 70
And two notes of the above returned as good by the   557 84
admr one on Tobias Broyles & one on Daniel Broyles to the
amount of $99 70 has since found out by the admr cannot   99 70

```
be collected.                                              $457 84
And find him charged with four hundred & fifty seven dollars
& eighty four cents and has produced vouchers to the amount
of two hundred and forty dollars and eleven cents          240 11
            In his hands                                   217 74
Given under our hands 12th January 1829
                            Wm Wilson     |
                            Wm Gilliland  |  Committee
                            Jno Link      |
```

Ordered by Court that Adam Broyles be allowed five per cent on $457 84 which will be $22 82. Year all-- William P Chester Cha filed at January sessions 1829 & ordered to be recorded

(p-95)   ELIZABETH BROWNS Estate

STATE OF TENNESSEE |
WASHINGTON COUNTY | May Sessions 1814 In persuance of an order of Court made & dated the above term we the undersigned Subscribers being appointed Commissioners to settle with Jacob Brown Senr administrator of the estate of Elizabeth Brown Decd do report & say that agreeable to vouchers as follows

	D	Cents	Mills
No 1	10	57	6
No 2	10	60	
No 3	4	16	3
No 4	9		
No 5		75	
	35	8	9
No 6 allowances & expenditures of said estate amounting to		9	96	
	45	5	9
And we find that the amount of the whole estate on examination is	51	4	7
The amount of debt expenditures &c	45	5	9
The amount of the whole	5	8	8

These are to certify that the above statement is just and true agreeable to the vouchers and Documents handed to us Given under our hands this 4th day of May 1814 filed May sessions 1814
```
                            Hy King      |
                            Wm Bayles    | Comt
                            John Patton  |
```

SUSANNAH JOHNSTON Estate

Agreeable to an order of Court to us directed we David Willson & John Strain (John Stephenson being absent) have proceeded to Settle with Thomas McMakin administrator of the estate of Susannah Johnson Decd,and having examined the documents belonging to said estate & ballance the debts & credits we find that said McMackin remains indebted to the said estate the sum of six dollars & forty eight cents the Court charges not settled for as there was no account came forward what said charges to certified by us the 13th day of January 1821
filed at January sessions 1821   David Wilson
                                        John Strain

(p-96)   MICHAEL WOODS Estate

1808   Michael Woods Jr admr of the estate of Michael Woods Decd of Washington County prays allowances for the following discharges

			D	C
Feb	15th	Paid William Brown see probate	4	--
Nov	18	Paid William Patton see note & receipt	33	75
		Paid Rebecca Moore see probate & recpt	3	56
		Paid William Patton see probate & recpt	4	--
	20	Paid Adam Harmon se probate & recpt	2	33
	21	Paid Jonathan Collom see probate & recpt	7	36
		Paid Thomas Gillispie see probate & recpt	4	--
		Paid Joseph Brown Sheff tax see recpt	5	97½
Dec	2	Paid Daniel Findley see probate & recpt	2	50
1809				
Jany	16	Paid Peter Earnest see note & recpt	106	25
	18	Paid Barnes Clark see probate & recpt		50
	19	Paid Wm P Chester Doctor see probate & recpt	5	--
	13	Paid William Miller see probate & recpt	6	7
Feby	15	Paid Jacob Gann see probate & recpt	3	50
	16	Paid John Clark see probate & recpt	23	9
		Paid Do Do See note & recpt	26	25
	17	Paid David Deaderick & Co See probate & recpt	72	40
		Paid Samuel Doak (Revd) see probate & recpt	4	--
		Paid Samuel Blackburn see probate & recpt	1	0-
		Paid James Miller see probate & recpt	2	--
		Paid Benjamin Blackburn see probate & recpt	9	84½
		Paid James Gray by the hands of Wm Gillaland see probate Recpt	1	38
	21	Paid Claudias Bustard see probate & recpt	6	4
Mar	1	Paid William Brown see note & recpt	436	--
Aug	8	Paid Ira Green see recpt	10	--
			$781	56

We the committee appointed by Court to Settle with Michael Woods administrator of Michael Woods Decd have examined his vouchers and find he has paid the amount of Seven hundred and eighty one dollars fifty six cents but as he is not ready for final Settlement we report this for February session 1810

                Wm Mitchell
                Wm Bayles
                Hy King

(p-97)   MICHAEL WOODS Estate

November session 1812 The within Committee being reappointed progress on Settlement & find $85 34 as shall appear by file No 5 of vouchers
                $85 34

Also expenditures as Shall appear by recpt in file No 6
                123 97½

Also allowances for time Spent during the time of administration which will appear by bill No 7
                115 --

Also report a final settlement and the ballance of the estate as shall appear by Inventory to be
                3491 36¼

filed at November Sessions 1812

                         Wm Mitchell
                         Wm Bayles   Committee
                         Hy King

ABIGAIL JOB Estate

STATE OF TENNESSEE

Where as the worshipfull Court of pleas & quarter sessions of Washington County at the January term 1822 Ordered and appointed James W Young and Henry King two of the acting Justices of the peace in & for said County of Washington to be a committee to settle with Joshua Job executor of Abigail Job Decd In persuance there of we the said James W Young & Henry King attended at the house of Abraham Job in said County on Saturday the Sixteenth of February A D 1822 and then & there made the following Settlement with Joshua Jobe the afforesaid executor--

The amount on the Inventory	$314 85
John A Aikens, Note (not returned with the inventory but now settled for by the afforesaid executor	122 --
Whole amount	436 85
Cash Disbursed, To Thomas P Ensor in full as pr voucher	347 47
Abraham Job Recpt on a note of hand for	20 --
James P Taylors fee for advice	5 --
James P Taylors fee for collecting money	12 --
John Saylor for coffin	4 --
For copy of the Inventory	75
Proving Testators will	93¾
Executors attendance and expences	21 --
Amount disbursed	$411 15¾
	25 69¼

(p-98)   ABIGAIL JOBS Estate

The amount due the legatees from the executor is $25 69¼
which sum being equally divided share & share between the six persons mentioned in the Copy of the will-- there is due each of them the sum of four dollars twenty eight cents and one mill & 5/6 of a mill-- And Abraham Job and John Jobs Receipts in full for their equal shares of the property devised to them by the afforesaid Abigail Job Decd were handed to us the Subscribers-- A true Statement. Given under our hands & seals the day and date above written.

                                 James W Young (Seal)
                                 Hy King (Seal)
                                 Committee

JOHN BERKLEYS Estate

Amt of monies paid out by administrators of John Berkley

	D	Cents
George Pursells a/c		25
Lewis Jordan for Crying sale	5	--
State Tax 1814	5	50

```
    Direct Tax  1814                                    4  4  5
    William K Vance a/c                                    .38
    Luke Carrol a/c                                         70
    James Sevier receipt                                  2 90
    Ephram Brabson a/c                                    2 29
    Doctor Bill                                          18 50
    Attendance at Court & sale & expences of Sale
    & expences of sale & funeral charges                 44 62½
                                       Amt               84 19
```

July sessions 1816 we the Committee appointed to settle with the administrators of John Berkley Decd do find on examination of the vouchers to us presented that the said estate with the monies recd amounts to $1912 31¾
And that the necessary expences amount to   84 19
And that the estate amounts to $1828 12¾
As far as we have examined witness our hands the date above
filed at July Sessions 1816

        Wm Bayles
        Wm Colyar   Committee
        James Parker

(p-99)   MARTIN FEAZELL Estate

We as a Committee appointed by the County Court of Washington County to Settle with John Bricker Guardean of the minor heirs of Martin Feazell Decd provided to examin the papers for and against the estate of said Feazell & find them as follows (to wit)

John Bricker Dr to one hundred dollars for money recd from sale of land
9th October 1824 $100 --
    To money Recd for sale of property at sundry times   53 7½
    Cr by   153 7½
    Proven recipt from Adam Broyles   11 92½
    By ballance due of settlement by a former Committee 24 14
    By a Judgt E West against the estate of Martin Feazell
    Decd   7 61½
    By money paid to John Stout as pr receipt   20 50
    By money paid to John Stephenson as pr receipt   12 29
    McGees receipt   4 --
    Susanna Bakers proven account   3 --
Judgt Henderson Clark agt Wm Patton & John Bricker admrs fe 12 75
Alexander Mathes Proven account   12 31
                                                        $108 53

Ballance due from John Bricker to the estate of Martin Feazell forty four dollars & fifty four & a half cents   44 54½
    January 26th 1827
filed at   Jacob Brown
                               Thos C Patton
                               Wm Wilson

(p-100)   WILLIAM TYLERS Estate

October Sessions 1828 We Jacob Brown Thomas C Patton & Joseph Longmire Justices of the peace appointed a Committee by Court to settle with William Bayles Guardean of Malinda Tyler William Tyler Phebee Tyler Minerva Tyler & Betsey Tyler minor children of William Tyler Decd do find that said William Bayles had in his hands at the last settlement four thousand three hundred & fifty six dollars thirty four & one fourth cents $4356 34¼

```
Interest on this til 14th instant                    $19 63½
Dividend on 10th March last $12330 interest
44 cents                                              12 74
Error in the three dividends in last settlement
30 cents each with interest                            1 --
         Amounting to                               $4566 11¾
```

We allow said Bayles the following sums Services fee
```
    Clerk of this Court on 17th January 1828          .62½
    Atto Finck on 26th January last                 12 50
    Atto Parson 13th March last                     25 --
```
And we allow the following as they have not been allowed in any former settlement

1825
```
April 23d       John Patton received $5 0 of Bayles       5 --
1826
March 11th      James Sevier $10 65                      10 65
       14th    Paid by Bayles to Henry Hoss $5            5 --
                Same day paid Daniel Kenney  $3           3 --
March 16th     Paid John Bricker $2 0                     2 --
Sept  13       Paid John McGee $21 88                    21 88
                2 years interest allowed on the six last
                items                                    5 64    $53 17
```
Services attending the Circuit Court & going home in January last nine days
at $2 per day   28 --
August last going to attending & going home fourteen
days at $2 per day   28 --
Said Bayles attendance at these three courts being thirty seven days for
which we allow him $74   74 --
Which with the rest of his credits or receipts make
127 17
                                                           53 17
                                                         $127 17

All of which being subtracted or deducted (p-101) from $4566 11¾
will leave in the hands or under the Controle of Said Wm Bayles a ballance
of four thousand four hundred and thirty eight dollars ninety four and three
fourth cents $4438 94¾

STATE OF TENNESSEE | William Bayles Guardean &c made oath before us that
WASHINGTON COUNTY | the accounts and Services rendered are Just and true
as Stands Stated.   Wm Bayles
Attest Jacob Brown Justice of the peace
        Thomas C Patton Justice of the peace
        Joseph Longmire Justice of the peace
Witness our hands and Seals this 14th day of October 1828.
                                    Jacob Brown (Seal)
                                    Thos C Patton (Seal)
Examined and approved by Court   Joseph Longmire (Seal)
October Session 1828   Committee

(p 101)
                        URIAH HUNTS Estate

STATE OF TENNESSEE |
WASHINGTON COUNTY | Pursuant to an order of the County Court of Said
County dated April Session 1828 and to us directed to settle with Smith &
Thomas Hunt administrators of Uriah Hunt Decd we the undersigned met in
Leesburgh at the house of Frederick Devault in the County afforesaid on the

WASHINGTON COUNTY, TENNESSEE

2 & 3d of May 1828 and after calling on the administrators for their papers the produced to us the following Inventories in the words & figures valuation of property of the estate of Uriah Hunt Decd. (Inventory 1st marked (A) October 16th 1824

40 Hogs	45 --
1 old red cow & Calf	12 50
1 Red Bull	8 --
1 Large Spotted heifer	11 --
1 Red Steer	7 --

(p-102)   URIAH HUNTS Estate

1 dark Red Heifer	6 --	
1 Red Heifer	5 50	
1 White Do	5 50	
1 Muley Cow & Calf	8 50	
1 Red & white	4 50	
1 Sorrel Horse	66 --	
1 Bay Horse	96 --	
1 Pair Horse Geers	9 --	
1 Saddle Bridle & Blanket	9 --	
1 Saddle	10 --	
1 Silver Watch	18 --	
1 Rifle Gun	18 --	
Thomas Hunts negroe Jack	105 --	
Richard Martins Do Zachariah	150 --	
Benjamin Hunt 4 Sheep	6 --	$592 50

Fifty dollars of Inventory marked (A) Transferred to Inventory marked (C) Sorrel horse--
Inventory marked (B) 3 notes on Elhiu Embree

1 note	$238 22½	
1 Do	150 --	
1 Do	230 50	$618 72½
1 note on Jno Gray du 1st February 1825	110 --	
1 Do on Wm Spurgin dated 5th May 1820	100 --	
	210 --	
due fifteen months after date Cr $18	18 --	
	192 --	192 -0
1 note on George Jinkin & David Robinson due 1824 1st Augt	57 50	
Cr by Cash $10 Do Sugar & Coffee $10 Do $4 37½ cr	24 37½	
	33 13½	33 13½
1 Note on Rees Bayles due Sept 1824 the amount	33 --	33 -0
		$1469 36

1 Do on John Epperson date April 5th 1814 $24 desperate

(p-103)   URIAH HUNTS Estate

		$1469 36
1 note on Sam Brison du October 19th 1813 $8 desperate		
1 Do on James Duncan due 14th Jany 1824 $25 cr $13 Interest	15 6	
Some wheat in the Barn Supposed to be 100 bushels & each heir received their part--		
1 note on Smith Hunt dated July 20th 1824	250 --	
1 Do Do Do dated September 21st 1824	33 --	
1 Do Oliver B Ross	99 34	$397 40

Some money on hands but not known how much as it never came into our hands

1 note on Mark Beane for $14" due 25th Decr 1823 all paid to our Father in his lifetime but a small sum & that part desperate

Book account on Benjamin Shipley $2 " desperate--

    Inventory (C) Wm Hunt Decd

1 note on Wm Hicks due 2d March 1825	$75 --	
1 Do on Jonathan Bacon for 100 bushels of corn each legatee received their part		
1 Sorrel Horse brought from Inventory (A)	50 --	
To 70 Doz oats each Legatee recd their part		
October 2d 1824 Jessee Hunt Dr	2 --	
To Cash on hands	14 26½	

October 1824 Recd Wm Hunt Decd his plantation to rent out until the death of our mother as agreed by a written article and each heir has recd his part of the rent to this date 2d May 1828   141 26½   141 26½

    Inventory Marked (D)

One two horse plough James Duncan	2 --
1 Scythe Do Do	85
1 Harrow Peter Hunt	5 --
1 Hoe James Duncan	35
1 Log chain Richard Martin	2 80
1 Wind Mill Peter Hunt	10 --
1 Cutting knife Benjamin Hunt	2 75
1 Horse Uriah Hunt	25 --
1 Him Smith Hunt	31¼

(p-104)   URIAH HUNTS Estate

1 Matax Benjamin Hunt	1 40	
1 Pair Geers Do Do	3 25	
1 Waggon Peter Hunt	51 --	
1 Cow Benjamin Hunt	14 --	
1 Chain & James Duncan	75	
1 Loom Smith Hunt	6 --	
1 ten Gallon pot Widow Hunt	1 19	
1 six Gallon Do Ryley Alford	2 25	
1 Large Oven Thomas Hunt	2 --	
	130 90¼	130 90¼
		$2138 92¼
1 small oven Ryley Alford	1 50	
1 drawing knife & Bell Jessee Hunt	12½	
1 Falling leaf table Benjamin Hunt	5 18¾	
1 Desk & Book cases James Duncan	24 25	
1 Bed Do Do	8 25	
1 Bed Benjamin Hunt	11 --	
1 Bed Dicey Hunt	8 --	
1 Bed & Stead James Duncan	5 45	
1 Stricher Thomas Hunt	1 25	
1 Shovel Plough Ryley Alford	2 --	
2,000 lb of plaister Paris Smith Hunt	7 --	
1 Tar Bucket Thomas Hunt	51	
1 Little wheel Richard Martin	1 82½	
1 Reel & anvil James Duncan	30	
1 Grind Stone Smith Hunt	50	

WASHINGTON COUNTY, TENNESSEE

```
1 Auger Thomas Hunt                                        .25
              Inventory Marked (E)                    77 39½    $77 39½
Amount of Bank Stock                                1500 --
Interest on the Bank Stock 3 years & six months
to the 2d May 1828                                   360 --
                                                    1860 --    $1860 --
                                                              $4076 32½
```

(p-105)   URIAH HUNTS Estate

```
        Amount Brot up                            $4076 32½
Inventory Marked (F)
The hire of a negroe woman Jane the price esti-
mated by John Stephenson & James Deakins @ $25
per year in the benefit of Thomas Hunt two years
one month & twenty two days dated 1st May 1828        53 50
                    Amt                             4129 82½
```

And the administrators produced to us the following vouchers in the words & figures following--

No		
1	February 27th 1828 Recd of Conrad Haws thirty eight dollars James Duncan	38 --
2	October 16th 1824 Recd of Thomas & Smith Hunt Admrs of Uriah Hunt Decd twenty eight dollars and fifty cents James Duncan	28 50
3	October 28th 1826 Recd of Thomas & Smith Hunt admrs of Uriah Hunt Decd forty two dollars & twenty cents James Duncan	42 20
4	January 13th 1825 Recd of Thomas & Smith Hunt admrs of Uriah Hunt Decd seventy dollars James Duncan	70 --
5	July 5th 1827 Then recd of Smith Hunt one of the admrs of Uriah Hunt five dollars on Embree	5 --
	James Duncan By Smith Hunt	
6	One day after date I promise to pay David Robinson the sum of twenty five dollars in current Bank notes for value recd of him this 14th Jany 1824 Cr Thirteen dollars & interest leaving a ballance James Duncan	15 6
7	Recd of Smith Hunt & Thomas Hunt admr of Uriah Hunt Decd ninety one dollars seventy five cents 2d May 1828 James Duncan	
		$290 51

(p-106)   URIAH HUNTS Estate

```
     Amount Brought over                           $290 51
No 8  October 16th 1824 Recd of Thomas &
      Smith Hunt eighteen dollars out of
      the estate of Uriah Hunt Decd                  18 --
                    Benja Hunt
```

SETTLEMENTS OF ESTATES, VOLUME 00, 1790-1841

9	Recd out of the estate of Uriah Hunt six dollars Benja Hunt	6 --	
10 & 11	April 21st 1827 Recd of Thomas & Smith Hunt admr of Uriah Hunt Decd forty seven Dollars & ten cents Benja Hunt	47 10	
	July 7th 1826 Recd of Thomas & Smith Hunt admr of Uriah Hunt Decd fifty six dollars Benja Hunt	56 --	
		$127 10	
		$417 61	$417 61
12	Recd of Thomas & Smith Hunt admrs of Uriah Hunt Decd thirty seven dollars fifty eight & three fourths of a cent October 28th 1826 Benja Hunt	37 58¾	
13 & 14	Recd of Smith Hunt the amount of tax due from the estate of Wm Hunt Dec for the year 1826 Jno Bricker D Shff	2 8	
	Recd of Sarah Hunt by the hands of Smith Hunt her tax for the year 1826. Jno Bricker D Shff	2 8	
15 & 16	Recd of Smith Hunt the amount of tax due from Wm Hunt for the years 1824 & 1825 Jno Bricker D Shff	5 1½	
	Recd of Smith Hunt the amount of the tax due from the estate of Uriah Hunt decd for the years 1824 & 1825 Jno Bricker D Shff	17 92	
		$64 68¼	$64 68¼
17	On the 13th Jany 1826 Then recd sixty dollars by the hands of Embree by order of Thos & Smith Hunt admr of Uriah Hunt Decd; Richard B Martin	60 --	
18 & 19	May 1st 1828 Then recd one note on John Melvin for five dollars	5 --	
	due 4th Feby 1826 & one note on S G Chester for eighty five dollars due May 28th 1828	85 --	
	Recd of Smith Hunt one of the admrs of Uriah Hunt Richard B Martin		
No 20 (p-107)	**URIAH HUNTS Estate**		
No 20	Recd of Thomas & Smith Hunt admrs of Uriah Hunt Decd four dollars sixty two & one half cents October 28th 1826. Richard B Martin	4 62½	
21	October 16th 1824 Recd of Thos & Smith Hunt one hundred and fifty dollars out of the estate of Uriah Hunt Decd Richard B Martin	150 --	
		$304 62½	$304 62½
22	January 13th 1826 Then recd of Thos & Smith Hunt admr of Uriah Hunt decd seventy five dollars Jessee Hunt	75 --	
23	Recd of Thos & Smith Hunt admrs of Uriah Hunt		

WASHINGTON COUNTY, TENNESSEE

	Decd twelve & one half cents October 28th 1826	.12½	
	Jessee Hunt		
24	October 16th 1824 Recd of Thos & Smith fifty dollars out of the estate of Uriah Hunt Decd	50 --	
		125 12½	$125 12½
			$912 4¼
25	October 16th 1824 Recd of Smith & Thos Hunt admr of the estate of Uriah Hunt Decd one Watch Valued to eighteen dollars-- Jessee Hunt	18 --	
26 & 27	Recd of Smith & Thos Hunt admrs of the estate of Uriah Hunt Decd seven dollars at John G Easons store for the use of Dicey Hunt now Dicey Squibb this 9th of April 1827	7 --	
	Jessee Hunt Gudn.		
	Recd of Smith & Thos Hunt admrs of the estate Uriah Hunt Decd Sixty dollars for the use of Dicey Hunt -- now Dicey Squibb August 1st 1827	60 --	
	Jessee Hunt Guardean		
28 & 29	Recd of Smith Hunt one of the admrs of Uriah Hunt Decd sixty nine dollars sixty five cents in a note on Wm Collom 15th Feby 1828,	69 65	
	Jessee Hunt		
	Also on recpt on Wat Hale for four dollars which recpt was paid out of Bank Stock	4 --	
	Jessee Hunt		

(p-108)   URIAH HUNTS Estate

No 30	February 17th 1827 Recd of Thomas & Smith Hunt eighty seven dollars in gold & silver and	87 --	
	eighty one dollars in bank notes by me	81 --	
	Joseph Duncan		
31	October 16th 1824 Recd of Thos & Smith Hunt admr of Uriah Hunt Do twenty six dollars	26 --	
	Peter Hunt		
		$352 65	$352 65
32	Recd of Thos & Smith Hunt admr of Uriah Hunt Decd sixty six dollars October 28th 1826	66 --	
	Peter Hunt		
33	On the 13th Jany 1826 Then recd of Smith Hunt & Thos Hunt Sixty dollars by the hand of Elijah Embree and also on the 7th July Recd	60 --	
	twenty dollars of said estate & April 1827	20 --	
	Recd of Smith Hunt & Thos Hunt admrs of Uriah Hunt Dec three dollars & Seventy five cents	3 75	
	Peter Hunt		
34	Recd of Smith Hunt fifty six & one fourth cent Executor of Wm Hunt Decd in full of his account for me May 31st 1826 Samuel Dougless	.56¼	
35	Febry 21st 1825 Recd of Smith Hunt agent of Uriah Hunt Decd two dollars & sixty two & a half cents that being my account in full against said estate. Recd by me	2 62½	
	Elisha Caskill		
36	April 16th 1826 Then paid Henry Hartman one dollar for breaking one auger of Hartman out		

SETTLEMENTS OF ESTATES, VOLUME 00, 1790-1841

   of the estate of Uriah Hunt   1 --
     Smith Hunt

                153 93¼ $153 93¾
                     $1418 63

37   Recd March 14th 1826 of Smith Hunt fifty
   four cents in full of an account against
   the estate of Uriah Hunt Decd. M Deaderick   .54
   & Son

38   One day after date I promise to pay Saml Greer
   three dollars six & one fourth cent for value
   recd Witness my hand & seal 1st day of Feby
   1828   Smith Hunt Admr (Seal)   3 6¼
       of Uriah Hunt Decd

(p-109)   URIAH HUNTS Estate

   Recd of Smith Hunt amount of this note likewise one dollar twelve & a half cents for
   the copy of Inventory & Copy record Committee to settle May 1st, 1828   1 12½
       Jas Sevier Clk
       By Saml Greer D C

39   Recd of Smith Hunt one dollar & fifty cents for
   publishing in the farmers Journal administrators
   notice of the estate of Uriah Hunt in the   1 50
   month of February 1826 May 1st 1828
       J Howard

40   Recd of Smith Hunt & Thomas Hunt admr of
   the estate of Uriah Hunt Decd one Bureau
   twenty two dollars seventy five cents, for
   the use of Dicey Hunt now Dicey Squibb   22 75
   16th October 1825   Jessee Hunt Guard

41   Recd of Smith Hunt & Thos Hunt admrs of
   the estate of Uriah Hunt Decd one Bed
   eight dollars October 8th 1826   8 --
       Jessee Hunt for the
   use of Dicey Hunt

42   February 28th 1820 Then Recd of Smith Hunt
   admrs of Uriah Hunt Decd Seventy eight dollars
   & fifty cents in notes   78 50
       Benja Hunt

43   Recd of Thos & Smith Hunt Admrs of Uriah
   Hunt Decd thirty five dollars which sum was
   agreed on with the heirs of said estate
   November 8th 1825   her   35 --
      Sarah   x   Hunt
        mark

44   By Letter & order from Joseph Duncan to
   Thos & Smith Hunt for Iron for forty seven
   dollars twelve and a half cents dated   47 12½
   16th May 1827
       Joseph Duncan

45   Elijah Embree proven account 12th October
   1825   68 50

46   James P Taylors recpt for getting administrators and Inventory 11th March 1828   10 --

WASHINGTON COUNTY, TENNESSEE

(p-110) URIAH HUNTS Estate

No 47	Thos Hunt has recd one Sorrel Horse at $66 & Jack a man of colour untill he is 35 years $171 -- of age at 105.66 $171-- Thos Hunt	
48	February 17th 1827 Joseph Duncan Dr to Smith & Thos Hunt admrs of Uriah Hunt Dec for discount on gold and Silver the amount $87 to one year two months & fifteen days @ 6 pr cent	6 53
	Smith Hunt } Thos Hunt } Admrs	
49	Doctor David Nelson proven account 29th Jany 1825	30 --
50	November 6th 1824 Recd of Thos Hunt four dollars of Uriah Hunt Decd estate I say recd by me, his Uriah Hunt mark	4 --
51	The heirs of Uriah Hunt Decd Dr to Thos Hunt for raising one black child 1 year six months for nursing doctoring & burying the same/child two years to finding necessary & nursing the black woman while in child bed	70 --

```
                                                 557  63¼
                                                1418  63
                                               $1976  26¼
```

52	October 16th 1824 Recd of Thos & Smith Hunt sixty four dollars twenty five cents out of the estate of Uriah Hunt Decd. Test John Stephenson Uriah Hunt His x mark	64 25	
53	Recd of Thomas & Smith Hunt admr of Uriah Hunt Decd twenty five dollars this 28th October 1826. His Uriah x Hunt Mark		
54	March 11th 1826 Recd of Smith Hunt admr of Uriah Hunt admr of Uriah Hunt Decd Sixty dollars in iron & nails out of the said estate this 17th December 1827	60 --	
		$2165 51½	
	Uriah Hunt his x mark		
55	David Nelson & D Kenney proven account	12 50	$2178 1¼

(p-111) URIAH HUNTS Estate

                          Amt Brot up $2178 1¼

56	Recd of Smith & Thos Hunt admrs of the estate of Uriah Hunt Decd two dollars for services rendered in Settlement of said estate 14th July 1828 Joseph McLin	2 --
57	Recd of Smith & Thos Hunt admrs of the estate of Uriah Hunt Decd Three dollars for services rendered in settlement of said, estate 14th	3 --

July 1828

Jno Link $2183 1¼

STATE OF TENNESSEE }
WASHINGTON COUNTY   }   We the undersigned appointed by Court to settle with the above named administrators find that they stand charged four thousand one hundred & twenty nine dollars eighty two & a half cents and produced to us vouchers to the amount of two thousand one hundred and eighty three and one fourth cents and find the administrators have in their hands nineteen hundred & forty six dollars eighty one and a fourth cents of which sum the administrators have in their hands notes and accounts and officers receipts to the amount of one thousand dollars in Lieu of bank Stock that the administrators Conveyed to Doctor David Nelson Given under our hands and seals 14th July 1828.

           John Link   (Seal)
           Jos McLin   (Seal)
           David Wilson (Seal)

(p-112)   JOHN LAWS Estate

1828   John Biddle Guardean of John Law Recd of Robert C
        Wilson for work and Labour done by Jno Law for said
        Wilson 36½ lb pounds of cotton @ 10 cents pr lb   3 65
        For work and labour done for Saml M Grayham by said
        Law one month   4 50
Cr paid by John Biddle Guardean $8 15
        By Cash paid to Samuel Greer deputy clerk   1 --
        By one pair of shoes   2 --
        By five dollars to John Bricker deputy Shff for
        Summoning a Jury to examin into the state of mind   5 --
        of sd Law   -- --
                                                              8 --
                                                           $ " 15

STATE OF TENNESSEE }
WASHINGTON COUNTY   }   Personally came before me John Link one of the Justices for Sd County John Biddle in open Court and made Oath that the account stated as above that came into his hands of Jno Law is Just and all the Credits is Justly given. Given under my hand & seal 13th April 1829 filed at April Session 1829
           John Biddle (Seal)

Test John Link <u>Justic</u> of the peace

JOSIAH FRANKLIN Estate

We the Commissioners appointed by Court april term 1829 to Settle with Col Jacob Brown Guardean of the minor heirs of Josiah Franklin Dec after <u>examining</u> his a/ find him indebted to said estate the sum of nine hundred & Seventy two dollars sixty cents & ¼ Given under our hands and Seals the 14th April 1829 filed at April Sessions 1829
           William P Chester (Seal)
           Thos C Patton (Seal)
           Wm Gillaland (Seal)

WASHINGTON COUNTY, TENNESSEE

(p-113)   DANIEL BAYLES Estate

We Joseph Longmire Jacob Hartsel & Jacob Brown Commissioners appointed by Court to settle with Jessee Bayles & Richard Bayles administrators of the estate of Daniel Bayles Decd We do find by the Clerks certificate &c amounting to nine hundred & ninety seven dollars & twenty four cents

		$997 24
And they produced the following vouchers (to wit)		239 86½
		$757 37½
No 1	John D Bayles Receipt	2 50
2	Joseph Kenners Receipt	3 --
3	Greenways & Jones note	6 41
4	Sheriff Rylands tax Receipt	1 87½
5	Beavers note	4 25
6	James Harveys account	10 85½
7	John G Easons account	14 23¼
8	Adam Mitchells account	4 --
9	William Irwins account	4 --
10	Robert Prestons account	3 --
11	Sheriff Hunts tax Receipt	1 84
12	Greenway & Jones account	41 76
13	James Young account	63
14	William Dossers Receipt	36 93
15	Greenways & Jones note	1 61
16	Michael Crouses account	1 75
17	Kleppers Receipt	2 70¼
18	Pattersons Receipt	2 --
19	Thomas T Youngs account	6 50
20	Samuel D Bayles Receipt	2 --
21	Beavers account proven by John D Bayles	4 --
22	Robert Cashedy account	60
23	Jacob Howards Reciept	1 50
24	John Andis account	1 --
25	Reuben D Bayles account	1 92
26	Clerks Service Receipt	5 --
27	A Finch <u>Counsill</u> Receipt	5 --
28	A legacy due Milly Harrell formerly Milly Deakins	70 --
	turn over	$239 86½

(p-114)   DANIEL BAYLES Estate

Amt Brot Over	$997 24
Amt Brot Over	$239 86½
	$757 37½

The whole amounting to two hundred and thirty nine dollars & eighty six and a half cents after being <u>reducted</u> from nine hundred & ninety Seven dollars & twenty four cents leaves Seven hundred & fifty seven dollars & thirty Seven & a half cents in the hands of the administrators except their Services for their trouble in said administration Given under our hands & seals this 23d Jany 1829

                         Joseph Longmire (Seal)
                         Jacob Brown (Seal)
                         Jacob Hartsell (Seal)
filed at April Session 1829   Commissioners

JOSEPH MERCERS Estate

STATE OF TENNESSEE
WASHINGTON COUNTY Persuant to an Order of the County Court of said County dated Janyary Sessions 1829--
And to us the undersigned directed to Settle with Thomas W Mercer admr. of Joseph Mercer Decd. We met at the house of John Stormer in the County aforesaid and after Calling on the administrator for his papers concerning the estate he produced to us a vendue bill marked (A)

Amount Charged	$65 42
Cash notes returned by the adminr in the Inventory	29 10¼
	$94 52¼

And produced vouchers

No		
1	Wm P Chester Constable recpt for Judgment in favour of Jno G Eason against Thos W Mercer admrs of Joseph Mercer Decd June 7th 1828	11 50
2	John Ingles Reciept for making coffin for Joseph Mercer Decd Dated 19th July 1828	5 --
3	William Bottles proven account	6 63
4	E L Mathes recpt for a Judge in favour of Henry Bottles	8 17
5	John A Aikens receipt	5 --

(p-115) JOSEPH MERCER Estate

6	James Sevier Clerk	1 62½
7	James Sevier clk for order for Settlement	50
8	Thomas C Patton Receipt	1 --
9	William Wilson Receipt	1 --
10	John Link Receipt	1 --
11	Ellenor Mercer recpt for her year provisions	29 30
12	Thos W Mercers account rendered for Services in Settling the estate 29 days	29 --
		$99 72½

STATE OF TENNESSEE
WASHINGTON COUNTY After examining the papers we find the administrator Charged with ninety four dollars fifty two and three fourth cents, and produced vouchers to the amount of ninety nine dollars Seventy two and a half cents and find the administrator paid five dollars and twenty cents more than fell in his hands-- Given under our hands 2d February 1829 fild at April Session 1829 Approved by Court

William P Chester Chairman,
Thos C Patton
Wm Wilson
Jno Link--

SAMUEL BITNERS Estate

We Jonathan Collom Jessee Payne & William Mitchell being appointed by Court to settle with Margaret Bitner administratrix of the estate of Samuel Bitner Decd find the amount of vouchers in file No 1 to be ₤ 33 4 0

And in file No 2 to be	$164 61½
Allowance for Mrs Bitners Services	15 --

```
        Amount of Inventory                        $122 66
        Ballance due Mrs Bitner                     167 63¼
        From which Subtract her sale bill which is   45 63½
        filed at July Sessions 1819                 $121 99¾
                        Jona Collom
                        Wm Mitchell
```

(p-116)   JACOB BROWN (WAGGONER) Estate
                                          to

The amount of the Sales and accounts due/the estate of Jacob Brown (Waggon-maker) as given to us by William Bayles & George Brown administrators of said estate is $397 98 1/6
Contrary. By Vouchers produced & expenses for services
by said administrators & also expenditures $132 93
                                                                       $265 5 1/6

We your Committee find that the above Statement of three hundred and ninety Seven dollars & ninety eight cents & one sixth of a cent agreeable to the papers Shewn to us is due to the said Estate and that by vouchers produced & expences & expenditures by said administrators they have paid one hundred and thirty two dollars and ninety three cents-- which leaves a ballance due the estate of two hundred and sixty five dollars & five cents & one sixth of a cent, But the administrators plead they have not fully administered. February 6th 1811 filed February Sessions 1811
                                      Joseph Britton
                                      Jacob Brown   Committee
                                      Jacob Hoss

                               HENRY WINKLES Estate

We the Committee appointed by Court have Settled in part with John Winkle administrator of the estate of Henry Winkle Decd and find the amount in hands of the administrator to be three hundred and ninety Seven dollars and eighty three cents and the amount paid out as shall appear by vouchers in file No 1 to be one hundred & twelve dollars & nintey two cents, Filed/February Sessions 1813.
                                    Jonathan Collom
                                    Jessee Payne
                                    Wm Mitchell

(p-117)   THOMAS YOUNGS Estate

May 7th Recd of Joseph Young administrator and Mary Young admrx of the Estate of Thomas Young Decd on behalf of the Court to be filed in the office one note for the sum of ten dollars & ninety cents, one Recpt of Daniel Bayles for eighty four cents two Receipts of Robert Anderson for four dollars one recipt of Joseph Brown for five dollars, One recipt, and Judgment Vallentine Sevier for three dollars, 68 cents one recipt of John Shields for two dollars fifty cents one recipt, of George Gillispie for ten dollars seven cents, one recpt of James Aiken for twenty eight dollars sixty two cents. Recd by us
                                    Joseph Brittin
                                    Wm Blair   Committee

WILLIAM TYLERS Estate

STATE OF TENNESSEE
WASHINGTON COUNTY } We the undersigned appointed a Committee by order of the County Court of said County to make an allowance to Wm Nelson a Guardean appointed to take care of & support Polly Tyler (an Idiot) daughter of William Tyler Decd are of the opinion that said Nelson as Guardean have and receive from the executors of said William Tyler Decd the sum of three hundred and fifty dollars for the term he has supported said girl which is one year & nine months, which is allowing the said Guardian two hundred dollars per annum, Given under our hands and seals this 18th day of January 1823 filed at January Sessions 1823.

        Saml Greer J Peace (Seal)
        D G Vance Justice of the peace (Seal)

(p-118)   JOHN EMBREE Estate

Mary Embree Dr To the estate of John Embree Dec--

To the amount of personal property	$415 --
To the amount due the said estate from Thomas Sellars note for	53 90
To one note on Michael Brown	5 --
	$473 90

Contra Cr.

By Sundry accounts paid to Sundry persons for the Estate as appears by Receipts filed		59 --
		$414 90
By her part of the sale of said estate which is ¼ of $414 90 after discounting all the debts paid one the account of the estate, which is		$103 17 1/3
due		$311 17 1/3
By Thomas McGinnes Recpt filed $89 30		89
By her trouble as admx of the said estate	20 --	
By Boarding and washing for two Children for two years untill this date November 7th 1805	60 --	
	169 30	169 30
Ballance due		$141 87 1/3

We being appointed by the Court to Settle the account of the estate of John Embree Decd with Mary Burns administratrix do find agreable to the different accounts produced we find the above ballance to be due the estate-- Given under our hands & seals this 7th November 1805.

        Jessee Payne Justice of the Sd County (Seal)
        Isaac Depew Justice of the peace (Seal)
        Thos Stuart Justice of the peace (Seal)

(p-119)   HENRY MARTINS Estate

STATE OF TENNESSEE
WASHINGTON COUNTY } Pursuant to an order of the County Court of said County dated January Sessions 1829 and to us the undersigned, directed to settle with John Martin Surviving executor of Henry Martin Decd. We met at the house of Ebenezer Berkley in the County aforesaid on the 3d of April

1829 and after Calling on the executor for his papers he produced to us a
copy of Inventory marked (A) charged with this amount $712 54
Note 1   Jacob Miller   117 50
     1   Do John G Eason   200 --
     1   Do James Deakins   50 --
     1   Do Elias Owens   12 12½
           due bill as Juror   2 --
           John Blairs note   60 --
           Thomas Brabson Do   131 93
           Abel Wiley Do   50 --
                                                                    $1336 9½

           John Sots Do desperate $7 00
           Do Do Do   2 75
                                              9 75

And the Executor produced vouchers to us
No 1   Charles Howels proven account $2 25
   2   Mathew Stephenson Do Do   81¼
   3   David Nelson Do   16 --
   4   John McCorcle Do   12 50
   5   E & E Embree by Jas S Johnston   6 75
   6   John Kotz proven account   10 25
   7   John Strain Do Do   2 96½
   8   Thos Brown Do Do   2 00
   9   John Berry Do   1 75
  10   Daniel Berkley & Eb Do   3 50
  11   Jacob Miller proven account   11 37½
  12   John Doane Do   40
  13   John Jones & Elizabeth his wife recpt   100 --

(p-120)   HENRY MARTINS Estate

  14   Cloe Martins receipt $100 --
  15   Richard B Martins Receipt   100 --
  16   Abell Marsh & Ann Marsh Do   72 75
  17   Caleb Martin Do   100 --
  18   Treacy Walker & John Walker Do   80 --
  19   John Martin proven account   8 --
  20   John Martin Do Do   19 55
  21   John Martin Recpt for the copy of Inventory   75
  22   Do Do for order of Settlement   50
  23   John Martin proven account   10 --
  24   John Link receipt   1 --
  25   Joseph Maclins Receipt   }   1 --
  26   Daniel Berkleys Receipt   } Committee   1 --
  27   John Walker Receipt   }   23 --
        Do Do   7 --
        Do Do   5 --
  28   John Wilds Elias Martin probate for payment of
        money
  29   Joseph Martin receipt   1 --
  30   John Link receipt   1 --
  31   Daniel Berkleys receipt   1 --
        Commissions on the sum of $1367 86½
        at five per cent is   68 39
                                       $1299 47½

STATE OF TENNESSEE }
WASHINGTON COUNTY } After examening the papers we find the Executor John
Martin, has received assets in his hands amounting to thirteen hundred and
sixty seven dollars & eighty six cents & one half one the 30th October 1821.
Including interes, on all notes to that date and find interest in his hands
the sum of fifty two dollars incurred we find debt and expences and executors commission five hundred & fifty four dollars nine cents & a half leaving a ballance in his hands of seven hundred and sixty five dollars and
Seventy Seven cents and a half and from Information of the executor there
are ten heirs and each heirs part being the sum of Seventy six dollars fifty seven cents & a half besides interest

(p-121)   HENRY MARTINS Estate

accruing to them untill paid and we find that the executor is yet indebted
to the estate the sum of three hundred & thirty five dollars and sixty eight
cents--

30th October 1821 Cloe Martin	$100	--
September Do Calib Martin	100	--
October 1824 Richard B Martin	100	--
October/1828 Abele Marsh	72	75
April 17th 1827 Tracy & John Walker	112	47
September 10th 1821 Jno B & Eliza Jones	100	--

And we find that the above named Legatees ought to have
recd.

Cloe Martin	76	57½
Caleb Martin	76	57½
Richd B Martin $95 35 including interest due him	95	35
Abel Marsh 108 34 including interest due him	108	34
Tracy & John Walker $97 94 including interest due him	97	94
John B & Elizabeth Jones	76	57

The above account was settled by us the undersigned Committee 14th April
1829-- Given under our hands & seals the date above filed in office April
Sessions 1829.

        Jno Link (Seal)
           (Seal)
           (Seal)
       Committee

(p-122)   JACOB GYRES Estate

	D	C
The amount of the list of Vouchers Produced		
One note of hand in the hands of Godfrey Carriger	257	56½
One note in the hands of Thomas Gray	50	--
One Receipt of Brice Blair Sheriff	663	47
One order of Wm Cock & receipt of payment	50	--
One note in the hands of George Gillispie	121	--
One proven account of Adam Slyger	6	32
One proven a/c of Thomas Scott	5	--
One proven a/c of John Brown	11	86½
One proven a/c of Mordicai Price	2	--
One proven a/c of Sebastian Hawn	6	66 2/3
One proven a/c of John McAlister	19	8
One proven a/c of Jacob Hunter	4	37½
One proven a/c of George Hawn	5	51

One Do a/c of Jarred Hodgease	$1 50
One Do a/c of Burjes Witt	8 --
One Do-- a/c of John Hunter	3 --
One Do a/c of James Stuart	22 94
One Do a/c of John Rinehart	19 59
One Judgment in favour of Wm McCutchen	4 --
One Receipt of Brice Blair Sheriff	9 --
One Receipt for direct tax R Thornton	9 18
One Receipt of Brice Blair Sheriff	42 19
One Receipt of Joseph Brown Sheriff	44 69
One Receipt of Joseph Crouch Shff	3 50
One Receipt of Joseph Brown Sherff	2 41½
One Receipt of George Williams	7 57½
One Receipt of Joseph Brown Sheff	2 42½
One Receipt of John McKinney	7 --
One Receipt of Joseph Crouch Sheff	3 25
One bill of costs John Rodgers vs Gyre	7 12½
One bill of costs Geo Gillespie vs J & Henry Gyre	3 82½
One bill of costs Thos Gillespie vs J & Henry Gyre	6 62½
One Receipt of Joseph Brown Sheff	2 41¼

(p-123) JACOB GYRES Estate

One Receipt of John Carter Master in equity	6 --
One Receipt of Joseph Crouch Sherff	3 --
One Copy of bill costs in equity	5 50
One Receipt of B Blair Sheriff	4 30
One Do	4 35
One bond in the hands of Jacob Gyre Jnr in Pensylvania	228 60
One Receipt of Judgment J Tadlock vs J Gyre	1758 8
One note in the hands of John Rhea	100 --
One Do	50 --
One Do in the hands of Jenken Whitesides for fees in suit vs W Cocke	50 --
One Do in the hands of John Kennedy in the Same Suit	50 --
One a/c of Jacob Gyre Jur	140 --
One proven a/c of Henry Gyre	22 33
For interest paid by Jacob & Henry Gyre	545 28
Allowance made the Services of the administrators	125 --
Total amt of monies paid out & allowance made &c	4505 48 5/12
Total amt of monies Received	1759 15
Ballance in favour of the administrators	2746 48 5/12
Amt of Sale	911 19
Judgment against Cocke	797 96
George North	19 --
Briant	31 --
Total amt of the estate recd by Jacob & Henry Gyre	1759 15

We the commissioners appointed to settle with Jacob & Henry Gyre administrators of the estate of Jacob Gyre Decd on examination find said estate to be worth seventeen hundred & fifty nine dollars & fifteen cents and that the money & services expended by said administrators amounts to four thousand five hundred & five dollars & sixty five cents five twelfths, which leaves a ballance in favour of the administrators is $2746 48 5/12
Given under our hands & seals this 11th day of August 1809 filed in office August Sessions 1809

Wm Bayles (Seal)
Jessee Payne (Seal)
Wm Colyar Justice of
the peace (Seal)

(p-124) THOMAS YOUNGS Estate

Bill of payments made by the within administrators   D   C
  To Joseph Hamilton Esqr atto at law (burnt)   8   --
  To John Ingle for sawing Do   5   16
  To John Bell for one Shovel Do   1   25
  To one certificate & county Seal to a duplicate warrant   62½
  To Joseph Young for Cash & brandy due him (burnt) 8   29
  To William Ward fr crying vendue (lost or Do)   2   --
  To Peter Bowman Do   1   92
  To Joseph Melvin ditto   2   50
  To John Ruble ditto   2   66
  To Thomas Miller ditto   41
  To Noah Hathorn ditto   1   50
  To Thomas Rodgers for Smith work ditto   3   55
  To William Hogart ditto   84
  To Robert Gillaland ditto   3   67
  To James Irwin ditto   7   18
  To costs of a Suit George James Aiken recpt exhibited   28   62
  To George Gillispie for taxes for 1795 ditto   10   7
  For County Seal never had any recpt   1   50
  To Judgment Valentine Sevier exhibited   3   68
  To costs of a warrant on account against John Cashedy   84
  To Robert Anderson ditto   4   --
  To John Shields for Surveying ditto   2   50
  To Joseph Brown ditto-- ditto   5   --
  To a note to the estate of Robert Young   10   90
                                                                116   66½
                Estate $2085   25
                Credit   114   66½
                          $1970   58½

WASHINGTON COUNTY
STATE OF TENNESSEE | We Joseph Britten William Bayles and William Blair being appointed a committee of the Court of said County to settle with Joseph Young and Mary Young administrator & administratrix of the estate of Thomas Young Decd report & say That we find that the said administrators are charged to the amount of two thousand and

(p-125) THOMAS YOUNGS Estate

eighty five dollars and twenty five cents, and that they ought to have credit for one hundred and fourteen dollars and sixty six & a half cents which leaves a ballance in favour of said estate of one thousand eight hundred and sixty nine dollars & ninety five & a half cents May 7th 1807 filed at May Court 1807
                        Joseph Britten
                        Wm Bayles   Committee
                        Wm Blair

GEORGE CLOUSE Estate

STATE OF TENNESSEE }
WASHINGTON COUNTY } February 3d 1813 we the Subscribers being appointed by Court as a Committee to settle with Clem Clouse administrator & Elizabeth Clouse administratrix of George Clouse Decd and we find the amount of the estate of the sd George Clouse is six hundred eighty nine dollars and twenty three cents -- $689 23

Voucher No 1		26 25
2		3 25
3		6 --
4		3 --
5 & 6		84
7		1$\bar{5}$ --
8		1$\bar{7}$ $\bar{75}$
9	3 75	$61 9

And we find that after Reducting the amount of the vouchers out of the whole amount there remains $628 14 cents $628 14
Given under our hands this 3d February 1813 filed at February sessions 1813

      Henry King }
      Nathan Shipley }
      George Swingle } Commissioners

(p-126)   JAMES GRAYHAMS Estate

Agreably to an Order of Court we Jessee Payne Jona Collom & William Mitchell Justices of the peace in& for Washington County being appointed a Committee to Settle with Ellenor Grayham executrix of the estate of James Grayham Decd have on this Seventeenth day of January 1818 Settled with said Ellenor Grayham and find the amount of sales of said estate to be $99 81¾

Amount of Grayhams wages, voucher as pr file	81 --
As pr Recpt pr Jessee Payne esqr in file No 1	12 --
As Pr note lost $25 in Do	25 --
Services by the Court	25 25
Amt of file No 1	94 28½
	$156 53½
The total amount of Dr is	180 81¼
The total of Crs is	156 28½
Ballance due is	$24 53

filed at April Sessions 1818

      Jessee Payne }
      Jona Collom } Justices of
      Wm Mitchell } the peace

SAMUEL ADAMS Estate

We Jonathan Collom John Stephenson & Nathan Shipley commissioners appointed by Court to settle with John Chester administrator of Samuel Adams Decd met at Jonesborough on the 23d day of April 1818 and made out the Schedule as followeth.

Amount of property sold at vendue $553 59
One bond on James Young & Wm Ore payable 1st April
1807 for   ₤ 34 12 --
One on James Young & Wm Ore payable April 1st 1806 for 27 4 6
One on Samuel Knox & Wm Wilson payable April 1st 1807

```
for                                                          $19 --
One on Samuel Knox & Wm Wilson payable 1806 for               19 --
2 bonds on James Wilson & Saml Knox payable April 1st
1807 for $15 each                                             30 --
                                                            ₤129 16 6

All collected as debt equal to  $346 20
                                 553 59
                                $899 79
              deducts            231 76
              Ballance due      $668  3
```

(p-127)　　　　　　　　　　　SAMUEL ADAMS Estate

	D	Cents
Amount of vouchers produced by the administrator		
Judgment in favour of Jno Brown Inkeeper	2	25
Paid John C Harris for an entry of land		50
William P Chester Proven account	26	12½
Simon Hunt Proven account	9	48
Joseph Brown Proven account	19	92
Dufty Jacobs for making coffin	4	--
Thomas Ball proven account	3	50
John Chester Bill for expences saving crop on the plantation	26	6¼
John Kennedy receipt for several services	20	--
James Sevier clerk fees for Copy	1	30
John C Harris for entry & record of land	1	12½
John McCracken for Crying sale	2	--
John Chester administrator for attending sales and management of estate, also two Journeys to Pensylvania collecting money for said estate	110	--
James Sevier Clerk for fees in office	3	--
	$231	76

Given under our hands the day above

filed July Sessions 1818　　　Nathan Shipley　}
　　　　　　　　　　　　　　　Jna Collom　　　} Commissioners
　　　　　　　　　　　　　　　John Stephenson }

(p-128)　　　　　　　　　　　SAMUEL BRISONS Estate

We John Stephenson Archabald Glasscock & Nathan Shipley having met according to appointment & by virtue of an order of the Court of Washington County to Settle Isabella McAdams alias Isabella Hale administratrix of Samuel Brison Decd do find by the list of Sale of the personal estate of said Samuel Brison Decd her chargeable with the sum　　　　　　　　　$158 91½

Out of which she has paid		
To the estate of Hugh McAdams Dec	37	3¼
To Peter Gardner by note recd	3	50
To Ballance on Andrew Duncans note	2	--
To Charles Bacon by proven account	2	50
To Spencer E Gibson Do	4	75
To John Kerts Do	4	50
To John Hartmant Do	9	--
To Elisha Cahile Do	1	96
To John McAlister Do	13	10
To John G Eason Do	8	7
To Joseph Duncan Do	2	50

To William Hope Do	$5 66 2/3
To John Rolston Do	3 25
To Mary Brown Do	1 83
To Thomas Brown for calling sale	1 50
To Mathew Stephenson for burying clothes	4 25
To William Walker by probate of a note lost	21 --
For coffin	8 --
To paid James Sevier for administrator	2 50
Allowance for expence of sale & collection and other Services	25 --
	$161 90

Given under our hands this 22d day of July 1819
filed at October 1819-

        Nathan Shipley
        Archabald Glascock
        John Stephenson

(p-129)   JACOB HOSS JR Estate

STATE OF TENNESSEE }
WASHINGTON COUNTY } Whereas the worshipfull Court of Said County appointed Henry King Jacob Ellis & Thomas Bacon esquires a Committee to settle with Mary Hoss administratrix of Jacob Hoss Junr Decd this 14th day of October 1819 we the Subscribers proceeded in the business assigned us.

	D Cents
John McAlister per voucher	$29 30
John Houston per ditto	1 7
James Nelson per ditto	5 83 1/3
Wm Kelley per ditto	5 --
David Deaderick per note	41 25½
Richard Deakins per ditto	3 --
David Deadericks act per voucher	20 3
James Long per ditto	91
Joseph Woolf per ditto	50
Joseph Bowman per ditto	9 46
Edward McKin per ditto	9 6
John Sailor per ditto	4 56
Mathew Aiken per ditto	3 75
John Kennedy per ditto	3 46
Philip Deeds per ditto	18 42
John Slagle per ditto	50
Lewis Hunt per ditto	1 --
Thomas Love per ditto	5 --
Isaac Hammers note	35 20
Elkanah R Dulaney per voucher	17 --
Abraham Hoss per voucher	1 50
John Norwoods Receipt for	284 10
Taxes	1 54
Joshua Boren for Crying the sale	1 50
Total amt	$502 95

filed at October Sessions 1819

        Hy King   }
        Jacob Ellis } Commissioners

SETTLEMENTS OF ESTATES, VOLUME 00, 1790-1841

(p-130)   EDWARD MILLION Estate

We Jacob Brown James Parker two of the Commissioners appointed by Court to settle with John Million & Robert Million admrs of Edward Million Decd do find that according to the Inventory to us produced of the personal estate to amount to be three hundred & sixty four dollars and seventy four cents, and the vouchers to us produced and the expences of administration to be sixty nine dollars & sixty eight cents and that the ballance of said estate after reducting said expences to be $295 6 cents to be for the use of the different Legatees the said vouchers is here with filed Certified by us the 8th day of October 1819   filed at October Sessions 1819
              Jacob Brown
              James Parker

MARTIN FEAZELS Estate

We Thomas C Patton William Wilson & Jacob Brown commissioners appointed by Court to settle with John Bricker Guardean of the minor heirs of Martin Feazel Decd we find him chargeable January 26th 1827 by a former Settlement

	$44 54½
Interest on the above Sum up to 11th July 1829	6 57
	$51 11½
Feazels note given to John Rimal principle & interest	26 40
Samuel B Cunningham Medical Bill	5 45
Jonathan Colloms receipt	1 --
Tax paid for Martin Feasels tax 1824 & 1825	2 68
Clerks receipts for recording Guardean bond & two Settlements	1 85
Browns & Pattons fees one dollar each	2 --
	$39 38

Ballance due from John Bricker to the estate of Martin Feasel Decd the Sum of eleven dollars Seventy three & a half cents   11 73½
John Bricker allowed eleven dollars Seventy three & a half cents   11 73½
approved by Court
filed July Sessions 1829

        William P Chester   Chairman,
        Thos C Patton   }
        Wm Wilson   }   Commissioners
        Jacob Brown   }

(p-131)   GEORGE FRAKERS Estate

STATE OF TENNESSEE }
WASHINGTON COUNTY   } Pursuant to order of the County Court of said County dated April Sessions 1829 and to us the undersigned directed to settle with Ellenor Fraker administratrix of George Fraker Decd we met at the house of Abraham Brown in the County aforesaid on the 27th of April 1829 & after Calling on the administratrix for her papers she produced to us Vendue bill

marked (A), charged with		$226 65
Running Geers of Waggon to D Deakins		20 --
Iron to Abraham Brown		10 --
Iron to Jacob Brown		4 50
John Pattons note		80 -- $341 65

And Produced vouchers to us on hands

No			
1	Robert Reeds note	$2	60
2	Alexander Campbell Do	2	91
3	Daniel Deakins Do	31	30
4	John Salts Do	26	--
5	Nicholes Pring Do	2	66½
6	Jessee Brown Do	2	46
7	Abraham Brown Jur Do	12	36
8	Abraham Brown Sen Do	13	80
9	Aaron Finch Do	6	53
10	Thomas C Patton Do	34	86¼
11	Hezekiah Bayles Do	17	85½
12	Jacob Brown Do	2	89
13	Jacob Brown Do	5	99
14	John Mitchell Do		39
15	John Patton Do ballance	14	90
		$178	51¼

And produced Vouchers

No			
1	Saml G Chesters proven account		56¼
2	Wm Bayles Recpt for services rendered in writing	1	--
3	Daniel Berkly note Receipted	2	37
4	Daniel Berkley Do Do	5	29
5	George Fraker Do	12	--

(p-132) GEORGE FRAKERS Estate

6	Daniel Berkleys note receipted	9	30
7	Daniel Berkleys note Do	13	44
8	Michael Fraker proven account	7	83 1/3
9	John G Eason Receipt	3	55
10	John Frakers proven account	3	50
11	Jacob Brown Receipt	5	--
12	David Nelsons Do	2	50
13	John Patton Proven account	1	50
14	Saml B Cunningham proven account	9	--
15	Mathew Stephenson Receipt	11	44
16	John G Eason proven Receipt	7	12½
17	John G Eason proven account	1	5
18	James Seviers Receipt	1	62½
19	Daniel Berkly Receipt	1	23
20	William Dosser Do		50
21	Mathew & John Stephenson proven account	1	50
22	Aaron Brown Receipt	3	--
23	James Sevier Recpt for a Committee		50
		$104	83¾

STATE OF TENNESSEE }
WASHINGTON COUNTY } After examining the papers laid before us by the administratrix we find her charged with three hundred and forty one dollars & sixty five cents & produced legal vouchers to the amount of one hundred & four dollars & eighty three & three fourth cents and find that the administratrix has in her hands the Sum of two hundred and thirty six dollars eighty one & a fourth cents. Given under our hands & seals 27th April 1829.

Charged with the Sum	$341	65
Paid out this sum	104	83¾
	$236	81¼

Widow allowed ten dollars for her Services $10 --
Approved by Court & filed July Sessions 1829.

                                           John Link (Seal)
                                           Hez Bayles (Seal)
                                           Thos C Patton (Seal)
                                           Commissioners

(p-133)   JOHN CROUCH Estate

A list of Vouchers produced by Samuel Hunt & Polly Crouch administrator and administratrix of the estate of John Crouch Deceased.

Jessee Hunt proven account	$19 --
Mathew Aiken Do	34 50
John McEfee Do	6 75
Joseph Bowman Do	4 --
David McNabb Do	2 75
James R Isbell Do	15 --
Samuel Bogart Do	87½
Abraham Tipton Do	77 25
Mary Brown Do	1 5
Benjamin Chapman Do	6 16¼
Adam McKee Do	21 46
John Wright Do	5 52½
Henson Hunt Do	60 --
Micajah Rust Do	1 --
Samuel McCracken Do	31 --
Abraham Tipton Do	37 --
Joseph Crouch Jr Do	192 2
Samuel Hunt Do	150 --
Jonathan Smalling note	12 --
Abraham Job Do	12 83
John Kennedy Receipt	10 --
Alfred M Carter Do	26 2½
Isaac Taylor Do	2 --
Abraham Tipton note	115 --
Tidence Lane Receipt	28 50
Samuel Lane Do	8 55
John Miller Do	4 --
Henry Slagle Do	4 --
John Adams Do	81¼
John McCraken Do	2 --
Mary Brown Do	1 5
David McNabb Do	1 37
	$893 48

(p-134)   JOHN CROUCHES Estate

      We the Committee appointed by the County Court of Washington County to Settle with Samuel Hunt administrator & Polly Crouch administratrix of the Estate of John Crouch Decd do find them chargeable to the Estate the sum of three thousand one hundred & twenty two dollars and thirty cents. Including two notes to the amount of six hundred and sixty five dollars belonging to said Estate in their hands, Yet uncollected and remains doubtfull whether said Sums can ever be collected by them and they have produced vouchers against Said Estate to the amount of eight hundred & ninety three dollars and forty eight cents, leaving a ballance in favour of said Estate to the a-

mount of two thousand two hundred and twenty eight dollars and eighty two cents. Including the six hundred and sixty five dollars as above Stated--
Given under our hands & seals the 12th day of July 1829.

Approved by the Court   Nathan Shipley (Seal)
July Session 1829   Joshua Boren (Seal)
and filed.   Richard Carr (Seal)
    Justices of the peace

ALEXANDER STUARTS Estate

We the undersigned being appointed Commissioners to settle with David Russell surviving administrator of Alexr Stuart Decd did proceed to Settle said estate in part & do find from the Inventories of the sale of said Estate returned that said administrator is Chargeable with the Sum of
    $454.96 cents

And Said admr Presented vouchers to the following amount

Wm Dosser recipt for ballance of Judgt Thos O Roberts Recovered against Alexr Stuart	10 99¾
Wm Dossers recipt for this amount	4 73
John Strains recpt for this Sum	2 --
James Seviers recpt for this Sum	62½
John Brickers recpt for this Sum	19 57
James Sevier recpt for this Sum	1 --
Nimrod C Willets for this Sum	10 --

(p-135)   ALEXANDER STUARTS Estate

Daniel Berkley recpt for this Sum	3 61¼
James Sevier recpt for this Sum	1 12½
John Stuarts recpt for this Sum	6 --
James Sevier recpt for this Sum	75
James Seviers recpt for this Sum	50
Thomas Brown recpt for this Sum	4 --
John Ryland recpt for this Sum	32 87½
Mathew & John Stephenson recpt for this Sum	20 --
Saml Greer agent of the bank of the State of Tennessee this Sum	24 92½
Mary Stuart recpt for this Sum	200 --
	$342 71
Amt with which charged	454 96
Amt of Vouchers	342 71
Ballance due by Sd admr to Said estate	$112 25

Given under our hands & seals this 13th June 1829.

    Samuel Greer (Seal)
Filed at July Sessions 1829   Justice of the peace
    William P Chester (Seal)
    Justice of the peace
    Heza Bayles (Seal)
    Justice of the peace

(p-136)   SAMUEL CULBERTSON Estate

A list of monies paid to the Creditors & Legatees of the estate of Samuel Culbertson Decd & every other expenditure incured in the management of Sd estate.

	D	C
Paid the clerk of Washington County Court for recording the Will	1	--
Paid the Sheriff of Washington for the tax of 1798 1799 & 1800	8	6
Paid Isaac Collet-- pr his deposition	2	50
Paid Clerk of Washington County Court for recording Inventory		60
Paid the Sheriffs of Washington County Court as pr their receipts	3	88½
Paid John McAlister for Stamped paper pr Sundry Receipt	3	60
Paid John Rhea for Counsil & for money paid printer for advertising	8	--
Paid Collector of direct tax	4	98
Paid John Herrold pr his deposition	5	92
Paid Gasper McInturff as pr order of Daniel McCray an executor	3	--
Paid Charles McCray as pr Order on Daniel McCray Executor	5	--
Paid Wm & David Pugh for whiskey for vendue	8	50
Paid Gutridge Garland pr his deposition & **recipt**	2	79
Paid Adam Hawn pr his deposition & Joseph Culbertson	15	92
Paid Charles Hutchings pr his deposition	7	62½
Paid James Cooper pr his deposition	4	25
Paid John Love pr book a/c & deposition	58	1
Paid Thomas McRenolds pr his deposition	1	75
Paid William P Chester for medecine pr his Receipt	1	79
Paid James Polly pr his deposition		93
Paid Joseph Barnes pr his order to John C Brown	5	--
Paid Joseph Pickens pr his deposition	4	--
Paid James Stuart esqr pr his deposition	30	--
Paid Josiah Culbertson a Legatee Pr Sundry Receipts	502	99 2/3
Paid Joseph Culbertson a Legatee pr Sundry Receipts 630	634	13½
Paid Joseph Culbertson the holder of a note of hand given to Jas Stuart	11	35 2/3
Paid Andrew Culbertson & his executor Saml Culbertson pr Sundry Receipts	50	10½
Paid Samuel Culbertson a Legatee pr Sundry receipts	502	4 1/3
Paid James Culbertson a Legatee pr Sundry receipts	503	1
Paid Jane Culbertson a Legatee now Jane Hill pr vendue book & receipts	510	14
Received by Daniel McCray one of the executors pr his Services	10	--

(p-137) SAMUEL CULBERTSON Estate

ditto assumed for Sundry persons	28	93 1/3
Paid to Abel Ewards for doing the business of a clerk for vendue	3	50
Paid to John Polly for Crying Vendue	2	50
Recd by Robert Love one of the Executors for his Services	60	--
ditto purchased at vendue as pr book after credit given as pr vendue book	3	55

$3953\ 31\frac{1}{2}$

Daniel McCray as an Executor charges the estate of
Samuel Culbertson Decd with Services of forty two
days   42 --
Robert Love as ditto charges with sixty days   60 --
Also for Surveying Sundry tracts of land belonging
to sd estate for satisfaction of the executor & pur-
chasers and for paper made use of in the management &
settlement of sd estate & for drawing deeds &c   10 --
  70 --

Jane Culbertson now Jane Hill as an Executrix charges $112 --
the estate of Samuel Culbertson Decd with the Services
of Seven days   7 --
Also for taking care of the Stock untill the day of sale   20 --
Also paid by Robert Love to Clerk pr returns of a Inventory & this Settlement   1 20

STATE OF TENNESSEE }
WASHINGTON COUNTY } We Our Committee appointed to Settle with the Executors of the Estate of Samuel Culbertson Decd and do find them Chargeable
with three thousand five hundred and sixty six dollars and Seventy eight
cents and that they have paid out to the different Creditors and Legatees
to the amount of three Thousand nine hundred and fifty four dollars and fifty one & a half cents which leave a ballance in favour of the said executors
to the amount of three hundred and ninety seven dollars seventy three & a
half cents which they suppose must have accrued from the interest on the
different sums while in their hands collecting which they kept no account
of-- Given under our hands the 4th day of May 1808.

                Joseph Britten
Filed at May Sessions 1808   Joseph Young
                Nathan Shipley

                Committee of the Court
                of Said County

(p-138)   PHILIP PARKES Estate

STATE OF TENNESSEE }
WASHINGTON COUNTY } We the Subscribers appointed by Court to settle with
Philip Parks administrator of Philip Parks Decd do find as follows
A Voucher No 1. $8 54
      2   1 $6\frac{1}{4}$
      3   2 --
      4   1 --
      5   1 --
      6   6 --
      7   2 50
      8   3 25
      9   4 --
     10   50 82
     11   5 56
               $85 $73\frac{1}{4}$

We the Subscribers appointed by Court as a Committee to settle with Philip
Parkes administrator of Philip Parks Decd do find the amount of the estate
to be two hundred and one dollars & thirty two cents & the vouchers laid in

by sd administrator for debt & costs paid by him & for trouble $85 73 cents and the ballance remaining is $115 59 cents. Given under our hands 2d day of February 1813

Filed at February Sessions 1813

Jacob Brown
Wm Colyar } Committee
Hy King

(p-139)   JOHN YOUNGS Estate

TENNESSEE STATE }
WASHINGTON COUNTY } We Joseph Britten William Bayles and William Blair being appointed a Committee of the Court of Said County to settle with Joseph Young & Jonathan Caruthers administrators of the estate of John Young Decd Report & say that we find that the said administrators are charged to the amount of one thousand four hundred & seventy eight dollars & forty nine cents and that they ought to have credit for two hundred dollars & fifty cents which leaves a ballance in favour of said estate of one thousand two hundred & seventy seven dollars & ninety nine cents May 7th 1807.

Filed at May Sessions 1807

$1478 49
 200 50
────────
$1277 99

Joseph Britton
Wm Bayles } Committee
Wm Blair

JOHN COFFMANS Estate

We the Committee appointed to settle with Col Brown administrator of John Coffman Decd find the estate of Coffman to be worth two hundred & ninety three dollars eighty five & fourth cents and find the money paid out and expenditures including the allowances to the administrator for services rendered to be forty seven dollars sixty one & a half cents which leaves the ballance of the estate to be two hundred forty six dollars twenty three & three fourth cents-- this is a final Settlement by the Committee appointed February term 1810 filed at May Sessions 1810

Wm Mitchell
Wm Bayles
Hy King

(p-140)   JOHN MCCLURES Estate

	D	Cents
William Patton Proven a/c note	7	16 2/3
Joseph Browns receipt	5	82
Alexander Mathes Do	4	8 1/3
Wm P Chester Do	9	66
Alexander McKie Do	2	46
Thomas Nelson Do	1	15
David Deaderick Do	1	--
Thomas C Patton Do	6	50

The Committee appointed to settle with the executor of John McClure estate have met and progressed this far and report to court August 10th 1810 filed at August Sessions 1810

Wm Mitchell

WASHINGTON COUNTY, TENNESSEE

James Parker
Wm Colyar

MICHAEL BROWNS Estate

STATE OF TENNESSEE
WASHINGTON COUNTY   Pursuant to an order of the County Court of sd County & to us the undersigned directed to settle with Michael Hoyl executor of Michael Brown Decd we met at the house of Wm Wilson esqr in the County afore said on 11th July 1829 & after calling on the executor for his papers he produced to us thru vendue bills

Vendue bill Marked (A)	$87 77¾
One note on James Falls	57 18½
One Ditto on Catharine Ramsey doubtfull	1 76
due Bill on Abraham Barnhert	3 --
Vendue Bill marked (B)	39 16½
Do Do Do (C)	22 41½
John Williams confesed account	5 18
Isaac Wilson Do Do	15 --
James F Broyles note on Henry Burghner	2 40
	$232 12½

(p-141)   MICHAEL BROWNS Estate

		D	C
	And produced Vouchers to us		
No 1	Peter Parson note vs Michael Brown	4	79
2	Joseph Snapp Do Do	20	10
3	John Williams proven account	10	40
4	James F Broyles proven account	7	50
5	Adam Harmon proven account		83 1/3
6	Henry Earnest & Co Do Do	22	47
7	Jacob Copp proven account	3	16½
8	George Brown Do Do	2	25
9	James Seviers receipt	6	12
10	James Seviers Do		62½
11	John McNeel Do	6	44
12	Wm Wilson for Services for Crying Sale	1	--
13	Wm Gillaland Do Do Do for Clerk at Sale	1	--
14	Wm Patton proven account	1	82
15	Michael Hoyle executor for furnishing whiskey	2	50
16	Wm Willson for Services rendered in Settling	1	--
17	John Link Do Do Do	1	--
18	Wm Gillaland Do Do Do	1	--
19	Jacob Hoyle receipt Do	4	--
		$98	1 1/3
	Executor allowed ten dollars for his Services	10	--
		$108	1 1/3

STATE OF TENNESSEE
WASHINGTON COUNTY   After examining the papers laid before us by the executor we find him charged with the Sum of $232 12½

and Produced legal Vouchers to the amount of $108 1½
And find that the executor has in his hands the
Sum of $104 2½
Given under our hands & seals 11th July 1829

                         Jno Link (Seal)
Approved by Court   Wm Willson (Seal)
July Sessions 1829   Wm Gillaland (Seal)
     William P Chester Cha.
not filed untill <u>untill</u> October Sessions 1829.

(p-142)   ALEXANDER STUARTS Estate

We the undersigned being a committee to Settle with David Russell admr of
Alexander Stuart <u>Ded</u> -- Do find that said Russell is chargeable with this
Sum being the ballance <u>du</u> on Settlement made 13th June 1829.
                                          $112 25
And also with this Sum being the amt of Supplementary
Inventory   421 70
              Amt of Said estate   533 95
from the Amt of Said estate this Sum is to be deducted
as returned in the inventory desperate   54 --
                                          $479 95
We find that said administrator has paid out as per
Vouchers Shewed to us this Sum   35 8
To this amount paid Wright for a bond on Alexr Stuart
for land in Bedford County <u>Ten</u>.   368 --
                                          403 8
To this amt allowed the admr for his Services   46 75
                                          $449 83
         Ballance due the estate $30 12
We find the ballance due as before Stated Given under hands & Seals this
5th day of October 1829.
                      Saml Greer Justice of the peace
                      Wm P Chester Justice of the peace
                      Hez Bayles Justice of the peace
Recd 5th October 1829 from David Russell two dollars for two days Service
to Settle with Sd Russell as administrator of Alexr Stuart estate
                      William P Chester
Recd 5th October 1829 from David Russell two dollars for two days Services
to Settle with Sd Russell as administrator of Alxr Stuarts estate.
                      Hez Bayles
Filed October Sessions 1829

(p-143)   JOHN WADDELLS Estate

STATE OF TENNESSEE }
WASHINGTON COUNTY } Pursuent to an order of the County Court of Sd County
Court of Sd County & to us directed dated July Session 1829 to Settle with
James Broyle & John Gray executors of John Waddell we met at the house of
William Wilson esqr in the County aforesaid on the 28th of September 1829 &
after calling on the executors for their papers they produced to us a schedule as follows marked A
     One note on William Wilson for $272 --
     One due bill on Wm Wilson   39 --
                                           $311 --

WASHINGTON COUNTY, TENNESSEE

find Credit on the above note to this ammount		$207 53½
		$103 46½

And find the Sum of one hundred & three dollars forty six & a half cent Interest on the one hundred & three dollars forty six and a half cents for one year & six months   9 27
                                                $112 73½

And produced vouchers as followeth

No			
1	Henry Burgners recpt for Coffin	10 --	
2	Adam Broyle proven account	9 16	
3	James F Broyle Do	3 50	
4	James Sevier recpt	2 37½	
5	William Garret Clerk of Cock County	70	
6	John Links rcpt	1 --	
7	Joseph McLin Do	1 --	
8	William Gillaland Do	1 --	
9	John Nelsons recpt for taxes	5 98½	
10	One note to Mary Fesel	3 60	
		$38 32	
			74 42

John Gray executor for 10 days lost in the above estate at 6/ pr day $10 00
for cash expended   2 12½
James Broyles Exr to 3 days at 6/2 per day   3 00   15 12½
                                 in hand this $59 30½

(p-144)   **JOHN WADDELLS Estate**

STATE OF TENNESSEE
WASHINGTON COUNTY   We have examined the papers of the within belonging to the estate that was laid before us and find that the Executors have in their hands fifty eight dollars and thirty cents Given under our hands 28th September 1829
filed at October Sessions 1829

                                      John Link
                                      Joseph McLin
Note the adition is wrong   Wm Gilleland
its $59 30

WILLIAM TYLERS Estate

A Settlement of William Bayles the Guardean of Malinda Tyler Phebee Tyler Minerva Tyler & Betsey Tyler minor heirs of Wm Tyler Decd as follows (viz)

Said Guardian had at last Settlement	$3456 72½
Interest on this Sum one year $207 40	207 40
	$3664 12½
October 14th 1829 Dividen at Knoxville	28 70
Interest on this till this day	43
Making in the whole $3693 25½	$3693 25½

William Bayles attending at Knoxville to see to drawing the dividend four days at $2 pr day $8 00
Coming attending & returning home in making this Settlement thirteen day at $2 pr day $26 00 for recording this Settlement   62½
                 $34 62½   34 62½
Which Sums deducted from $3693 25½ leave in the hands   3658 63

```
of sd Bayles thirty Six hundred and fifty eight
dollars & Sixty three cents                                    $7 25
                                                              $3651 38
January 14th 1830 After which receipts from S H Doak
and J N Doak amounting to $7 25 come in, which leaves  8 --
only thirty six hundred & fifty one dollars &                 _____
thirty eight cents in the hands of William Bayles   $3643 38
Charges by Committee, Thos C Patton $5.  Wm P Chester
$1 O Daniel Berkley $2 O making $8 -- Nathan Shipley $2 00 which leaves in
```

(p-145)   WILLIAM TYLERS Estate

the hand of said Wm Bayles $3641 38
Examined and approved by us
                            Daniel Berkley)
                            Thos C Patton   ) Committee
January 14th 1830   Nathan Shipley)

BARNEY FORDS Estate

STATE OF TENNESSEE)
WASHINGTON COUNTY) We Henry King Jacob Hoss & Jacob Hunter Justices of
the peace being appointed by the Court of Said County to Settle with Mary
Ford administratrix of Barny Ford Decd do find the whole amount together
with the amount arising from the sale (after the Said administratrix has
paid all demands against said estate) is six hundred sixty two dollars and
Eighty two cents-- There is eleven legatees which sum being equally divided
among them there is sixty dollars & twenty cents and Seven elevenths of a
cent to each-- Given under our hands and Seals this 30th day of December
in the year 1809

                            Henry King Justice of peace (Seal)
Filed February 1810   Jacob Hoss Justice of peace (Seal)
                            Jacob Hunter Justice of peace (Seal)

(p-146)   JOSEPH TUCKERS Estate

April 8th 1830 Return of Property in inventory that fell into the hands of
John Tucker & Abraham Tucker Executors of the estate of Joseph Tucker Decd.
                                                     D   C
2 year old calves 4 Sheep 6 Hoggs cash on hand   2   --
1 Lot furr Sold for $5   5   --
Recd of Martha Payne on account 50 cents   50
Due bill on John Britten $3 57   3   57
Due Bill on Jacob Taylor for Blacksmith work   4   92
of Thomas C Roberts 50 cents   50
     Vouchers Received $17   9
John Clarks Receipt for   8   --
John Murrs Recpt   3   25
Barbary Zettey Recpt   2   --
Mathew & John Stephenson   1   27
Ballance of George Pursels note   1   40
William Dosser Recpt   2   --
Elizabeth Browns Recpt for 2 Sheep 3 hoggs & one
Calf Patience Murr & John Murr Recpt for 2 Sheep 3
hoggs & 1 calf, Reece Tuckers Recpt for all his part

of tools & farming utensels Mentioned in the will, John
Birkly D Sheriff Green County $1 41
                                                            $19 33
32 cents given to get Silver for Clocks debt   32
Clerk Greers Recpt   1 50
Wm Dossers Recpt for Browns Judgment   12 50
Berkley Committee Recpt   1 --
Jas W Wiley Recpt as attorney   5 --
                                                            $39 65

We the Committee appointed by the Court to Settle with John Tucker & Abraham Tucker executors of the estate of Joseph Tucker Decd have examined all laid before us in Sd Settlement by the executors of Said estate & do find them Standing Dr & Credit as above Stated Given under our hands this 12th day of April 1830.

Approved by Court   Daniel Berkley
& filed at April   Hez Bayles   Committee
Sessions 1830   Joseph McLin

(p-147)   ISAAC RUBLES Estate

We the undersigned being a committee appointed by order of the Court of pleas &c for the County of Washington & State of Tennessee at the April term of said Court to Settle with John G Ruble administrator of Isaac Ruble Decd after due examination we find Said administrator Chargable as fellows pr Inventory of Sale for this Amt $49 32 cents

We find said admr has paid by vouchers this day Shown
to us
No 1 To James Sevier $2 50
   2 John G Ruble proven account   29 --
   3 To Docr John C Harris   29 75
   4 John Parker   1 --
   5 Henry E Ruble   1 --
   6 Greenways & Jones   22 59
   7 Greenway & Jones   1 37½
   8 James Sevier   1 87½
                                                            $89 9

Given under our hands & Seals this 13th July 1830
                                Saml Greer (Seal)
                                Justice of the peace
Filed at July Sessions 1830   Jacob Hartsell (Seal)
                                Justice of the peace
                                Daniel Berkly (Seal)
                                Justice of the peace

(p-148)   MARY WRIGHTS Estate

STATE OF TENNESSEE
WASHINGTON COUNTY   We Thomas C Patton William Colyar and Daniel Berkley a Committee appointed to Settle with Jacob Brown Security for Charles Davis, Administrator of Mary Wright Decd do find that he Brown as as Security for said Davis is Chargeable with this Sum $19 98
And have disbursed and paid Clerks fees   2 27½
    Jacob Varners proven account   87½
                                                             $3 15

```
                                                     $16 83
After allowing 2 years for Settling we find the In-
terest to be                                           5 50
July 12th 1830                                       $22 33
                        Daniel Berkley
                        Thomas C Patton
                        Wm Colyar
```

GEORGE LITTLE Estate

```
We have examined the estate of George Little Decd & find the whole amount
to be Debts against the estate              L100  5  3
debts against  | No 1                            10  3
the estate     | No 2                         1   2  -
                 No 3                         2   5  -
                                             96   8  3
           Errors excepted Widows dowery     32   2  9

                   Orphant part             L-64  5  6
```

Filed February Session 1796   William Nelson J P
                                 Joseph Young J P

(p-149)   JESSEE BILLINGSLEY Estate

		D	Cents
1	William B Childers receipt	70	--
2	Thomas Barrons note	37	--
3	Jacob Range do	73	18
4	Nathan Grage do	37	--
5	E & E Embree do	34	15
6	John Baskets Judgment	155	25
7	Isaac B McClellens recpt	94	32
8	Wm Deareys recpt	30	--
9	Saml Hunts Sheff recpt	10	50
10	John Gates note	161	20
11	Samuel Watsons note	2	83
12	Christopher Murreys note	62	70
13	James Fitsgarrel	25	32
14	John Chesters Judgment	134	84
15	Robert Stuarts proven account	4	25
16	Jonathan Leslie recpt	10	--
17	Thomas Pattons recpt	9	53
18	George Hale note	28	50
19	Martin Kitsmiller note	33	35
20	Peter Cable note	35	--
21	Samuel Hunt Shff recpt	8	15
22	Saml Greer agent of the bank of the State of Tennessee	80	--
		$1137	7

We the Committee appointed to Settle with Nathan Shipley and Jacob Billingsley administrators of the Estate of Jessee Billings Decd do find that they have received of the Said estate one thousand and twenty six dollars sixty six & three fourth cents and that they have paid out by the vouchers produced to us the Sum of eleven hundred and thirty Seven dollars and Seven cents witness our hands the 16th day of October 1822.

WASHINGTON COUNTY, TENNESSEE

filed at October Sessions 1822

Jacob Brown
Wm Bayles
Thos C Patton

(p-150)   PETER EPPERSONS Estate

A list of bond notes & proven accounts brought before us this 7th day of August 1804

	D	Cents
Jonathan Bacons proven account	99	--
John Brown Do	5	44½
Hues Cade Do	55	--
Lott Gott Do	60	--
James Brown Do	6	--
John Gifford Do	73	25
Wm Jackson Do	14	50
Benjamin Rector Do	25	--
Henry Tiffin Clerk of Sale	6	--
Recpts from Jos Brown D Sheriff	8	20
James Johnston for part of proven account	57	16 1/3
Henry Tiffin proven account	2	-
Thomas Haws part of a proven acct	50	83
Thos Haws Do	65	--
Martin Holland Do	55	--
Hues Cade Do	58	--
Joseph Hale Do	46	50
George Jackson Do	199	--
Thomas Haws Do	75	--
John Haws Do	67	8
Robert Allisons Bond	350	--
Sarah Matlocks note	50	--
Uriah Hunts proven acct	95	--
Joseph Hale Do	66	66
Thomas Ford Do	27	70 1/3
Archl Glasscock for bringing a waggon & team from Baltimore	47	71
John Chesters proven account	60	--
James English Note	12	½
Jos Denton Do	9	--
Wm Jackson Ballance of a note	16	--
George Kincheloe proven acct	15	--
John Chester Do	9	51

(p-151)   PETER EPPERSONS Estate

	D	Cents
Jacob Kibler Do	15	--
Bird Deatheridge part of a note	32	--
Arthur Flin ballance of a note	11	75
Richard Basket	6	--
Arthur Flin note	20	--
Wm Epperson bond for a negroe value by Edmond Beane & David Stuart to be worth	283	33 2/3
John Haws bond	208	--
Hues Cade recpt for money borrowed of Thos Stuart	13	--
Martha Epperson admx of Peter Epperson Decd for Selling & other expences	117	75

Abraham Campbell note	$53	75
John Kennedy proven account	60	--
Mathew Aikens Judgment	26	25
Thos Stuart recpt on a Judgment obtained by McKinsey	443	--
John K Wheelock of Peter Eppersons Coffin	3	--
Orders from W P Chester	89	33
Proven account from Do	67	24
Do from Nathan Shipley	2	--
Errors excepted	$3240	19½
Amount of Inventory	718	52½
Amount of Sale	2827	76
	$3546	28½
Ballance	306	9½

We the Committee appointed to Settle with Martha Epperson administratrix of Peter Epperson Decd do certify the within Schedule to be a true return of the bonds notes & proven accounts brought before us. Given under our hands the above date.

Filed at August
Sessions 1804

Nathan Shipley
Archl Glasscock
James Patterson
William Colyar

(p-152)   ALEXANDER M NELSON Estate

STATE OF TENNESSEE
WASHINGTON COUNTY   Pursuant to an order of the County Court of Said County and to us directed to Settle with the executors of Alexr M Nelson Decd we met at the house of John Nelson Decd on the 27th of September 1830 and after Calling on the executor and Administratrix of John Nelson Decd who was one of the executors of the above estate of Alexander M Nelson the administration of John Nelson Decd has passed into the hands of Ebenezer L Mathis Guardean of the minor heirs of Alexander M Nelson Decd the following notes to wit

Notes	D Cents		
Saml G Chester	300 --	due 3d May 1828	
Adam Broyles	15--	due August 7th 1823 Cr August 18th 1825	$3 75
Lewis Jordan	2 --	March 8th 1823	
Adam Broyles	28 50	March 23d 1825 cr Augt 10th 1829	$45 --
Jessee Smith	135 --	December 12th 1821 cr Feby 18th 1823	42 --
John Nelson Senr	50 --	December 25th 1822 also May 6th 1825	71 --
William Colyar	17 94	July 21st 1821 Desperate	
Isaac Wilson	105 --	October 24th 1822	
Thomas Brabson	184 93	Sepr 23 1828 - -	
Ervin McClure	223 -	Febry 12th 1827	
James Broyles	75 --	May 3d 1823 May 1824	$17 --
James Gillispie	25 --	March 13th 1827	
Abraham Looney	40 25	May 13th 1823 Desperate	
Abraham Looney	8 50	May 13th 1823 Desperate	
George Smith	14 --	May 18th 1821	
Joseph Patton	15 --	March 17th 1827	
Ephraim Drake	9 --	Sepr 14th 1822 Desperate	
Lewis Jordan	132 50	Sepr 4th 1823 - - -	
Wm K Vaner	20 90	October 30th 1828	
Robert Wilson	9 --	January 4th 1829 - -	

Elbert Sevier	$60 --	August 29, 1820 $6- - -
Richd Greenway	100 --	October 1st, 1829
Ebeneze L Mathis Exr Doak estate	363 75	April 3d, 1829
James Sevier	600 --	July 18th 1826 - - -
Henry Gyre	120 --	Sepr 6th 1829

(p-153) ALEXANDER M. NELSONS Estate

James Patterson	153 50	May 23d 1827 Desperate
Wm Wilson	60 --	due September 19th 1826
Jessee Payne	30 --	September 30th 1826
Gabriel McCraw	96 --	May 13th 1823
Daniel Barkley	54 --	April 27th 1825
William Carmicle	50 --	Sepr 12th 1826
Nathan Shipley	12 15	November 3d 1823
Hezekiah Bayles	270 --	February 16th 1829
David R Holts	23 --	November 12th 1827
Jacob Brown	30 --	June 23d 1827 Cr 4th November 1823 $20 --
George McCray	20 --	April 23d 1823
Jessee Payne	25 59	July 23d 1824
David McCord	119 50	July 30th 1823 Jany 25th 1826 $ 7 00
John Sevier	11 37½	June 14th 1822 Desperate
John Humphreys	127 65	March 4th 1828
Elijah Embree	50 --	March 31st 1821
E & E Embree	400 --	Cr November 26th 1818 $24 -- July 22d 1819 $24 --

June 14th 1820 $24 -- September 1821 $20 and the remainder of E & E Embrees Note Doubtfull - - -
George T Gillispie & T
Gillispie   400 -- June 12th 1821 to Cr Recvd 11th June
$48 -- August 30th 1825 $30 September 26th 1826 $18 25 May 1st 1829 $10 0
May 11th 1829 $25 0
James Allen   1885 -- September 28th 1829 payable in four years after date with interest Supposed to be Credited thirty or forty dollars and Secured by mortgage Doubtfull

James Guinn	35 --	October 1st 1827
Lewis Fondwill	57 35½	October 1st 1830
Wm K Vance	15 87½	Sepr 22d 1830
Accpt agt John Nelson Decd	50 --	

And we also find that the Items Specified in the will of Alexander M Nelson for his children the administratrix of John Nelson Decd delivered them unto the hands of the Guardean of the heirs--

(p-154) ALEXANDER M NELSONS Estate

Minerva G Nelson administratrix of John Nelson Decd Exhibited an account that the estate of John Nelson has against the Estate of Alexr M Nelson Decd for raising boarding Clothing and tuition for Alexander from April 1821 to April 1830 $450 Nancy Nelson 1822 to April 1830 for as above Stated--
    400 --Keeping a negro woman & four children 16 months
     25 -- $875 --
NB the above account of the administratrix do not include twenty two dollars & Seventy five cents for tuition within the above time paid by Ebenezer L Mathis Guardean--

And we find that the amount of the estate of Alexander M Nelson in notes w which came into executor John Nelson hands was from the best information before us about four thousand dollars Some doubtfull & some desperate and on account of rent for a house and lot in Greeneville after deducting repairs two hundred & thirty Six dollars & ninety cents-- and it appears Satisfactory to us that none of the estate of Alexander M Nelson ever came into the hands of Mathew Stephenson one of the executors and it appears Satisfactory to us that the administratrix has accounted for all that came into her hands Given under our hands and Seals 27th September 1830

         Jno Link
         Wm Gillaland   Commissioners
October Sessions 1830   Joseph McLin
 Approved by Court
 and filed--   William P Chester Chairman

(p-155)   WILLIAM DELANEY Estate

STATE OF TENNESSEE
WASHINGTON COUNTY   We the undersigned being appointed a Committee of Court to make Settlement, with Rebeccah Delaney administratrix of James Delaney Decd who was administrator of William Delaney Decd we find the Said admrs Chargeable with the following amounts. Amount of Sale when Said William Delaney property was Sold $122 9¼
Out of which Sum said administratrix is entitled to the
following Credits as per vouchers--

1	Alexander Harvey	$24 --
1	Elijah Brown	3 50
1	John Ryland	4 41½
1	John Ryland	8 63
1	William Dosser	30 --
1	James Sevier	2 72½
1	William Dosser	7 45
1	William Dosser	1 15
1	William Dosser	1 --
1	Samuel Crawford	3 4
1	David Rogers	6 10
1	Samuel Crawford	18 56
1	Rachel Melvin	17 --
1	William Dosser	69
1	James W Young	6 37½
		$134 93½

Given under our hands and Seals this 24th of September 1830--
        Richard Carr Justice of the peace (Seal)
Filed at October Sessions   Jacob Hartsell Justice of the peace (Seal)
1830

(p-156)   JOSIAH FRANKLINS Estate

Bird Brown Guardian of the minor heirs of Josiah Franklin Decd Dr October 13th 1830.
 To this Sum due the wards being the amount of principal & interest up
to this date $1060 13 cents
Cr by this Sum paid the wards at different times   42 75
Leaving the ballance due $1017 38

WASHINGTON COUNTY, TENNESSEE

October Sessions 1830 Personally came into open Court Jacob Brown and made Oath that he made the above payments a agent for the above Guardean.

           Jacob Brown
Test Jas Sevier Clk   for
filed at October Sessions   Bird Brown
1830

RICHARD ROBERTS Estate

Nacky Roberts Guardean of the minor heirs of of Richd Roberts (to wit) Sarah Roberts Nancy Roberts Eliza Roberts Elbert Roberts and Nicky Roberts- to this Sum Recd as Guardian from George Hendley administrator of Richd Roberts Decd at Sundry times, as well as can now be recolected in cash and other articles such as Corn & Salt and Store goods between the years 1823 & 1827 as I believe, amounting to the Sum of one hundred and fifty eight Say $158. The above wards to wit Sarah Nancy, Eliza, Elbert & Nacky have been raised by me Boarded Cloathed & Schooled out of the above Sum Since March 1820 to this date Oct 1830 except Elbert which died in the year 1826 which Sum has not been any thing like a reasonable Compensation October Session 1830 Sworn to in open Court Filed at October Session 1830
               Nacky Roberts

(p-157)   JOHN WILLIAMS Estate

STATE OF TENNESSEE
WASHINGTON COUNTY   Pursuant to an Order of the County Court of Said County dated July Sessions & to us directed to Settle with John Williams and Ann Williams administrator & administratrix of John Williamd Decd on 4th of October 1830 and after Calling on the administrators for there papers they produced to us the amount of John Williams Decd as returned into the office by them Signed Jas Sevier Clk

           Amount $258 91½

Notes produced to us by the administrators not return- ed into the office on Jeremiah Farnsworth 4th October 1830
                 67 19
Do on John Davis   3 66
                $329 76½

No	Name	Amount
1	James F Broyles	4 50
2	John D Guinn	8 --
3	John J Seehorn	3 --
4	Thomas Brown Recpt for Crying Sale	2 --
5	Saml Greer Dpty Clerk for fees of Office	2 62½
6	James Seviers Recpt	1 --
7	William Seehorn Do	20 90
8	Saml Williams Do	15 34¼
9	Williams Allison Do	16 81¼
10	James Williams Do	20 83¾
11	Thomas Williams Do	20 86¾
12	Samuel Byerly Do	25 44
13	Peggy Williams Do	24 75
14	Benjamin Williams Do	24 75
15	Jama Williams Do	24 75
16	Nancy Hope Do	14 33
17	John M Crawford Do	1 --
18	John Link Do	1 --

19	John & Ann Williams Share in the personal estate	$48 36
20	Do Do for Services in Settling Do	16 48
		$296 74

And we find that the administrator and administratrix Charged with the sum of three hundred & twenty nine dollars Seventy (p-158) JOHN WILLIAMS Estate six & a half cents and have produced vouchers to the amount two hundred ninety six dollars Seventy four Cents leaving in their hands thirty three dollars two & a half cents Given under our hands & Seal 4th October 1830

        Jno Link   (Seal)
        J M Crawford (Seal)
        Joseph McLin (Seal)
        Commissioners

Approved of by Court
Filed at October Sessions 1830 William P Chester Chairman

THOMAS BROWNS Estate

Agreeably to an order of the County Court of Washington County January Sessions 1831 and to us the undersigned directed to Settle with the Executors of Thos Brown decd We met in the Court house of Said County on the 11th January 1831 and after Calling on the Executors for their papers <u>the</u> Produced to us a Sale bill Exhibit A which we find them Charged with this Sum

                    $317 11

And produced to Legal Vouchers

No 1	Wm Slemmons receipt	-- 66
No 2	James V Anderson Do	18¾
No 3	Nathan Shipley Do	1 37½
No 4	Enos Campbell Do	2 75
No 5	Jno A Wilds Do	3 00
No 6	Jno Bricker Do Do	7 60½
No 7	Nathan Shipley Surveying Do	10 00
No 8	James Sevier Do	1 25
No 9	William P Chester Conet Do	34 44

(p-159)   THOMAS BROWNS Estate

No 10	James Acton Do	2 00
No 11	William Miller Do	5 00
No 12	Isaac Hartsell Do	2 00
No 13	John P Chester Do	31 75
No 14	William Dosser Conet Do	26 83
No 15	William Dosser Do	6 50
No 16	Robert McKee Do	150 80
No 17	John Kennedy Do	15 00
No 18	James Sevier Do	1 50
No 19	<u>Samel</u> G Bayles & Jacob Brown for <u>Servces renderd</u>	26 50
No 20	Daniel Barkley Jon Link and William P Chester Commissioners	3 00
		$342 14¾

 We find the Executors Charged with Three hundred
 and Seventeen dollars and Eleven Cents $317 11 cents
 and produced to us Legal vouchers to this amount $342 14¾

WASHINGTON COUNTY, TENNESSEE

    Given under our hands and seal the 11th January 1831
                           Danel Barkly (Seal)
                            John Link (Seal)
                            William P Chester (Seal)
                            Commissioners
Approved by Court   Wm P Chester Chairman
<u>Filled</u> at January Sessions 1831

(p-160)   WM BAYLES GUARDIAN &C

Note: the following enclosed ( ) has been marked out in the original Volume.
(Six and a half cents and have produced vouchers to the amount two hundred and ninety six dollars, & Seventy four cents leaving in their hands thirty three dollars two & a half cents
Given under our hands & Seals 4th October 1830.
                        JNO Link
                        John M Crawford
Filed at October   Joseph McLin
Sessions 1830   Commissioners).

           WILLIAM BAYLES GUARDEAN OF TYLERS HEIRS

    January Sessions 1831
    William Bayles Guardien of Milinda Tyler Phebe Tyler
    Minerva Tyler and Betsey Tyler minor heirs of William
    Tyler deceased this day appeared had accounts examined
    and made settlements in manner following that is he had
    in his hands or under his direction at the last Settle-
    ment $3641 38
    Interest in this sum one year that is the 14
    instant   218 48
Oct 25th 1830 Then received dividends at Knox   25 54
    Interest on this Till the 14th instant   33
    making in the whole $3884 73
    allowance to William Balylis for drawing the
    dividend at Knoxville 2 days at $2 per day   4 --
    Coming attending and returning home in making this
    settlement twelve days at two dollars per day   24 --
    for recording the settlement   62½
    Charges of Committee
    Viz Daniel Barkly 1 day $1 00
        Thos C Patton 1 "   1 00
        John Stephenson 1 "   1 --   3 --

(p-161)   WILLIAM BAYLES <u>GARDIAN</u> OF <u>TAYLER</u> Hair

    All which make   31 62½
    leaving in the hands of said <u>guardien</u> against the
    14 instant $3853 10½
    Examined by the Committee in open Court and ap-
    proved January 10th 1831.
                          Danl Barkley
    Approved by Court   Thos C Paton   Committee
January 1831   John Stephenson
Wm P Chester Chairman
    of the Court &c. Filed at January Sessions 1831.

JACOB GYRES Estate

Agreeably to an order of Court Issued at April Term 1831 appointing Jacob Hartsell Wm Colyeer & Wm P Chester Esqr to settle with Charles Quillon administrator of Jacob Gyre Decd Met on the 11th day of April 1831 as follows

No		
1	Proven account Jacob Gyre to Alex Mathes	$0 72
2	Do Jacob Gyre To Wm Colyeer	4 00
3	Do Do Jacob Hartsell	7 75
4	Do Do Saml Greer	25
5	Do Do Ditto	1 12½
6	Constable recd Rogers Do Wm Nelson	35 30
7	Constable Do Chester Do Anderson	50
8	Proven account Do David Robeson	2 50
9	Saml Greer recd for Copy of Inventory	75
10	Do for Registration of Deed	1 12½
11	Proven account Jacob Gyre to Claburn Nelson	5 37½
12	Jacob Gyre to Abraham Hicks & Rect	2 28
13	Wm Nelson Rect for attendance G M H vs J G	3 00
14	Jas Sevier rect for Letters of administration on other Suit	10 17½

(p-162) JACOB GYRES Estate

15	McKinny } Taylor vs Quillon by note for Estate	12 50
16	Thos Brown decd by S Bayles Exr of Thos Brown	17 50
17	John Blair Proven account vs J Gyre	50 00
18	Jas V Anderson rect for costs of Suit Gyre vs May	14 00
19	Aaran Finch proven account vs J Gyre	25 00
20	Phillip Parks Do	10 00
21	Wm P Chester Do	3 61
22	Crawford Jones Do	3 00
23	Lwois Anderson Do	9 00
24	John Nelson by W Willitt recd for tax	5 50
25	Wm Wilson rect for attendance G Vs May	26 50
26	John Damran rect for Judge vs J Gyre	14 41
27	Henry Gyre Rect for attendance Jonas Gyer &c	7 00
28	Jas Acton account for Coffin	3 00
29	John P Chester Prove account for Medicine	1 00
30	Amount of Feeding Stock of Decd	16 00
31	To fifty days attendance at Court fifteen days	
32	at one dollar pr day & thirty five days while	
33	at Scott County one dollar & fifty cents per	
34	day }	67 50
35	Amount of Jacob Hartsell Wm Colyeer & Wm P	
36	Chester account Commissioners appointed to Settle with Charles Quillon adr of Jacob Gyre Decd one dollar each	3 00

$374 69½

By amount of Sale as pr Inventory   62 99½
By amount of Sale of Iron to John Blair   142 25
& Henry McCray   50 10
$255 44½

By Amt of Iron Sold Quillion
By 200 lb Iron to Par   6 00
$261 44½
$113 45

WASHINGTON COUNTY, TENNESSEE

(p-163)   JACOB GYRE Estate

We Wm Colyeer Jacob Hartsell Wm P Chester Commissioners to Settle with Charles Quillon administrator of Jacob Gyre decd and find that the Estate of Said Gyre is Indebted to him the above Sum of one hundred and thirteen dollars & forty five cents as is Stated by Vouchers Sworn to before me the 11th day of April 1831

                         Charles Qullon Ad (Seal)

Wm P Chester
Jacob Hartsell   Commissioners
Wm Colyeer
Filed at April Session 1831

WM NELSONS Estate

STATE OF TENNESSEE
WASHINGTON COUNTY   We Daniel Barkly Jacob Hartsell & Jacob Brown being a Committee to Settle with Wm & Mark W Nelson Exctrs of the Estate of Wm Nelson decd do find that he has vouchers as follows

14	James Sevier Rect	$-- 62½
15	James Carothers	1 55
16	Cunningham & Kinnys rect	10 00
	Clerk fee for recording this	62½
		$12 80
Mark W Nelsons account for attending two days		2 00
Commissioners		3 00
		$17 80

     Daniel Barkly Jacob Hartsell & Jacob Brown Commissioners
Filled at April Sessions 1831

(p-164)   JACOB CLAWSONS Estate

Agreeable to an Order of Court of Washington County Passed at July Sessions 1831 to us directed as Commissioners of Said Court to Settle with Samuel Clawson administrator of the Estate of Jacob Clawson decd. After Examining all the documents laid before us by said adrs respecting Said Estate we the undersigned Committee report as follows

	$ ¢
The amount of two Sales of Said Estate	162 08
To one note on Wm P Chester Bal due	104 73
To one Note on Aaron Jones	20 20
Do on John Chester	7 88

All of which notes are Counted doubtful

To one note on Saml Clawson to be paid in Iron at 5 cents per lb due April 7th 1832	40 00
Do on Do for two notes to be paid in horses valued as Iron at 5 cents per lb the one due in March 1832 and the other in March 1835	400 00
	$735 09

Paid out of the above amount the following orders

To James Sevier one Order ¢¢ ¢¢ ¢¢	2 75
Do/to Do	1 12½
Do to John Sherfy for Coffin	5 00
Do to Jeremiah Keys for Calling on Sale	75
Do to John T Smith for Clerk at Sd Sale	75
To Joseph Bail Calling Second Sale	75

Matthew & John Stephenson account   -- 75
                  $12 37½
                  $722 72½

Given under our hands & Seals this 6th day of October 1831.
         John Strain (Seal)
Filled at October   John Stephenson (Seal)
Sessions 1831   Joseph McLin (Seal)

(p-165)   THOS BROWNS Estate

STATE OF TENNESSEE }
WASHINGTON COUNTY } Agreeable to an Order of the County Court dated July Sessions 1831 and to us the undersigned directed to Settle with Jacob Brown Samuel G Bayles Executors of Thos Brown decd we met in _Jonesbro_ on the 11th July 1831 and after Calling on the Executors for thier Papers The produced to us Papers for money paid & Services $ ¢
No 1 Saml Greer receipt for   62½
  2 Do Do   62½
  3 Do Do   62½
  4 Proven account Services rendered by Exrs 7 00
    Wm P Chester for Services rendered   1 00
    John Link for Services rendered   1 00
    Wm Colyeer for Services rendered   1 00
                    $11 87½

Cr by Saml Kennedy $9 09

STATE OF TENNESSEE }
WASHINGTON COUNTY } We Do Certify that we find that the Executors paid out Eleven dollars Eighty Seven and a half Cents and find that they recd nine dollars & nine cents Given under our hands & Seals 11th July 1831.
         Jno Link (Seal)
Filled at July   Wm P Chester (Seal)
Sessions 1831.   Wm Colyeer (Seal)

(p-166)   WM FLETCHERS Estate

We Richd Carr Levi Bowers & Danl Barkley a Committee appointed by Court to Settle with Jacob Hartsell administrator of Wm Fletcher decd have this day Examined and make report of the Same.
  We Fletcher is Chargable with the Sum $109 81¼
And has produced the following vouchers
No 1   Clerk Certificate for Six perf dd   2 37½
  2   McBrides rect   4 00
  3   Wm Sligars rect   6 47
  4   Charles Davis Do   8 08
  5   Wm Browns Do   7 20
  6   Saml Templin Do   33
  7   G Henley Do   7 00
  8   Clerk rect   1 62½
  9   Charles Hartsell Do   8 80
 10   Wm Bottles Do   10 00
 11   Bend Brown rect for Judgt   29 62½
 12   Isaac Hartsell Do   20 65
 13   Wm Dosser Do   12 71
 14   Isaac Hartsell Do   1 01½

```
15      Danl Deakins rec                         1 05
16      Wilson Scotts Rect                       1 00
17      Jacob Hartsell Do                       41 40
                                               143 33½
```

                        Danl Barkley
Filled at Oct Sessions Richd Carr
1831.

(p-167)   ADAM WATERBARGERS Estate

STATE OF TENNESSEE }
WASHINGTON COUNTY } Pursuant to an Order of the County Court of Said County dated July Session 1831 and to us the under signed directed to Settle with Christian Zetty & Frederick Fensalaer Excer of Adam Waterbarger decd We met in Leesburgh 24th September 1831 and after Calling on Frederick Fensalaer one of the Executors we find him Charged with John Spradlings account $3 62

We find a Paper purporting to be a Judgt with a credit of Thirty six dollars and Eighteen & three fourth cents made on Execution on Thos Mitchell Senr   57 75

Peter Waterbargers note for fifty five pounds of Cotton due 4th Novr. 1824

One note on Wm Waterbarger due 17th Augt 1826 Doubtful   17 66 1/3

One Do Christian Lightner du 9th August 1824 Doubtful   30 00

& Produced vouchers to the amount
Peter Waterbarger rect for 42 lb @ 5c pr lb   2 10
for his account   2 58   4 68

and Christian Zetty one of the Executors Produced Legal vouchers that he has paid Sarah Waterbarger rect for fifty dollars agreably to the will   50 00
One Do Sarah Waterbarger   13 00
Jacob Waterbarger Receipt   13 00
Wm Waterbarger Do   13 00
Adam Waterbarger Do   13 00
Jessee Brown Do   13 00
Jessee Brown Do agreeable to the will   50 00
Wm Waterbarger Do   46 50
John D Gwinn Do   1 00
Wm McPheters Do   5 80

(p-168)   ADAM WATERBARGERS Estate

Jas V Anderson Do   22 00
Wm McPheters Do   4 00
Jas Sevier Do   50
Sol Waterbarger Do   13 00
John Bricker DS Do   1 72
Michael Waterbarger Do   13 00
John Bricker DS Do   3 61½
Frederick DaVault Wm Wilson & John Link Rect   3 16¼
John McGhee Rect   2 00
Jessee Brown Do   51 50
John Nelson Receipt   49 79
                                                    $382 50¼

SETTLEMENTS OF ESTATES, VOLUME 00, 1790-1841

John M Crawford Joseph McLin John Link $3 00
                                                          $385 50¼

And we find that Christian Zetty one of the Executors has paid out three hundred and Eighty five dollars and fifty cents & one fourth Given under our hands & Seals 24th Sept 1831

$385 50   John Link (Seal)
$ 5   Joseph McLin (Seal)
$1927 50 at 5 per cent   John M Crawford (Seal)
Filled at October Sessions 1831.

JONATHAN BACONS Estate

STATE OF TENNESSEE }
WASHINGTON COUNTY }   Agreeably to an Order of the County Court of the County Court of Said County dated April Sessions 1831 and to us the undersigned directing to Settle with Jonathan Bacon decd we met in Jonesboro 11th July 1831 and after Calling on the administrator for his papers a copy of an Inventory and find (p-169) JONATHAN BACONS Estate him charged with this amount

this amount	$141 89¾
Hay & Grain not canued out adr ackno	51 08
Notes amounting to	66 72
	$259 69¾

And Produced Vouchers

Jas Bacons Receipt	1 37
Sol Miller Do	3 00
John Hartman Proven acct Do	2 50
Matthew Stephenson Receipt	2 00
Sarah Erwin Do	2 00
Joseph Sheilds Do	5 00
Jos Bacon Do	3 00
Joseph & Nancy Shields Do	8 00
Sarah Irwin Do	7 65
Jas Arturburn Do	2 00
Sol Miller Do	7 98
Rial Phillips Do	8 82½
Jas Bacon Do	15 46
Sol Miller Do	2 50
Alen Erwn Do	6 82
John Bacon note Lifted	8 28
Cunningham & Kenney Rect	2 25
John Bricker Shff Do	1 12½
John Kennedy Do	10 00
Charles Bacon Do	2 00
Saml Greer Do	2 00
John Hartman Do	10 00
Saml Greer Do	61¼
John G Eason Do	4 06¼
Rial Phillips Do	12 71¼
Sarah Erwin Do	3 00
Jas Sevar Do	1 25
Sol Miller Do	4 00
Alexr Erwin Do	35 00

(p-170)   JONATHAN BACONS Estate

James Bacon receipt	72 50

Saml Greer Do	$ 1.25
Wm P Chester Danl Barkley Jno Link	3 00
Jonathan Bacon Proven account	25 00
	$276 14¾

STATE OF TENNESSEE }
WASHINGTON COUNTY } We do Certify that we have Examined the papers and find the administrator Charged with two hundred and fifty nine dollars and Sixty nine ¾ cents and Produced Vouchers to the amount of two hundred and Seventy six dollars and fourteen and three fourth cents and find that the administrator has paid Sixteen dollars forty five cents over & above the assets in his hands Given under our hands & Seals 11th July 1831.

<u>Filled</u> at July Session 1831

John Link (Seal)
Wm P Chester (Seal)
Danl Barkley (Seal)

ELIAS BOWMANS Estate

Agreeable to an order of the County Court of Washington County appointing us the undersigned a Committee of said Court to settle with the administrator of the Estate of Elias Bowman decd and after duly Examining the Documents respecting the proceedings of the administrator we report as follows
The Property Sold at two sales the one on the 18th day of December 1829 amounted to $210 30½
The other on the 10th day of April 1830 amounted to   201 00
                    The whole $411 30½
Out of which he has paid as follows to wit
To Jos W Wyly his counsel $5 00
To Funeral Expenses for Coffin to L Campbell $7 00

(p-171)   ELIAS BOWMANS Estate

For M & J Stephenson proven acct for Linen	$5 68¾	$411 30½
To Jas Sevier rect	2 25	
One Do	1 50	
One Do	62½	
Another Do	50	
To one proven account by Seth Smith	4 31¾	
To M Smith Jr proven account	3 00	
To Thos Brown rect for calling first sale	2 00	
To John T Smith rect for calling Second sale	50	
To John T Smith rect for clerk first sale	50	
Shff rect John Bricker for Taxes	1 60½	
To one proven acct of S D Boman	36 00	
		75 08¾
Remainder ---		$340 22¾

Given under our hands and Seals at the house of Saml D Bowman in Washington County & State of Tennessee on the first day of Oct 1831.

<u>Filled</u> at Oct. Session 1831.

John Strain (Seal)
John Stephenson (Seal)
Joseph McLin (Seal)

SETTLEMENTS OF ESTATES, VOLUME 00, 1790-1841

A M NELSON'S Estate

STATE OF TENNESSEE }
WASHINGTON COUNTY } Agreeably to an order of the County Court bearing date July Session 1831 and to us the undersigned directed to Settle with E L Matthis Guardian of the minor heirs of A. M. Nelson decd and to Correct Errors that the Guardian may have made to the July Court 1830 on returning the Inventory We met in Jonesboro 11th July 1830 and after Examining the notes we find them thus

(p-172) A M NELSONS Estate

Note S. G. Chester due 3rd May 1828 & at this time 11 July		$357 30
Do L Jordon Jr		3 00
Do A Broyles		9 88½
Do Jessie Smith on this note find a mistake against Guardian $43 41		18 53½
Do John Nelson Senr		75 62½
Do Wm Colyar Desperate		28 70
Do Isaac Wilson		159 89½
Do Thos Brabson		215 40
Do Ewing McClure		282 09½
Do James Broyles		87 50
Do James Gillespie		31 50
Do Abraham Looney two notes Desperate amount		72 59½
Do George Smith		23 31¼
Do Joseph Patton		18 87¼
Do Ephraim Drake desperate		13 76½
Do Lewis Jordon Sr		194 90
Do William K Vance		24 28
Do Robert C Wilson a mistake $4 87 against the guardian		7 91
Do Elbert F Sevier		99 12
Do Richard Greenway		110 66½
Do E L Mathis		412 26
Do James Sevier		779 23
Do Henry Guyer		133 30
Do James Patterson desperate		246 87½
Do Wm Wilson		77 31
Do Jesse Payne		38 60½
Do Gabrial McGrace	$143 02½	3665 47¼
Do Daniel Barkley		78 11½
Do William Carmichael		64 50
Do Nathan Shipley		17 75½
Do Hezekiah Bayles		308 88
Do Daniel B Holt		28 80
Do Jacob Brown		15 26

(p-173) A. M. NELSONS Estate

Do George McCray Desperate	29 86
Do Jesse Payne Esqr	37 14
Do Daniel McCorel	173 00½
Do John Humphreys	153 33½
Do John Sevier desperate	17 54½
Do Elijah Embree doubtfull	80 75½

Do E & E Embree doubtfull $651 69½
Do George T Gillespie 500 81¼
$5818 93¼

In the above sum we find seven hundred and thirty two dollars and forty five cents returned by the guardian as doubtfull also the sum of five hundred and nine dollars thirty three and half cents returned as desperate. And the guardian produced to us the following Vouchers.

No 1	Greenway & Jones receipt	$53 82
No 2	Minerva G Nelson Do	5 00
No 3	Wallace & Co Do	29 96
No 4	Jonathan H Collum Do	8 50
No 5	John A McKenny Do	7 08
No 6	John Link Do	1 00
No 8	Doctor Hoyle Do	6 50
No 9	Jno G Eason & Co Do	8 79
No 7	Wm M Cunningham Do	16 00
No 10	Frederick F Huskal Do	15 75
No 11	Ann McCampbell Do	31 25
No 12	J. H. Howard Do	3 00
No 13	Joseph McLin Do	2 50
No 14	Wm Gillaland Do	2 50
No 15	Jno Link Do	1 50
		$188 25

For services and the expenses rendered by the guardian for keeping Philis and two children of colour belonging to the Heirs of A. M. Nelson three months and bestowing the necessary

(p-174)   A M NELSONS Estate

attention while lying in child bead	17 00
Also expences and six days loss of time taken Nancy Nelson one of the heirs of A. M. Nelson to Knoxville	10 00
Also four days rendered by the guardian in May 1830	4 00
June two Do Do Do	2 00
July two Do Do Do	2 00
Septr one Do Do Do	1 00
June 1831 one Do Do	1 00
July do two Do Do	2 00
Commission on $188 100 @ 5 per cent	9 40
15	
	$48 40

STATE OF TENNESSEE }
WASHINGTON COUNTY } We do certify that we have examined the papers laid before us by the guardian and find him chargeably the sum of five thousand eight hundred and eighteen dollars and ninety three and half cents and of the above named sum we find seven hundred and thirty two dollars and forty five cents returned also the sum of four hundred and nine dollars and thirty three and half cents <u>desterate</u> given under our hands and seals 12th July 1831.

NB the guardian produced legal vouchers to the amount of one hundred and eighty eight dollars & fifteen cents also the allowance made to the guardian and of service rendered and his commission forty eight dollars and forty cents to be substracted from the above sum.

Jno Link (Seal)
Joseph McLin (Seal)
Wm Gilleyland (Seal)

ABRAHAM SMITH'S Estate

October Sessions 1827. Martha Smith and Isaac Smith Guardians for Elija Smith and Levi Smith minor Heirs of Abraham Smith Deceased here this day filed in the Clerks office Elijah Smith's receipt for the

(p-175) ABRAHAM SMITH'S Estate

amount due to him in a portion left in his father Abraham Smith's will to him it being for the sale of a stud horse and land. Also Martha Smiths account against Levi Smith for $342 00 the amount due to sd Levi Smith on a portion left in his Father Abraham Smith's will, it being for the sale of a stud horse and land.

In pursuance of an order of Court to us directed to Settle with Martha Smith and Isaac Smith, Guardians for Elijah Smith and Levi Smith minor heirs of Abraham Smith Deceased, have this day examined the papers relative to the settlement, and find that they have sufficient vouchers for the portion due to those Heirs.

                                Daniel Barkley (Seal)
                                Justice of the Peace
                                W. P. Chester (Seal)
                                Justice of the Peace
                                Wm Colyar (Seal)
                                Justice of the Peace

EPHRAIM OVERHULSERS Estate

STATE OF TENNESSEE
WASHINGTON COUNTY   Pursuant to an order of the County Court dated October Sessions 1832 and to us the undersigned directed to Settle with Saml McKeean administrator of Ephraim Overhulser Decd We met in Jonesborough 21st of January 1832. and called on the administrator-- he produced to us an inventory and find him charged with this sum $60 12¼ and produced vouchers to the amount of $10 19½ and find that the administrator has over paid eighty cents and half. Given under our hand and seals the date above written.

                          John Link   seal
      Joseph McLin Seal   J. M. Crawford seal

(p-176) WILLIAM TYLERS Estate

January Sessions 1832. E. L. Mathes the guardian of William Tyler one of the minor heirs of William Tyler Decd this day appeard had accounts examined and made settlement in manner following (that is) he had in his hands (or under his control) as appears of record $997 71
Interest on the above amount for three years up to
this date Janry 9th 1832.   9 50
Due of the Bank   1186 79
Allowance to E. L. Mathes 62½ cents clerks fee   62½
And Three dollars for the Committee   3 00
that made settlement with the Guardian   3 62½

And we find remaining in the hands of the Guardian the sum of one thousand one hundred and eighty six dollars and sixteen cents and a half. Given under our hands as we have examined in open Court this 9th day of January 1832.

WASHINGTON COUNTY, TENNESSEE

William Gilleyland
John Humphreys } Committee
Joseph McLin

F. ANDES Estate

We the Commissioners appointed October Sessions 1831(to wit) Jacob Brown, Jacob Hartsell & Jacob Hunter to settle with John Andes administrator of Frederick Andes Decd do find that he is charged with the amount of Two Hundred & thirty dollars and ninety nine cents by the Inventory to us produced.

The amt of Sales	$230 99
Vouchers No 1 Balance on a note of hand given to John G Eason	75
No 2 Clerks Receipt	3 25
No 3 E Linster receipt	1 00

(p-177) FREDERICK ANDES Estate

No 4 John Rulands Receipt	99¾
No 5 Henry Taylors Receipt	50
No 6 Jacob Hunters account proved the Balance of which leaves due Hunter	6 01
No 7 David Hunters Receipt as clerk	1 50
No 8 Clerks fee for Recording will and Letters of Administration	3 25
	$17 26¾

We find that hath paid out by the Vouchers to us produced for expenses and debt paid by said Administrator Seventeen dollars and and twenty six and three quarter cents.

The amt of the Inventory	$230 99
Money paid out by the Administrator	17 26¾
Amt of the estate in his hand	213 72¼
Allowance made by us for the Administrator	16 00
Received from the administrator for our fee as commissioners one dollar each	3 00
this 6th Jany. 1832	19 00
	194 72¼

The ballance in his hands is one hundred and seventy two and a quarter cents. Given under our hands and seals this 6th Jany 1832.

                Jacob Hartsell (Seal)
                Jacob Hunter (seal)
                Jacob Brown (Seal)

THOMAS C PATTONS Estate

STATE OF TENNESSEE } October Sessions 1831--
WASHINGTON COUNTY } Pursuant to an order of the County Court of said County and directed to the undersigned to settle with John McGhee administrator of Thomas C Patton Decd, we met at the house of John McGhee on the 6th January

(p-178) THOMAS C PATTONS Estate

1832 in the County aforesaid and after calling on the administrator for the

✱ (See Errata for correction)

papers we find him charged by an Inventory to this amount	$438 08¼
On the 5th day Jany confessed account on George Hensley which he promised 28th May next	3 00
To a Cann of Lard 36 lb @ 6¾ per	2 28
One note on John Cloyd returned in the Inventory desperate and since recovered	7 50
	$450 86¼
One note on Sample Ore returned desperate for paid in castings	20 00
One note on Sion Price	5 25
And the administrator produced Vouchers to us for this amt as followeth	
No. 1 John Patton proven act for funeral expenses	7 93¾
No. 2 Receipt Saml Greer agent for the Bank of the state of Tennessee for Washington County	243 50
Allowing the Administrator interest and Blank until the sale notes become due two months and three days	2 82¾
No. 3 John C. Harris County Treasurer Receipt for note	24 30
Interest on said note	1 52½
No. 4 Elener Fraker by John Smith her husband by note	41 00
Interest until the sale notes come due	1 35
No. 4 E. L. Mathes note guardian for the minor heirs of A. M. Nelson Decd	30 29
No. 6 Mary Patton widow of Thos. C. Patton Decd Receipt widow dower	16 25

(p-179) THOMAS C PATTONS Estate

No. 7	John Kennedy Receipt for counsel fee	5 00
No. 8	James Sevier Clerk	2 12½
No. 9	Do Do Do	3 87½
No. 10	Jacob Howard receipt for publishing in the Journal for crediter & crediters to come forward	1 00
No. 11	A note executed to Catharine Stormer and assigned to John Patton P ✱	11 00
No. 12	William Gilleyland Hezekiah Bayles and John Links receipt for	6 00
	For services rendered by the administrator	22 05
	This amt $441 8¼ cents at 5 per cent	
No. 13	Jas Seviers receipt	37½
No. 14	John Million receipt for part of two Judgts	28 69½
		450 86¼

And we find that the administrator stands charged with four Hundred and fifty Dollars eighty six and one fourth cents, and produced legal vouchers to the above amount, and by the Inventory we find the administrator charged with two notes returned desperate. One on Sample Ore for twenty dollars for castings payable Oct. 1st 1824. One on Sion Price for five dollars and twenty five cents due 9th November 1825, and we find the administrator has fully administered and paid out all the assets that came into his hands. Given under our hands and seals 9th January 1832.

Wm. Gilleyland seal
Hez Bayles seal
John Link seal
Commissioners

WASHINGTON COUNTY, TENNESSEE

(p-180) PETER BURGNER'S Estate

STATE OF TENNESSEE
WASHINGTON COUNTY Pursuant to an order of Court of said County dated October Sessions 1831 and to us the undersigned directed to settle with Jonathan Waddle and Eve Broyles formerly Eve Burgner Executor and Executrix of Peter Burgner Decd, we met at the house of Jacob Broyles in the County aforesaid on the 29th of October 1831--- and after calling on the executor and executrix for the papers of Jonathan Waddel the executor produced the amount of Inventory signed James Sevier Clerk $154 02½

And the executor produced vouchers as followeth

No. 1	William Patton proven account	1 99
No. 2	Saml W. Doak Do Do	5 00
No. 3	Henry Burgner Do Do	4 12½
No. 4	Peter Burgner note	58 87
No. 5	John Kennedy receipt	2 50
No. 6	Minerva G. Nelson Exe of Jno Nelson receipt	2 00
No. 7	Jos Broyles Jr. Receipt	2 50
No. 8	Jos Sevier Do	1 12½
No. 9	Peter Burgner proven account	0 87½
No. 10	Jacob Eimel note	2 16½
No. 11	Jas Broyles Sr. note	1 13
No. 12	Jno Link Hez Bayles & Wm Gilleyland receipts	3 00
		85 28
	For the executors services	4 87½
		90 15½

We find that the Executor Jonathan Waddel done the whole business of the estate and he has in his hands sixty three dollars and eighty seven cents. Given under our hands and seals 29th October 1832

                         John Link (Seal)
                         Hez. Bayles (Seal)
                         Wm. Gilleyland (Seal)
                         Committee

(p-181) WILLIAM TYLER'S Estate

January Sessions 1832 William Broyles the guardian of Malinda Tyler Phebe Tyler Minerva Tyler and Betsey Tyler minor heirs of William Tyler Deceased this day appeared had accounts examined and made settlement in manner and form following (that is) he had in his hands (or under his direction) at his last settlement, as appears of record $3853 10½
Interest on this up to the 14th this month   231 18½
                                                   4084 29

Allowance to M. M. Bayles for coming attending and returning home in making this settlement twelve days at two dollars per day $24 00
For recording this settlement   62½ $30 62½
Paid Jno Kennedy by Jno Bayles   5 00
Paid W. P. Chester Esq by sd Bayles   1 00
And paid for Malinda Tyler to John P Chester for medicine and attendance   14 87½
To D. D. Andrew for medical aid by D. Doak   4 00
To Wm Bricker for coffin   4 00
To pd Andrew for Burying cloths   4 88   27 75
Making this settlement   3 00
All these allowances &c &c make twenty twentyseven dollars   61 37½

and seventy five cents of this is to be charged to Malinda Tylers share of
the estate. And we find that said Wm. Bayles has in his hands (on County
interest to the 14th of this month) Four thousand Twenty Two Dollars ninety
one and half cents. $4022 91½
Given under our hands as we have examined open Court this 9th day of Jany
1831.

        Wm Gilleyland seal
        Jno Humphreys seal
        Joseph McLin seal

(p-182)   JAMES DELANEY'S Estate

March 31 day 1832. Pursuant to an order from Court last October We Jacob
Hunter & Jacob Hartsell a committee met at the house to settle with Rebecca
Delaney Administrator of James James Delaney Decd and find that the sales
of the personal estate amounts to $23 49

We find by Vouchers produced
No. 1	David Seates probate	$11 66
No. 2	Henry Slagle probate	4 40¾
No. 3	Jacob Hunter a/c accepted	7 00
No. 4	John Harvey probate	66 1/3
No. 5	Andrew Brummit probate	4 37½
No. 6	Richard Peoples probate	3 50
		31 61
		23 49
	Leave ballance of	8 12

Mrs. Delaney was allowed thirty Dollars by the
Committee   30 00
After striking a balance leaves   21 88
due the widow

 This is a true statement of the settlement of the personal Estate of
James Delaney Decd, as witness our hands and seals this 31 march 1832.
          Jacob Humphreys seal
          Justice of the Peace
         Jacob Hartsell seal
         Justice of the Peace

PETER BURGNER'S Estate

STATE OF TENNESSEE }
WASHINGTON COUNTY } Pursuant to an order of the Court of said County dated
Jany Sessions 1832 and to us we the

(p-183)   PETER BURGNER'S Estate

undersigned directed to settle with Jacob Broyles Guardian of the minor
heirs of Peter Burgner Decd we met at the house of sd Broyles in the County
aforesaid on the 28th January 1832 and from the papers submitted to us by
the Guardian we find him indebted to the heirs as followeth--
No. 1	One note on Jacob Broyles Guardian	$7 66 2/3
No. 2	One note on Jacob Broyles Do due 30th October 1831	51 02½
No. 3	One Do on Jacob Reymal due 6th January 1831	2 16½
No. 4	One Do on James Broyles	1 13

	due 6th January 1831	
No. 5	One Do on Jacob Broyles Guardian due 25th November 1831	$29 93
No. 6	One Do on Jacob Broyles Do due 26th Nov. 1832	30 55

Interest Calculated to 28th Jany on the above   1 10

               Charged with this $123 56 2/3

No. 7   One note on William McAdams for one Hundred and twenty Bushels corn due 25 November 1832 desperate

No. 8   One note on William McAdams for one Hundred and twenty Bushel of Corn due 25 November 1833 desperate

No. 9   One Do on Wm McAdams for 120 Bushels corn due 25th November 1834 desperate

Jas Sevier receipt for   1 12½

John Link & Wm Gilleyland receipt   2 00

Jacob Broyles Guardian for raising schooling and clothing two children two years one month and twenty five days to 28 January 1832   50 00

(p-184)   PETER BURGNER'S Estate

This sum subtracted from the above sum   53 12½

                                          $70 44¼

And we find in the hands of the Guardian the sum of seventy dollars forty four and one fourth cents the corn notes on Wm McAdams not included. Given under our hands and seals 28th Jany 1832.

                               John Link   seal
                               Hez Bayles seal
                               Wm Gilleyland seal
                               committee

                             JOSEPH CROUCH'S Estate

STATE OF TENNESSEE }

WASHINGTON COUNTY }   In pursuance of an order of the County Court at January Sessions appointing Wm Gilleyland Jno Humphreys and E. L. Mathes a committee to settle with Wm Nelson administrator on the estate of Joseph Crouch Decd, on examination we find in the hands of the above named Administrator as follows (viz) The amount of sale as returned in Inventory Seventy three dollars six three fourth $73 06¾

The amt of property sold at Knoxville by Robt. King viz.

One Flat bottom Boat twenty dollars   20 00

9 Barrels of Flour at $5 pr Barrel   27 00

cash found in Pocket Book $3 27¾   3 27¾

Notes of hand on George Henly for forty six dollars & ninety six and one half cent   46 93½

An a/c against Jesse Clark $1 27   1 27

Also notes on Geo Henly principal and interest up to this date   19 09¾

                                             190 64¼

(p-185)   JOSEPH CROUCH'S Estate

Also corn sold by sd Administrator		$7 10
added		197 74¾

Credit
Money paid out by the administrator
On D. McIntosh a/c

Funeral expenses (viz) for twelve dollars	No 1.	12 00
Mrs. McGiffeys a/c twelve dollars	No. 2	12 00
Geo. Might a/c	No. 3	6 50
Robt Kings a/c one dollar seventy five	No. 4	1 75
Saml Newman's receipt for two dollars 50¢ from Robt King of Knoxville	No. 5	2 50
Saml Greers receipt as agent of the Bank for Washington County No. 6 for seventy nine dollars and fifty five cents		79 55
County Clerk receipt for services		3 21½
Jacob Howard's receipt No. 8 for one dollar & fifty cents		1 50
Atto McKinny & Taylor a/c and receipt for twenty five dollars No. 9		25 00
County Clerks receipt for one dollar & twenty five cents No. 10		1 25
		145 26½
Robt King's account of Knoxville for services rendered (viz) hauling, storage sales and disbursing the same three dollars and sixty		3 60
One note of hand given by Joseph Crouch to Wm Nelson principal & Interest amounting to five hundred dollars and sixty four and ½ cents. No. 11		500 64½
Robert McKees note on sd Crouch principal and interest for seventy five ninety six cents No. 12		75 96

E. L. Mathes Guardian for A. M. Nelson

(p-186)   JOSEPH CROUCH'S Estate

due him for thirteen dollars and ninety two cents No. 13	13 92
Wm Nelson note prin & In nine dollars fifty six cents No. 14	9 56
James McAlester note on sd Crouch principle and interest yet remaining thirty five dollars and eighty one cents-- No. 15.	35 81
Wm Nelson proven a/c for twenty four dollars and 31 cents-- No. 16	24 31
We allowed said Admr thirty dollars for his services	30 00
Two dollars to the Committee	2 00

On an examination of the above papers laid before us we find that the administrator has secured one hundred and ninety seven dollars and seventy four cents and 3/4   197 74¾
And that he has paid out eight hundred eleven dollars and five cents   811 05
And that he has paid out six hundred and thirteen dollars and thirty cents   613 30
more than came into his hands; including the thirty dollars allowed for his services the estate is justly indebted six hundred and forty three dollars

WASHINGTON COUNTY, TENNESSEE

to the administrator.

                            Wm Gilleyland
                            John Humphreys
                            E. L. Mathes
April 14, 1832   Committee

CONROD KYKER'S Estate

We the undersigned being appointed to settle with Conrod Kyker Executor of Conrod Kyker Decd was ordered to report to April Sessions 1832, we find that by the Inventories of said estate said Conrod Kyker

(p-187)   CONROD KYKERS Estate

Executor is chargeable with this sum	$1768 33¾
And chargeable with this sum being the amt of interest that has accrued	283 60
And by receipts and vouchers produced by said Executor We find that he has expended this sum	95 31
Said Executor having boarded, washed for and found his mother all attention necessary for an aged person fire wood and light in a separate house from his own, by herself from the 2nd November 1826 to the 27th January 1832 making five years and almost three months, for which we have allowed him sixty dollars per year for the first two years making	$120 00
Sixty five dollars per year for the next two years	130 00
And one hundred and twenty five dollars per year for the balance of the time making	156 25
And interest on the above sums for annually up to this date	46 34½
And we allowed the Executor for his services as Executor five per cent on the amount with which he is charged	102 58
	$650 49
We find this balance in the hands of the Executor	1401 24¾

Given under our hands and seals this 16 day of April 1832.
                            Saml Greer   (seal) J. P
                            Danl Barkly (seal) J. P   Comm.
                            W. P. Chester (seal) J P

(p-188)   JOHN KLEPPER Estate

STATE OF TENNESSEE }
WASHINGTON COUNTY } We the undersigned being appointed by an order of Court at January Sessions 1832 to settle with Jacob Klepper administrator of the Estate of John Klepper deceased of which we find the administrator chargeable with the following sums to wit:--

Amount of sale	$500 25
Out of which sum the administrator is entitled to the following credits as pr receipts.	
For issuing order for settlement	0 50
For planking waggon bed & finding plank	2 50
Clerks fee at sale	2 00
Liquor for use of sale	3 00
Paid for coffin to Bowman	6 00
Paid to L. Williams for crying sale	4 21½

Paid John Hoss proven a/c against estate	$1 50
Paid J. Sevier administrator fee	1 62½
Paid Do Do cost	25
Paid Do for expense of Estate	1 12½
Paid Do for order for widows dower	50
Paid T. T. Young medical Bill	1 50
Paid J. G. Eason proven account	15 12½
Paid Hunt & Clem bal proven account	1 05
To 3 days hauling Crockery ware from G County	9 00
By sd admr for use of sd estate	
To 1 day taking Iron and wood work of waggon to shop	1 50
To 1 day at Court administering on sd Estate	50
" Hauling a new waggon from the shop	1 00
" 3 days hauling crockery ware from G County	9 00
" Collecting the property together	50
Attorney Taylors fee	5 00
	67 39

(p-189)   JOHN KLEPPERS Estate

Balance due the Estate $432 86
Given under our hands and seals this 15th March 1832.
                              Levi Bowers   seal
April Term 1832   Richd Carr   seal
Approved by Court and   Jacob Ellis   seal
Administrator allowed 5 per cent on the sum and one dollar for each Commissioner.

RACHAEL MERCER'S Estate

We the undersigned appointed to settle with Thos Mercer Administrator of Rachael Mercer Decd do find said Administrator chargeable with this sum being the amount of said estate $119 08¾
And said Administrator produced vouchers to satisfy us he has paid out of said estate this sum   62 34½
And said administrator is allowed for settling said estate   7 00
                                                                         69 34½
We find this sum in the hands of the administrator   49 74¼
Except the slave of Saml McCracken and wife, Abner Mercer & Rebecca Gran who have receipted said administrator in full for their respective shares of said Estate. Given under our hands and seals this 12th day of April 1832.
                              Saml Greer   seal J P.
                              John G. Eason seal J P.
                              William Chester seal J P

WILLIAM RUSSELL'S Estate

STATE OF TENNESSEE }
WASHINGTON COUNTY   } Pursuant to an order of the County Court of

(p-190)   WILLIAM RUSSELL'S Estate

said County dated April Sessions 1832 and to us the undersigned directed to settle with James Russell and Robert Russell Executors of Wm Russell Deceased. We met in Leesburgh on the 16th of June 1832 and after calling on the Executors for the papers James Russell one of the Ex. produced the following papers to wit:

The following notes on hands and due at the time the/Executors were qualified July Sessions 1826.

			to the above date
Bank note on hand after deducting the percent at par money	$26 10	Interest 9 13½	
One note on George Hale	15 10	-	4 65
Do on Jas & Jno Depew	5 10	-	1 81
Do Isaac and Jacob Hare	12 50	-	4 43
Do Isaac Horton & Glasscock	2 00	-	71
Do Danl Kinney	65 00	-	23 07½
Do Isaac Sands & Isaac Horton	5 00	-	1 77
	128 80		45 38
			$174 38
Part in price of a stud Horse	46 50	Interest 15 11	
600 lb Iron	18 00	"	5 40
1 saddle	4 50		1 35
1 Trade note on L. Kerl	4 00		
1 note on Wm Terry	3 60		1 27
	76 60		23 13 $99 23
Horse sold to Isaac Hare	50 00	"	13 25 63 25
For Grain sold to John Sherfey fell due March 9, 1830	5 25	"	70 5 95
Grain sold and money came due Oct 1831	12 00		45 12 45
Grain sold and money came due April 1831	5 12½		30 5 42½
			$361 18½

And produced to us Vouchers to this amount--

(p-191)   WILLIAM RUSSELLS Estate

No. 1	John G. Eason proven a/c	2 40
No. 2	David Nelson Do	14 00
No. 3	John D. Guinn a/c	4 00
No. 4	Saml B. Cunningham a/c proven	9 00
No. 5	Jno Hartman receipt for a coffin	8 00
No. 6	Aaron Finch Do	2 00
No. 7	Jos Sevier Do	1 00
No. 8	Do Do Do	3 62½
No. 9	Jeremiah Keyes Do	50
No. 10	Joseph Bales Do	16½
No. 11	Jeremiah Keyes Do	50
No. 12	Glasscock, Link Barkly receipt as com	3 00
	For Interest overcharged	5 00
	For money paid for the support of Amanda Jean and services rendered up to the above date proven account	73 00
		126 19

And we find the Executor charged with the sum of three hundred and sixty one dollars and eighteen and half cents and produced vouchers to the amount of one hundred and twenty six dollars and nineteen cents, leaving in the hands of James Russell Two hundred and thirty four dollars ninety nine and half cents. Given under our hands and seals 19th June 1832.

        John Link Seal
        Danl Barkly Seal
        Archd Glasscock Seal

DAVID LEMMON'S Estate

STATE OF TENNESSEE
WASHINGTON COUNTY } Pursuant to an order of the County Court dated April Sessions 1832 and to us the undersigned directed to settle with John Million Executor of the Estate of David Lemmons

(p-192)   DAVID LEMMONS Estate

Deceased we met at the house of said Million on the 14th of July 1832 and after calling on the Executor for the papers he laid before us the following papers (to wit)

Charged on Inventory of debts due the Estate	$238 62
And produced to us vouchers to wit:	
No. 1 John Bricker receipt	56½
No. 2 Jos Sevier Clk do	1 12½
No. 3 Do Do Do	2 12½
By one Hundred dollars taken out of the hands of Jno Million by Executor W. Brown plff vs John Cole one of the heirs	100 00
	$103 81¼
One Hundred dollars in trade on horse equal to Iron at 6 d per pound, which said Million received and sold at public sale which brought in cash	33 02
which the Executor was charged in the inventory with one hundred dollars cr. with John Million Ex charged	66 98
with five dollars in the Inventory which has proven to be desperate	5 00
John Million Executor for services rendered settling estate	22 00
Jno Link Hez Bayles Wm Colyar receipt	3 00
	130 00
Amt Brot under	103 81¼
	233 81¼

And we find Jno Million Ex charged with two hundred and thirty eight dollars and sixty two cents and produced vouchers to the amount of two hundred and thirty three dollars eighty one and one fourth cents leaving a ballance in the hands of the Executor four dollars eighty and three fourth cents.

Given under our hands and seals

(p-193)   DAVID MILLIONS Estate

the date above written.

John Link Seal
Wm Colyar Seal
Hez Bayles Seal
Committee

WILLIAM NELSON (GUARDIAN OF POLLY TYLER)

STATE OF TENNESSEE
WASHINGTON COUNTY } In pursuant to an order of the County Court at April Sessions 1832 directed to us the undersigned a Committee to settle with William Nelson guardian of Polly Tyler (an idiot) we met at the house of E. L Mathes on the 14th of July 1832 after calling on the guardian he produced a statement from Jas V. Anderson (Clerk of the Circuit Court) from which he is charged and is liable to the amount of Eight hundred and sixty eight dol-

lars and sixty six cents principle and interest, up to the present date, and the guardian produced the following vouchers (to wit) from No. 1 to No. 12 amounting in all to the sum of five hundred and fifty seven dollars fifty four cents $557 54
We believe the guardian is entitled to the sum of twenty eight dollars and forty cents for his trouble & as guardian and ten dollars paid to the committee
      28 40
    $585 94

From the above statement of the charge against the guardian and credit by vouchers we find that there is in the hands of the guardian two hundred and eighty two dollars and seventy two cents. Given under our hands the day and date above written.

        E. L. Mathes
        Wm Gilleyland   Committee
        John Humphreys

(p-194)   ROBERT MCLIN'S Estate

Agreeable to an order of Court passed at January Sessions 1832 to us directed we have examined the document belonging to the estate of Robert McLin Deceased and report as follows from the vouchers to us shewn.

The amount of an Inventory returned by Thos Nelson administrator by a certificate of the clerk is	$503 10
And some articles unsold	
Paid by the admr Thomas Nelson	
To 1 proven a/c to Leroy Taylor	7 14
To receipt by Thomas McLin	60 00
To 2 receipts by John Ferguson	52 72
To 1 receipt by John Charlten	54 00
Do by Clench McLin	55 00
Do by W. Mathes for his wifes share	67 35
Do by R. D. McLin for himself and the heirs of John McLin Deceased	72 77
Matthew Stephenson proven a/c	9 56 2½
One receipt by John Strain for acting as clerk at the sale	2 00
Ditto by Thos Brown for crying the sale	2 00
The administrator Thomas Nelson retains	$383 24.2½
in his own hands his wife's share of the said estate she being one of the heirs	50 00

The above certified by us this 14th day of My 1832.
        John Strain
        John Stephenson
        Joseph McLin

        JOHN GUYER'S Estate

STATE OF TENNESSEE
WASHINGTON COUNTY   In pursuance of an order of the Court of Pleas and Quarter Sessions held in Jonesborough on the 3rd Monday of July 1832 appointing Jacob Brown John G Eason and E. L. Mathes a Committee to settle with   (p-195) Jonas Guyer Administrator of John Guyer Deceased having met on the 4th day of October 1832 at the store house of John G. Eason and the said Guyer administrator produced from the clerk of the County Court a

certificate certifying that the amount of the Inventory returned to Court
by said Administrator amounted to two Hundred and forty five dollars and
sixteen cents $245 16
Also debts collected in behalf of the estate amount-
ing to $55 69   55 69
                                                                 $ 300 85
And sd Administrator produced vouchers as follows viz
No1.   Greenway & Jones receipt and Judgt amounting to   25 57½
No. 2 John Ryland sheriff receipt on a Judgement   45 82
No. 3 Isaac Allen receipt on a Judgt.   60 36
No. 4 Receipt on a note of hand given to Jos White   2 75
No. 5 David C. Hunter receipt clerk of sale   1 50
No. 6 Wm C. Smith proven a/c   5 00
No. 7 Robt Johnsons proven a/c   1 00
No. 8 John Bricker D Sheriff receipt   13 00
No. 9 Isaac Hartsell for crying the sale   2 50
No. 10 Nicholas Linebarger proven a/c   7 00
No. 11 Charles Hartsell proven a/c   12 13½
No. 13 John Mays receipt on Circuit Clk certifi   11 00
No. 12 Isaac Hartsell proven a/c balance   11 09
No. 15 J. M. Thompson for making coffin   8 00
No. 14 J. G. Eason proven a/c   24 90
No. 16 David Click note of hand   15 73
No. 17 Wm Slyger note of hand rcd   23 20

(p-196)   JOHN GUYER'S Estate

No. 18 & 19 John Green 2 notes of hand receipted   30 00
No. 20   Bird Brown proven a/c receipted   35 98¾
No. 21 22 & 23 William Dosser receipt   20 44½
No. 24   William P. Chester receipt as const   13 25
No. 25   Wilson Scott receipt Do   2 50
No. 26   Hannah Hartsell proven a/c   3 75
No. 27   Saml Early proven a/c receipted   12 41
No. 28   John Ryland sheriff receipt   15 60
No. 29   W. C. Sliger proven a/c   5 41
No. 30   Joseph Booth proven a/c   5 57
No. 31   James Sevier note of hand   20 37
No. 32   John Green receipt & Judgment   86 99
No. 33   David Deaderick note of hand   8 68
No 34   Gabriel Brown proven a/c   3 00
No. 35   Saml Greer note of hand   6 60
No. 36   Jonas Guyer proven a/c   335 20
No. 37   Note of hand for forty eight dollars   48 00
                           12 $519 43
                              48 00
           page 1   356 99½
                             934 42¼
                             300 85½
                             633 56¾

We as a Committee believe sd administrator is Justly entitled to forty dollars for his services in settling up the estate. From the above statement
we find that the administrator has received and is charged with the sum of
three hundred dollars and eighty five cents ½ and that the sd administrator
has paid out nine hundred thirty four dollars and forty two ¼ cents-- It appears that the Administrator has paid out six hundred thirty three dollars

and fifty six ¾ cents more than the amount

(p-197)   JOHN GUYER'S Estate

of the assets which came into his hands which sum added to his allowance will make the sum of six hundred and seventy three dollars and fifty six ¾ cents which is due said Administrator from the estate of John Guyer Deceased

             Jacob Brown
             John G. Eason
             E. L. Mathes, Com

WILLIAM CARSON'S Estate

Agreeable to an order of the County Court of Washington County to us directed we have caused to come before us John M. Crawford and John Strain who were appointed by Court to settle with John Stephenson and William Walker Administrators of the estate of William Carson Decd and have proceeded as follows (to wit.)

The amt of the property sold at the sale of the estate of said Wm Carson Deceased	$184 55
Received of the administrators of his fathers estate	59 00
Received of his <u>wasges</u> for services in the late war	48 50
Received on a note of hand on Jesse Mullens and John Grimsly	14 00
The admrs are charged with the amt of	306 05
out of which they have paid the following sums	
To one receipt from Lawyer Kennedy	5 00
Do from Jos Sevier	2 40
Proven a/c by John Robertson	2 75
Proven a/c from Margaret Carson	1 00
Proven a/c from John Stuart	2 23
Do from Joseph Duncan	1 00
Cr by direct Tax pd by administrators	2 16

(p-198)   WILLIAM CARSONS Estate

Receipt from Jos Sevier for order for commissioners	50
For five Gallons and half of whiskey for the sale	2 81½
Money paid to the <u>crier</u> at the sale	2 00
To one paid to Lawyer Kennedy for counsel	1 00
Amt	22 91½
	306 05
	22 91
Amt of estate after paying all debts	283 14

     Given under our hands this 2nd day of Oct. 1832
                 John M Crawford Seal
                 John Strain Seal

THOMAS PRICE'S Estate

We the undersigned being appointed to settle with James W. Young admr of Thomas Price Deceased met the 11th day of October 1832.
From the Inventory returned and of Record said admr is chargeable with this sum $174 91½

Cash received of D. Thompson $ 9.55
                                                                    $184 46½
We find that said administrator by vouchers presented
has paid out from No 1 to No 30 This sum   193 94½
Amount charged   184 46½
Leaving the ballance due the admr   9 47½
He having paid out more than he had assets in his hands. Given under our
hands and seals this 11th Oct. 1832.
        Saml Greer seal JP
        Jacob Hartsell seal J P
        Joshua Boren seal J P

(p-199)   WILLIAM BAYLES GUARDIAN (Tyler heirs)

October Sessions 1832. William Bayles the guardian of Molinda Tyler Pheobe
Tyler Minerva Tyler and Betsey Tyler appeared in open Court and as he wishes
to pass over said wards Estate to another guardian and exhibits the settle-
ment by him made in this Court at the last January Sessions which shows that
on the 14th of said January he was chargeable on account of said wards Four
Thousand Twenty Two Dollars and ninety one and half cents $4022 91½
Interest on this sum up to 14th inst.   181 03
Making the sum of   4203 94½
And we allow said William Bayles for coming attending and returning home in
making this settlement twelve days at two dollars pr day $24.
For recording this settlement 62½ and Three dollars to the Committee for
making this settlement $3 00   27 62½
      Ballance $4176 32
We the Committee have examined the foregoing and find that there is now remaining in the hands of said Bayles as guardian four thousand one hundred
and seventy six dollars and thirty two cents, and that the sum of twenty seven dollars and seventy four cents allowed said Bayles in a settlement in
the January Session of this Court in 1832 for medicine, medical attendance
(or aid) Coffin and burying clothes for Malinda Tyler deceased, is allowed
to be taken exclusively out of her share or part of the estate. Examined
and given under our hands in open court this 16th day of Oct. 1832.
        W. P. Chester
        Jacob Hartsell   Comm.
        Richd Carr

(p-200)   JOSEPH YOUNG Estate

We find undersigned being appointed a Committee to settle with James W.
Young and Esther Young Executor and Executrix of Joseph Young Deceased met
on the 11th day of October 1832.
From amount of Inventories returned by said Executor and Executrix we find
them chargeable with this sum $1756 78½
And with this sum being the amt of property received
from James Gray   259 15½
                                                           $2015 94
Cash on hand   40 00
Debt due by Jas W. Young   35 00
                                                           $2090 94
We find that said Executor and Executrix has expended as per vouchers exhib-
ited this sum from No. 1 to No. 38 $1694 50½
And that said Executor and Executrix has paid in interest

on a note held by Chaney Boring dated 16th day of June
1821 this sum $113 16¾
And on a note given to Wilkins Young dated 22nd July
1818 this sum   391 00
And on a note given to Rebecca Irvin administratrix of Charles
Young deceased dated 16th October 1815 this sum   16 00
                                                            $2216 67¼

And that said Executor lifted a note given to John Chester
by his Testator which now amounts to this sum   128 37
This sum allowed the Executor Jos M. Young for cash
expended   22 12
For 164 days services at $1 00 per day   164 00
                                                            $2531 16¼
Amount charged   2090 94

(p-201)   JOSEPH YOUNGS Estate

Leaving this balance expended by   440 22½
the Executor over and above the assets which came into
their hands.

    Given under our hands and seals this 11th Oct. 1832.
                        Saml Greer seal   J P
                        Jacob Hartsell seal J. P.
                        Joshua Boring seal J P

SAMUEL B. LOVE'S Estate

A list of debts paid as the administrator of the Estate of Saml B. Love on
the behalf and for the said estate (to wit).

No.		$
1	paid Saml Hunt as shff of Washington an Execution in silver	$267 41
2	On a note of hand paid John McInturff	80 00
3	On a note paid Gammon & Crawford	138 16
4	Paid John M. Fain proven account	12 90
5	Paid James Guinn proven account	25 50
6	Paid Ganum C McBee proven account	47 00
7	Paid John Kennedys account	22 77
8	Paid Gammon & Crawford a note for	116 24
9	Paid Maj. Ryland on an execution for Dockins	39 68
10	Paid H. Harris on two notes given by Saml B. Love	80 00
11	Paid S. Crawford & C. Principal	23 83
12	Paid Gammon & Crawford a proven account	15 44¾
13	Paid Samuel Hunt for Taxes	6 06¼
14	Paid Samuel Hunt for Taxes in part for 1821 & 1822	23 67
15	Paid John Ryland in part of Taxes for 1827, 1828 & 1829	15 00
16	Paid Wm Erwin on a note	18 32
17	Paid Samuel Hunt for Taxes in part	5 00
18	Paid John Ryland for Taxes of 1827, 1828 & 1829	7 50
19	Paid Daniel Barkley on a proven a/c of Hiram Glass	10 00

                        Amt. Taken over $

(p-202)   SAML B. LOVES Estate

                        Amt Brot over $

SETTLEMENTS OF ESTATES, VOLUME 00, 1790-1841

⚜ (See Errata for correction)

20	Paid G & Crawford on a note J. McInturff for Iron	$26 00
21	Paid Saml Crawford & Co on a note	24 12½
22	Paid Jno Ryland for James Gaynn on a note	1 66
23	Paid George Williams on a note	10 00
24	Paid Isreal McInturff on a protested order	3 00
25	Paid John Ryland on an Exedution in favor of Rebecca Rogeown	15 00
26	Paid Rebin Rogers on an Execution in favour of Baxter Bean	3 25
27	Paid John S. Williams part of a Judgement	5 00
28	Paid E. S. Howel for Teaching the Heirs of Saml B. Love Decd.	6 00
29	Paid Jonathan Carauthers on a note & Judgement	8 83½
30	Paid Jonathan Caruthers a Balance on a note & Judgement in	5 75
31	Paid Saml Hunt for Taxes paid/1825. Say half	38 13½
32	Paid James H Young on a note	8 00
33	Paid Jonathan Suter an execution in favor of T. Stuart & V. B. Ross	10 00
34	Paid David Carden due Bill	5 00
35	Paid John Ryland on a note & warrant for O. B. Ross	6 07½
36	Paid Daniel Barkleys proven account	10 00
37	Paid D. Nelson on a note due 24th day of June 1823 & Int. from date	11 00
38	Paid the Hon John Blair for the use of W. K. Vance	31 00
39	Pd. G. Slagle $3 00 on a due Bill due 9th Septr 1822 It to 12th March 1827	3 25
40	Paid Wm Brown agreaable to an award of arbitration	141 18
41	Paid Saml Greer for registration fees	1 81¼
42	Paid for Schooling	2 00
43	Paid Gammon & Crawford on a note to Thos Lackey	3 00
44	Paid a proven account of William Henderson	3 00
45	Paid J. N. Hadden for Schooling	6 20
46	Paid Wm B. Carters proven account	5 00
47	Paid Wm Browns proven account	5 00
48	Paid Jno Ryland on a note & Execution to Saml Maxwell	7 31
49	Paid John Hise an account	1 00
50	Paid David S. Mitchel Shff of White County the costs of a Suit brought by Saml B. Love against the Securities of Thos Taylor former shff of W. County	25 75
	Amt Taken up $	

(p-203) SAML B LOVES Estate

51	Paid Jacob Ranges proven account	1 53¾
52	Paid Saml Crawfords Debt against P. S. Love	20 00
53	Paid John G. Eason on an Execution P. S. Love	12 14½
54	Paid John G. Eason a proven account against Polly S. Love	4 50
55	Paid Gammon & Son for P. S. Love on a note & account	10 91½
56	Paid Nelson & Kenny proven account against P. S. Love	12 50
57	Paid James W. Young proven account against P. S. Love	3 62½
58	Paid Col. N. Edmonson for money Recd from Embree by	

59	Paid Joshua Swonger for Smith work for the farm	$ 2	25
60	Paid Juball Massey for Smith work for the farm	4	87½
61	Paid Printer for printing advertisement Say	3	00
62	Paid John Wilds proven account		50
63	Paid Clerks fee on Administration	1	20
64	Paid Clerks fee on Inventory		60
65	Paid Col. James Taylor on Notes of hand with Interest	25	09½
66	Paid H. Wells cost and warrant taken against John Love and note		50
	Also paid Samuel Hunt on an Execution	8	00
	Paid Col. James Taylor as an atto for attendance as a fee	15	00
	Paid Alfred Taylor in a Joint fee with Saml B. Love in the case of Edmonson against Embree in Equity	5	00
	Paid Doct J. E. Cossin	4	25
		$1560	72

Robert Love has Exhibited Vouchers for all the Interest contained in the foregoing account amounting to fifteen hundred & Sixty Dollars Seventy two cents, from the above deduct amount of Debts due the Estate of Saml B. Love Deceased which Robert Love administrator considers   516 25
himself accountable for   1044 47
                 Deduct for over charged   10 00
Balance due to Robert Love administrator aforesaid $1034 47
as appears from the foregoing Statement amounting to the Sum of Ten hundred thirty four dollars and forty Seven cents, and we further find that Robert Love has received of the estate of Samuel (p-204) B. Love, has received of the Estate Six *negros* which said six *negros* we find has been received by the Heirs of Samuel Love from said Robert with their Increase which is four *negros* making all Ten *negros*. We the undersigned do certify that we have Examined the account of Robert Love Administrator of Samuel B. Love Estate & we find Robert Love chargeable with the foregoing amount as Stated, credited with aforesaid credits Given under our hands this 16th day of October 1832.

                        Daniel Barkley
                        Jacob Brown   Commissioners
                        Terry White

WILLIAM TYLER Estate

As Guardian of Phebe Tyler, Elizabeth Tyler & Minerva Tyler, minor Heirs of Wm. Tyler Deceast, I received (for me Guardian of the above named Heirs) Two notes of hand one on Said Wm Bayless John Bayless John Blair & Nathan Shipley for Two thousand Six hundred & Eighty Eight dollars 67/100 Supposed to be good $2688 67
& one note on John Blair for Nine Hundred & Seventeen
Dollars & Eighty four cents, supposed to be Good   917 84
Making in all Three thousand Six hundred and & Six 3606 54
Dollars & fifty four cents. Bearing Interest from the day of October 1832.

                    E. L. Mathis Guardian

Settlement with the Court at January Session of 1833, as Guardian of Wm. Tyler minor heir of Wm. Tyler Deceast up to this date there is in hands Twelve Hundred & fifty Seven Dollars & thirty three cents 1257 33
five days Services on attending on this Estate Since it came into

SETTLEMENTS OF ESTATES, VOLUME 00, 1790-1841

my hands which will be   5 00
Due said ward Twelve Hundred & fifty Two Dollars $1252 33
and thirty three cents

                           Ebenezer L. Mathis
                           Guardian of
                           Wm Tyler

(p-205)   THOMAS TILFORDS Estate

STATE OF TENNESSEE }
WASHINGTON COUNTY }   Pursuant to an order of the County Court of County dated October Session 1832 and to us the undersigned directed to Settle with George W. Tilford & E. L. Mathis and Miram Tilford Executors and Executrix of Thomas Tilford Deceast, we met at the House of George W. Tilford on 19th of January 1833 and after cawling for the papers, they produced and Inventory and find them charged with this amount   3 $2710 67½
      Mill wood account
$903 55 of third of the Valuable Sum   903 55
  16 66 one third of a Lawyers fee $50. in Broyles Suit
$886 89
177 36 Interest for three years & 4 months
1064 25
665 07 one third of the cost of the Law Suit also five hundred
399 18 dollars Recd by Mile Wood
117 70 Interest at four year & Eleven months
516 88
272 00 Received by M. Wood
244 88
 21 66 one third of Loss by A Finch & fee
223 22
 73 59 Interest five years & Six months
295 81
174 25 Received by M. Wood
122 56
 41 00 One third Loss Sustained in McNees land
 82 56
 43 08 One third of $129 26 notes on Saml & G. G. McNees
 39 48
  3 12 Interest for one year & four months
 42 60 $16 00 paid to Elisabeth Tilford in the year 1817 by account
       14 40 Interest on the above Sum to the present date.
 30 40   30 40
 12 20
    66 One third of Commissioners fees
$11 54   Taken over

(p-206)   THOMAS TILFORDS Estate

$11 54
  3 66 One third of McNees Suit
  7 88 Allowed for G. W. Tilford Executor for his Services one third out
        of $108 16 Equals $36 05
                                                              7 88
M. Wood due G. W. Tilford this sum 19th Jany 1833   28 17 cents
  3   $2710 67½   J Hannah a/c
        903 55 one third of the available Sum

$16 16   one third of $50 Lawyers fee in the Broyles Suit
886 89
177 36   Interest for 3 years & 4 months
1064 25
165 07   One third of the cost of the law Suit
899 18
215 76   Interest for 4 years
1114 94
330 00 Received of J. Hannah
784 94
 18 80 One third of a Loss by A. Finch & fee
766 14
102 13 Interest for 2 years 2 months & 20 Days up to Jany 21st 1826
868 27
152 00 Received of J. Hannah
716 27
 14 32 Interest for 4 months
730 59
 51 00 Received J. Hannah
679 59
 30 55 Interest for 9 months up to 2nd March 1827
710 14
 82 00   Received of J. Hannah
628 14
 18 84 Interest for 6 months up 5th Sept 1827
646 98

(p-207)   THOMAS TILFORDS Estate

646 98
150 00 Received by J. Hannah
496 98
 29 76 Interest for one year
526 74
 69 21 Received by Grace Hannah
457 53
 15 99 Interest for 9 months
473 52
112 60 Received by H. Hannah
360 92
 21 60 Interest for one year
382 52
 40 00 Loss Sustained by McNess land
342 52
 43 08   One third of $129 26 notes on Saml & G. A. G. McNees
299 44
  5 66 Loss Sustained in McNees Suit
293 78
   66   One third of Commissioners fees
293 12
 36 16 One third of Executors Services
256 96 This Sum Due Grace Hannah 25th August 1830.

STATE OF TENNESSEE }
WASHINGTON COUNTY } We the undersigned do find that G. W. Tilford Executor has over paid Mils Wood twenty Eight Dollars & Seventeen Cts of the available funds, and the Executor is due to John Hannah 25th August 1830 to

which time we calculated the sum of Two Hundred and fifty Six Dollars &
Ninety Six cents, Given under our hands and Seals 19th January 1833

         John Link (Seal)
             (Seal) Commissioners

Notes on hand & returned in Inventory
Desperate and not collected.

157 80	Cornelius Broyles & Scott Kennedy		
159 80	Do Do		
213 12½	Do Do	129 26	notes on Saml & G. A. G. McNees Doubtful but if
90 40	on Peter Sterns		can be collected Each to have his proportional
11 31	on Do Do		part & the Finch Debt if it can be collected Each to have his part--

(p-208)   WALKER BOONES Estate

STATE OF TENNESSEE
WASHINGTON COUNTY Pursuant to an order of Court we John Gott, Nathan
Shipley & Jacob Ellis Esqrs. a Committee appointed to Settle with Thomas
Barnes Executor of the Estate of Walker Barnes Deceast, have proceeded and
found the Executor chargeable with amount of Sale.

	$847 91½
One note on Samuel Job for	10 00
One note on John Bowser for	20 00
One due Bill on Wm Kellow for	5 00
One note on Roland P. Murray for	6 47
One note on Jacob Barron for	6 50
One note on John Douglass for	37 50
One due Bill on John Douglass for	1 00
One note on John Douglass for	37 50
	971 88½
Vouchers paid by the Executor	
John Stephensons proved a/c	3 50
Bricker takes Receipts	14 07½
Clerks fees	4 62½
Funeral Expenses	5 62½
Gammon a/c	1 25
Hulse's a/c for Crying Sale	2 00
Fitzgerrald a/c for crying Sale	1 15
proveing and recording Grant	1 25
	33 47½

Allowed the Executor for Services rendered $50 00

Given under our hands this 12th day of July 1833.
         Jacob Ellis
         John Gott
         Nathan Shipley

(p-209)   E. L. MATHES, GUARDIAN

Annual Settlement of the accounts between myself & Wards as Guardian of Nancy
& Alexr Nelson minor heirs of A. M. Nelson Deceast for the year Ending July
Term 1833. See Settlement July Session 1832. Total amount in good funds
Forty four hundred and fifty three Dollars and ninety five cents $4453 95
Five hundred & twenty four Dollars & 73 cents on G. T. Gillespie 524 73
And two hundred fifty three Dollars & Eighty cents on James Pat- 253 80

terson Deceased. Both in Green County which Sums I have received no Interest Since Settlement 1832. $3675 42
Two hundred Twenty Dollars & fifty two cents interest on 220 52
the above Sum for one year to be added
Twenty Dollars half of Beckly & Vilet, here added 20 00
Add Seven Hundred Seventy Eight Dollars & fifty 3 cents on 778 53
Gillespie & Patterson in Green County $4694 05
Add Twenty four Dollars for a bed & corn sold 24 50
Paid out Since the Settlement of 1832. $4718 55
No. 1 Mrs. Howards account $16 71 408 39
No. 2 Deadricks & Kinneys account $120 94 $4310 18
No. 3 Greenways & Jones account 207 75
No. 4 Guardians account for slaves
clothing & Services rendered
since Settlement 1832 19 52
Paid James McLin for schooling 24 50
Good & Co. advanced the wards 18 97
five pr cent on the sum paid out $408 39
Disbursed by Said Guardian his compen
returned for Services & Expenses as Such last Sums deducted leaves in said Guardian's hands of Good funds, Forty three hundred & ten Dollars Eighteen cents, The Seven Hundred thirty two dollars & forty five cents, & the Debt on James Allen remains as in last Settlement.

E. L. Mathis
Guardian of the minor
Ordered by Court that this within Settle- heirs of A. M. Nelson Decd.
ment be recorded.
Levi Bowers Chairman Protem

(p-210) JOHN W. DOAKS Estate

STATE OF TENNESSEE
WASHINGTON COUNTY Pursuant to an order of the County Court of said County Dated April Session 1833, and to us the undersigned Directed to Settle with Ebenezer Mathis Surviving Executor of John W. Doak Deceased, we met at the House of Jane Doak on 13th of July 1833, and after calling on the Executor for his papers he produced an Inventory and other papers, find him charged with this sum $2693 93
And produced vouchers to this amount 2913 00
And we find that E. L. Mathis Executor has paid two Hundred and Twenty Dollars thirty four cents over and above what came into his hands, and are opinion that the above named Executor is entitled to one hundred and fifty dollars for the percent in money collected and paid out and other Services Vending on Sales & Suits which adding to the Twenty Six Dollars & Seventy cents for attending to Suits making one hundred & Seventy Six Dollars & Seventy cents 176 70
Given under our hands & Seals the date above written.

John Link (Seal)
John Humphreys (Seal)
Joseph McLin (Seal) Committee

And we the undersigned Heirs of Jno W. Doak deceased being present at the within Settlement and having examined the Inventory and vouchers produced by the Executor and are of opinion he has acted, he has done it in good faith, and one note Saml Lyle and John Damron for four hundred & fifty Dollars in Brick work, Two thirds of said note belongs to the Estate, paid Several notes and a/cs returned on the Inventory Desperate which is yet in the hands of the Executor and the Executor agrees to receive and act on any legal Instructions from said heirs to collect the said notes and accounts, and Said Executor holds himself ready at any time if their should be a mistake in the within Settlement to correct it, and are all satisfyed that the court receive the Settlement as good and valid. Given under our hands and Seals 13th July 1833

(p-211)

Interlined before Signed	John N. Doak (Seal)
Test	John S. Waddle (Seal)
John Link	William W. Bovell (Seal)
John Humphreys	Alexander C. Mathis (Seal)
	Jone A. Doak (Seal)
	Archibald A. Doak (Seal)
July Session 1833 approved by Court	
	Levi Bowers Chairmen Protem

JOHN MELVINS Estate

Pursuant to an order of Court we Richard Carr and Jacob Ellis and Jacob Hartsell being appointed to Settle with James Melvin Administrator of John Melvin Deceast we met the 13th day of April 1833. We find the administrator chargeable by the Sale papers $156 59½

Produced Vouchers

1	Receipt for Eleven dollars pd Rachael Melvin 4th March 1824	11 00
2	By Recpt paid Rachael Melvin August 1823	34 02
3	James Sevier clerks receipt 1833	50
4	Money pd over to Rachael Melvin Guardian April 12th 1833	22 88
5	Money pd over to Rachael Melvin Guardian	57 08
6	Amt acknowledged by Guardian to be paid the administrator 1824	32 40
	Produced vouchers to the amount	$157 88

which leaves a balance due to the administrator the amount of one Dollar and Twenty Eight cents due. Given under our hands & Seals this 13th day of April 1833.

Jacob Hartsell (Seal)
Justice of Peace
Richard Carr (Seal)
Justice of Peace
Jacob Ellis (Seal)
Justice of Peace

(p-212) Annual Settlement of the accounts between myself & wards as Guardian of Alexander Nelson for the year Ending July Session 1834. See Settlement 1833. Total amount in good funds Four thousand three hundred and ten Dollars 18/100 $4310 18
of this Sum there is five hundred & twenty four Dollars & 73 cents in Green County on G. T. Gillespie on   524 73
                                                                                                         3785 45
which I have received no Interest Since Settlement 1833
Add two hundred & twenty Seven Dollars 12/100 Interest   227 12
Add Twenty Dollars & fifty cents half Servant Hire   20 50
Add fifteen Dollars 22. Interest on J. Pattersons note

WASHINGTON COUNTY, TENNESSEE

for the year 1833 $15 28
                                                                        $4048 29

Add Gillispies five hundred twenty four Dollars &
Seventy three cents.   524 73
Paid out since Settlement 1833   4573 02
1   J. Boyds a/c Twenty Dollars & Interest $20 60   199 77
2. Brickers receipt for Tax   9 61   4373 25
3   Hinkels a/c & Interest   8 92
4   Atkinsons account   11 69
5   Deadricks a/c   17 86
6   Gammons account 12 & Interest   32 25
7   Eason & Co Account   32 71
8   Guardians a/c for Shoes clothing & Ser-
    vices rendered since Settlement 1833   27 87
9   Jones & Greenways a/c of Greenville   11 49
10 Doct S. B. Cunninghams account   17 25
                                             190 25

    five per cent on this Sum Nine Dollars
    & fifty two cts.   9 52
                                             199 77

Disbursed by Said Guardian his Compensation for Services & Expenses as Such
which last Sum deducted leaves in the hands of said Guardian of Good funds
or common currency Four thousand three hundred Seventy three Dollars twenty
five cents, The Debt on James Allen & E. Embree remain as in last Settlement.
                                            E. L. Mathis
July Session 1834 approved by   Guardian &c.
Court
Jacob Brown Chareman Protem

(p-213)   REUBIN BAYLESS Estate

STATE OF TENNESSEE
WASHINGTON COUNTY   We the Committee appointed by Court to Settle with
the Executors of the Estate of Reubin Bayless Deceast, on the 29th January
1834. And we find the amount of the personal Estate in the hands of James
White one of the Executors of Said Estate to be $5213 14
                Vouchers as below   44 67
                                                           5168 47
                Extra drawn for Rebecca   300 00
                                                           4868 47
Executors Commission at 5 pr cent   260 65
                                                          $4607 82
And he produced the following Vouchers for money pd out by him.
1   James Sevier Receipt   .50
2   James Sevier Receipt   62½
3   Andrew Taylors Receipt $2 00
4   Andrew Taylors Receipt   1 00
5   James Acton   6 75
6   Richard Bayless   4 00
7   Alfred M. Carter   25
8   William Gott Receipt   4 14
9   William Gott Receipt   2 25
10   Alfred M. Carters Receipt   1 00
11   William P. Chesters Judgement   6 50
12   James Seviers Receipt   50

13	James Seviers Receipt	$1 50
14	Isaac Hartsell proved a/c	6 00
15	Wm Carter Rct. from Sheriff of Carter County	7 66
		$44 67

We also find that Daniel L. Bayless hath in his hand the amount of Banks Stock in his hand belonging to the Estate of the said Reubin Bayless Dect. three hundred & forty Dollars & 35/100 $340 35
For Services produced   17 01
There appears to be in the hands of Daniel L. Bay-   323 34
less of the Bank Stock this amount

(p-214)   REUBIN BAYLESS Estate

We likewise find that there is in hands of Daniel L. Bayless and Isaac Hendly the amount of the rents belonging to the Estate of the said Reubin Bayless Deceast, to be three hundred & forty three Dollars and Twenty two cents $343 22
There appears to be in the hands of Daniel L. Bayless   74 36
& Isaac Hendly of the rents of the said plantation this
amount $268 86

Daniel L. Bayless produced the following Vouchers & Receipts

No. 1	James Sevier Receipt	1 00
No. 2	John Brickers Receipt	10 00
3	Adam Mays Receipt	1 00
4	John Brickers Receipt	2 25½
5	William Colyars Receipt	7 31
6	John Brickers Receipt	1 56¼
7	John Brickers Receipt	1 56¼
8	Isaac Hartsels Receipt	2 00
9	paid Spirits at Sales this amount	1 87½
		$28 56½

We also find that James White, Daniel L. Bayless & Isaac Hendly done the following work & labor on the plantation of the said Deceast which they <u>clame</u> out of the rents of the said plantation

Daniel L. Bayless	$16 15
James White	8 00
Isaac Hendly	4 50
	$28 65

Amount forwarded $4607 82

We find that there is returned in the Inventory and note on James White for $12 92 and also one on James Campbell for thirty five Dollars which was returned Desperate and cannot be collected and ought to be deducted $47 92

And there is note on Nashvill Bank $12 00 Sold for $2 00   10 00
   $4549 90

Taken up

(p-215)   REUBIN BAYLESS Estate

Amt Brot up $4549 90
Commissioners Receipts for Services performed   9.

This appears to be the balance in the hands $1065 64
of James White one of the Executor of Estate of
Reubin Bayless Deceast.
We find that James White hath in his hands Receipts
& vouchers of the different Legatees to this amount

We the Committees appointed by Court to Settle with the Executors of Reubin
Bayless Dect, James White, Daniel L. Bayless & Isaac Hendly, proceeded to
Examine the papers of vouchers belonging to Said Estate and do find that
there is in the hands of James White, one thousand & Sixty five dollars &
Sixty four cents after deducting his vouchers & Services, and in the hands
of Daniel L. Bayless of the Bank Stock Two hundred & ninety four Dollars and
Seventy Eight cents, and we also find that there is in the hands of Daniel
L. Bayless & Isaac Hendly. Two hundred & ninety Seven Dollars & fifty Seven
cents of the rents of the plantation of Said Deceast - Given under our
hands this 11th March 1834.

                              Jacob Brown
The Sum of one thousand   Wm Colyar   Committee
& Sixty five Dollars & Sixty   John Humphreys
four cents under the aracurd

E. L. MATHIS (GUARDIAN OF WM TYLER)

January Session 1834
Annual Settlement with E. L. Mathis & his ward William Tyler minor heir of
Wm. Tyler Deceast, at a Settlement January Session 1833. there was Twelve
hundred Dollars & thirty three cents $1225 33
Interest on that is Seventy three Dollars & fifty cents   73 50
Makeing Twelve hundred Ninety Eight Dollars 83/100   1298 83

Received from Isaac Overall a administrator in Va. Three hundred Sixteen Dollars Twenty five cents   316 25
Take $31 25 out for my Services two trips to Va   31 25
One to Woodstock & one to Winchester   285 00

(p-216)   E. L. MATHES (GUARDIAN OF WM TYLER)

                              Amt Brot over $1298 83
                            Second amount " "   291 32
                                                 $1590 15
                            $285 00
Received $66 57 out of the Kox Bank, take $2 00
My Services going to Knoxville attending to $64 59
Business leaves $64 57 added makes $349 57   349 57
Paid out to Deadrick $5 50   58 25
To Naff   13 50   291 32
To James McLin   21 00
To Reubin Bayless   4 00
To L. J. Lucky   14 25
                  $58 25

From the above Statement there is in my hands at this date fifteen hundred
ninety Dollars & fifteen cents, Except Some clerks fees not paid out yet.
January Session 1834, approved of   E. L. Mathis
by Court John Link Chairman Protem   Guardian of Wm Tyler

E. L. MATHIS GUARDIAN of the MISS TYLER &C.

January Session 1834

E. L. Mathis Guardian of Phebe, Minerva & Elizabeth Tyler, Minor heirs of Wm Tyler Deceast. at January Session 1833.

I reported Three thousand Six hundred & Six Dollars 54/100	$3606 54
Two and one half pr cent out of that	108 19
leaves Three thousand four hundred ninety Eight Dollars	3498 35
& thirty Seven cents	
Interest on that amount for 15 months	262 37
Received nine Hundred forty Eight Dollars 75/100 from	$3760 72
Isaac Overall, Virginia, Take ninety three dollars 75/100	829 93
my Services (viz) one trip to Woodstock, Va. in 1830	90 35
& one trip to Winchester, Va. 1833	4681 00
	42 75
	$4638 25

(p-217)   E. L. MATHIS (GUARDIAN of the MISS TYLERS)

leaves Eight hundred fifty five Dollars, Two & a half pr cent out of that is $25 65 leaves Eight hundred twenty nine Dollars & thirty five cents-- Received twenty nine Dollars and Seventy three cents out of the Bank of Knoxville U. S. Money take Six dollars out of that for my going to Knoxville, attending to said money & two Dollars & Eighty Eight cents, the two & a half pr cent retained, leaves ninety Dollars & ninety three cents, added makes four thousand Six hundred Eighty one Dollars paid forty two Dollars & Seventy five cents out of the above to L. J. W. Lucky clerk of the Supreme Court (Subtracted) leaves in my hands at this time Four thousand Six hundred thirty Eight Dollars and twenty five cents $4638 25

            E. L. Mathis
            Guardian of Phebe,
January Session 1834   Minerva & Elizabeth Tyler
Approved of by Court
John Link
Chairman Protem

JOHN BRICKER (GUARDIAN OF ALEXANDER DOAK)

STATE OF TENNESSEE
WASHINGTON COUNTY   Pursuant to an order of the County Court of said County dated Oct. Session 1833, and to us the undersigned directed to Settle with John Bricker (Guardian of Alexander Doak, we met at Jacksons School House on the 9th November 1833, and after calling on the Guardian he produced

to us the following papers and find him charged with this Sum		$90 91¼
And produced legal vouchers to this amount		38 73¼
1 Note Jane Doak & Wm McGee due 23rd June 1831	$35 20	52 17¼
Account agains Doak for wheat	6 02	
Also account against the same for corn	8 18¼	
For receiving and paying out $90 91¼		49 40¼
for paying out 38 73¼		
129 64½		
Commission on the above Sum		3 24
		$52 64¼

WASHINGTON COUNTY, TENNESSEE

(p-218)   JOHN BRICKER (GUARDIAN OF ALEXANDER DOAK)

And we find that the Guardian has paid forty Seven cents, and notes on hand more than came to his hands. Given under our hands and Seals 9th November 1833.

                                                       John Link   (Seal)
                                                     E. L. Mathis (Seal)

Returned at January Session 1834   John Humphreys (Seal)

JOHN RANGE'S Estate

STATE OF TENNESSEE
WASHINGTON COUNTY   We the undersigned Justices of the peace for Said County being appointed a Committee to Settle with John Wright Administrator and Abigal Range Administratrix of John Range Deceast, of Said County, and after duly Examming and Enquiring into the whole matter and appurtenances of the said Estate, being now on the premises, March 31st day 1834.

By the list of the Sale	$861 66¾
To 1 note on John G. Eason with $40 credited	208 80
(Interest from the 30th May 1828	
To cash on hand (and Interest)	256 56½
Two notes on James Caruthers (and Interest)	29 91
One note on John Saylor No 1	28 50
One note Martin Kitsmiller	188 25
One note on James Young (Balance	50
One note Thomas King	36 30
One note on Joseph Bell	1 78
One note on William & George King	35 72
One note James & William Houston	22 40
One note on Ephraim Ganes	1 50
One note on John Humphreys No 2	4 40
One note on John Fulmer	1 15
One note on Valentine Bowers	1 12
One order on John Wilcox (four hundred lb	12 00
One due Bill on Mark Reeve & Son	20 67
One note on Sheriff for Beauro	18 00
	$1729 23¼

(p-219)   JOHN RANGE Estate

Amt Brot up	$1729 23¼
One note on A. A. Kincannan (Desperate No. 4	101 25
One note David Kitsmiller	62 74
One note on Jacob Hair (Desperate (No 5	17 50
One note on Braxton Bary for 46 lb Coffee (Desperate)	
One note on John Wooldridge (Desperate No 6	112 40
One Do Do Do No. 7	12 33
One Do Do Do No. 8	4 80
One note on Joseph & Thomas Bacon (Desperate No. 9	91 25
One note on Joseph & Thomas Bacon (Desperate No. 10	60 00
One Do Do Do No. 11	20 00
One Note on Henry Jones 163½ lb Iron (Desperate No 12	
Two notes on Mark Reeves & Son (Desperate No 13	110 05
Bal. of note on S. Q. Sherfey for Iron (Desperate No 15	1 00

One on Jacob Miller No 16	$20 16
One Do Do No. 17	2 00
One note on Joseph Shell & Halfacre, Desperate No. 18	80 00
One due Bill on Thomas Dunworth (Desperate No. 19	
One note on Peter Emmert (Desperate No. 20	2 00
One note on Henry Miller (for 32 Bushels corn) allowed for the year of the widow	
One note on John Deckard Dect-	
Constable Recd for David & Ab Scotts notes (Desperate No. 21	
	$150 00
J. Worley, R. C. J. James Desperate No. 22	5 50
Jefferson Ranges Receipt No. 44	125 50
Zachariah & Susannah Butler Receipt No. 43	54 57
Balance on the old Book account	45 98
Amt of Interest on the Sale money up to the present date	$2808 67 1/3
	120 63
	$2929 30 1/3

On Examining of the a/c I am charged with a Rect No. 43 for $54 57 but it should of been No. 29 for $170. this must be corrected on next Settlement, make-ing a mistake of $115 43 in property.

         J. Wright

(p-220)   JOHN RANGES Estate

And we find them Intitled to the following Crt with Interest from the payments up to this date as we have charged & counted Interest on the debtor Side to the Same---

By John G. Easons proven account No. 23	$19 30
" Jefferson Rages Receipt No. 24	174 75
" John & Elizabeth Longmires No. 25	179 16
" Jacob Rangs account No. 26	58 65
" Susannah Ranges Receipt No. 27	109 50
" Hugh Manes proven account No. 28	15 60
" Zachariah & Susannah Buttler No. 29	170 00
" William White Receipt No. 30	1 20
" D. Sellers receipt for cost No. 31	2 25
" Wm. Stockhouses Receipt No. 32	8 00
" John Parkers School Receipt No. 33	7 63
" Tax Receipt No. 34	9 00
" D. Sellers Cost Receipt No. 35	1 12½
" James Seviers Receipt No. 36	1 42
" George Littles proven account No. 37	2 92
" Doctor Bill No. 38	21 83
" John Malonee proven account No. 39	3 91
" John Saylors proven account No. 40	13 53
" William & George G. Kings proven account No. 41	15 84
" Abegal Ranges (Receipt No. 42	171 00
" Zachariah & Susannah Butler Receipt No. 43	54 57
"	6 00
" John Williams Receipt	4 75
" John Worleys Receipt	2 37½
" Jefferson Ranges Receipt No. 44	125 50
" Jefferson Ranges Receipt No. 45	6 50
" Abigal Ranges Receipt No. 46	12 00
" paying (carpenters) H. Worley for repairing & doing to the House on premises 48	
Taken up	$77 22

(p-221)   JOHN RANGES Estate

                           Amt Brot up $
John & Elizabeth Longmires Receipt 47   6 00
Sarah Ranges Receipt No. 49   53 50
                                                  $1335 03

STATE OF TENNESSEE }
WASHINGTON COUNTY } We the undersigned a committee appointed by Court to
Settle with John Wright, Administrator and Abigal Range, Administratrix, of
the Estate of John Range Deceast, do find the administrator & Administratrix
chargeable as above stated with $2929 30 1/3
And having produced vouchers to the amount of 1335 03
Leaving a Balance of $1594 27 1/3
As we believe to be correct. Given under our hands this 1st day of April
1834.

                            Jacob Ellis
                            Justice of Peace
              Committee   Joshua Boren
                            Justice of the Peace
                            Henry King
                            Justice of the Peace

                        JAMES YOUNGS Estate

STATE OF TENNESSEE }
WASHINGTON COUNTY } This day agreeable to an order of Court at April
Session 1834. We as a Committee appointed by Said Court to Settle with
William H. Young and James Gillispie, Executors of James Young, Deceast,
Guardian of Catheran Young, met at the house of James Young, Deceast on the
27th day of June 1834.
    We find Catharan Young in possession of the following property. Three
head of Horses, Two Cows, five young Cattle, Two Black Men, one negro Girl,
one negro man Sold at five Hundred Dollars, and the money appropriated to
the youse of James W. Young Deceast, in 1834, after taken

(p-222)   JAMES YOUNGS Estate

into consideration the age of the negros from one year and five months old
and upwards, and Sise of her farm being so Small that said Catharine Young
should have no Interest on the above Sold negro $500 00
We find James W. Young Deceast charged with five Hundred Dollars
We find in the possession of James W. Young Deceast the following Vouchers
for money paid out by her proportionable part paid into Ewin Young for the
Land She now Lives on $113 00
No. 2   80 1/2
    #3   3 00
     4   1 37
     5   5 39
     6   3 38
     7   5 29 1/2
     8   4 06
     9   4 28
    10   2 64
    11   7 41
    12   5 29 1/2

No. 13	$1 49½
14	2 66
15	2 30½
16	3 49
17	25 00
18	1 25
19	13 00
20	42 50
21	22 49
22	21 50
23	1 56¼
24	1 00

Taken up $

(p-223)   JAMES YOUNGS Estate

No. 25	1 06¼
26	60
27	50
28	60
29	60
30	60
31	2 00
32	2 68
33	4 49
34	3 75
35	6 00
36	7 00
37 for Direct Tax 1814	5 92½
38 for Direct Tax 1815	14 28½
39 for our Services on Settlement	3 00
	$347 30

We find James W. Young Deceast charged with after Deducting the above account from the five hundred Dollars $152 70
Whereunto We Set our hands the day and date above written

                                   Henry King
                                   Justice of the Peace
July Session 1834 approved of by   Joshua Boren
Court   Justice of the Peace
     Jacob Brown   Jacob Hartsell
     <u>Chareman</u> protem   Justice of the Peace

THOMAS BROWNS Estate

STATE OF TENNESSEE
WASHINGTON COUNTY   Agreeable to an order of the County <u>County</u> Court, dated July Session 1834. And to us directed to Settle with Jacob Brown, and

(p-224)   THOMAS BROWNS Estate

Samuel G. Bayless, Executors of Thomas Brown, Deceast, We met in Jonesborough on July 1834 and after calling on the Executors for their papers they produced to us Legal vouchers for money paid & Services rendered--

| No. 1 | Clerks Receipt | $ .62½ |
| 2 | Recording Settlement | 62½ |

WASHINGTON COUNTY, TENNESSEE

No. 3   S. G. Bayless for Services $4 00

                                                 $5 25

And find them charged with four Dollars & fifty Cents as by Inventory retained by Court, Given under our hands & Seals 21st July 1834.

	E. L. Mathis (Seal)
July Session 1834 allowed	Jacob Hartsell (Seal)
by Court Jacob Brown	Wm. S. Erwin (Seal)
Chareman protem	

THOMAS BEARDS Estate

STATE OF TENNESSEE
WASHINGTON COUNTY   In pursuance to an order of Court made at April Session 1834, Appointing Nathan Shipley, Henry King & E. L. Mathis, a Committe to Settle with Daniel Deakins, & James Beard, administrators of Robert Beard Deceast, & return this Settlement to the present term, the Committee met in Jonesborough on the 24th April 1834, after calling on the administrators for the papers they produced an Inventory of Sale amounting to Six hundred Dollars & Seventy one cents $600 71

Which Sum Said administrators are chargeable with, also for the hire of negros one hundred & Eleven Dollars & twenty Six cents   111 26
Which sum will be due the 5th Novr. 1834   711 97
And the Said Admrs produced the following vouchers

(p-225)   THOMAS BEARDS Estate

No. 1	Dossers receipt as cryer	$1 00
2	Thos D. Greer clerk receipt	2 00
3	Richard Deacons	2 00
4	Do Do	1 00
5	Clerks Receipt	2 00
6	Dossers receipt for crying the sale	2 00
7	Daniel Deacons account	3 00
8	Martha Beards receipt for nessacerries furnished	22 12½
9	By Daniel Deacons administrator	10 00
"	" Kennedys Receipt ten Dollars	10 00
"	" James Beards as Adr charged for ten days Service	
"	" Danl Deacons as adr charged for Eight days Service	8 00
		$63 12½

We the Committee appointed do find the said Admrs chargeable
with the sum of $711 97
And the vouchers which they produced & received amounting to Sixty three dollars 12½ cents   63 12½
Leaving a Balance in favor of the Estate of Six Hundred
& forty eight dollars & eighty four cents $648 84½
Due Nov. 1834   Nathan Shipley
                                Henry King   Committee
                                E. L. Mathis

E. L. MATHIS, GUARDIAN OF A. NELSON & M. G. KINNEY

SETTLEMENTS OF ESTATES, VOLUME 00, 1790-1841

✶ (See Errata for Correction)

STATE OF TENNESSEE
WASHINGTON COUNTY   Septr 10th, 1834

We E. L. Mathis, Guardian of Alexander Nelson & M. G. Kinney, administratrix of the Estate of Col. John Nelson Deceast, met for the purpose of Settling the Business of Said Estate as the Committee appointed by the County Court(could not Settle with Sd Administratrix from the Inventory returned by her) on Examination of the Books of said administratrix I do find that sd administratrix has received the Sum of Eleven hundred ninety Six Dollars & ninety nine cents & from said Books & vouchers Sd administratrix

(p-226)   E. L. MATHES, GUARDIAN OF A. NELSON & M. G. KINNEY

has paid out the sum of Eleven hundred Eighty four Dollars and Twenty Eight cents leaving in the hands of the administratrix Twelve Dollars & Seventy one cents, allowing Said administratrix fifty nine Dollars & Twenty one cents 5 pr cent on the above Sum of $1184 28 paid out, leaves a Balance due Said adx forty Six Dollars & fifty cents, besides leaving in the hands of Said adx Several notes of hand on Wm Colyar, Robt Strain & others which are considered Desperate or at least Doubtful but if any part of them Said admx is to receive the remainder of the present which is $46 50 & divide the residue if any, I believe the Books above alluded to was correctly kept & was the only criterion We could come at to make a Just Settlement as the Inventory which was returned by Said admx was in correct, Given under my hand the day and date above written

          E. L. Mathis
          Guardian & co.

REESE BAYLESS, GUARDIAN OF THE HEIRS OF D. BAYLESS DECEAST

Pursuant to an order of Court we have <u>proceded</u> to make a Settlement with Reese Bayless, Guardian of the minor heirs of Daniel Bayless Deceast (have from vouchers to us Shown found that Said Guardian has received into his hands of said Estate in money Interest vouchers &c. $166 22 which being divided between the two heirs will be $83 11 to Each out of which we find that he has paid to Young Bayless $71 12½ and that he has paid to Joseph Bayless ✶ of $14 36. Given under our hands this 21st day of July 1834.

          John Stephenson
          Wm. Gilleland

We recommended to the Court that they allow Reese Bayless the Guardian of the minor heirs Daniel Bayless Deceast the

(p-227)   REES BAYLESS GUARDIAN OF THE HEIRS OF D. BAYLESS DECT.

Interest of their <u>claimes</u> amounting to 28 Dollars for a compensation for his Services as Guardian for renting and Settling rents for five years and other Services relative to the Estate.

          John Stephenson
          Wm. Gilleland

ROBT. S. MCCALLS Estate

We the undersigned being appointed to Settle with Jamima McCall administratrix of Robt S. McCall, Deceast, met this day November 1835, We find Said administratrix chargeable as pr Inventories rendered with this amount, Seven hundred Eighty nine Dollars fifty four cents $789 54

And we find By examination of vouchers from No. 1 to No. 25
Inclusive Said Administratrix has paid out this sum $485 66½
Leaving this Sum in hands of Administratrix $303 87½

                             Saml Greer
                             John Stephenson   Committee
                             Saml Conley

JACOB ACRES Estate

We the under assigned being appointed by Court to Settle with Henry March Senr as administrator of the Estate of Jacob Acre Deceast, having met & called uppon him for his vouchers & he presented the following (viz)--
Cash in the hands of Acre at his Death together with check received from the pension agent $105 55
Against which the said March presents an off Sett for Cash paid out for Funeral & other Expenses (viz)
For Coffin $5 00
Doctors Bills   1 25
                                    Taken over

(p-228)   JACOB ACRES Estate

                     Amt Brot over $
Clerks fee for administration $3 00
Pare of Stockings for Burying   62½
Expenses Geting Pension from Knoxville   75
Two Clerks for Geting Pension   25
Boarding from the 22nd of July to 18th of January at
the rates of $70 pr year   64 00
Paid for nursing him in his Sickness   20 00
Additional Trouble during his Sickness & Funeral   10 65½
                                                       $105 53

After having Examined the vouchers aforesaid we find the Estate fully administered and nothing remaining in the hands of the Administrator. Given under our hands this 17th of October 1835.
                                   John Stephenson
                                   Ebenezer Barkley
                                   Saml Conley

SOLOMON KROUSES Estate

We the undersigned being appointed by order of Court to Settle with Daniel Krouse & Susannah Krouse, administrator & administratrix of Solomon Krouse Deceast, met on the 15th October 1835. And after an Examination of the Inventories of said Estate find the administrator & administratrix of Said Estate chargeable with this amount in Good Debts $998 23

We also find said Adr & adx has paid out as pr vouchers and receipts from No 1 to No. 15 Inclusive for Debts due by the Estate & Funeral Expenses this
Sum   99 75
And we think Daniel Krouse the above administrator Should
be allowed for his Services this Sum $75 00 $174 75

```
                                    Taken up        $823 48
(p-229)              SOLOMON KROUSE'S Estate

                                    Amt Brot up     $823 48
Said adr & adx has yet in their hand the note on the   5 00
Cheraw Bank                                         $818 48
```
We also find Said adr & adx has Balance paid to the Guardian of the Children
as pr receipts from No116 to No. 22 Inclusive this Sum $691 51½
To Sunnah Krouse widow of the Intestate her part being
one Sixth of Sd Estate this sum $136 41½   827 93
Said admr & admx having out over the assets which have
come into their hands as yet this Sum   9 45
We find yet from the Inventory there is yet unsettled of Bad and Desperate
Debts which are on Insolvent persons and persons moved out of the County in
Small Sums this amount $42 05
We do hereby certify the above Settlement to have been made by us on the 15th
October 1835. Given under our hand and Seals this 15th October 1835.

                                    Saml Greer (Seal)
                                    Justice of the Peace
                                    Jacob Hartsell (Seal)
                                    Justice of the Peace
                                    Levi Bowers (Seal)
                                    Justice of the Peace

                    SETH McCLARYS Estate

STATE OF TENNESSEE }
WASHINGTON COUNTY   } October Session 1835
My report as Guardian of Wm & Jesse McClary, minor heirs of Seth McClary
Deceast, there is in my hands fourteen hundred & Sixty two Dollars
                                                    $1462 00
Including what I will have to pay out to Nathan Barnes for accompaning me to
and from the state of Mississippi, my part out of that will be one half a-
greeable to the laws of the State of Mississippi
                                    Over - - - -

(p-230)   SETH McCLARY'S Estate

Which will leave in my hands Belonging to Said Wm & Jesse Minor heirs of
Seth McClary Deceast Seven hundred and thirty one Dollars $731 00
Including half which I will have to pay to N. Barnes
October 22, 1835.
E. L. Mathes   Sarah McClary
Sworn to in open Court   Guardian &c.
at Oct. Session 1835.
    S. Greer D. C.

              E. L. MATHES (Guardian for the MISS TYLER &C)

Annual Settlement of the accounts between my self as Guardian & wards,
Phebe, Minerva & Elisabeth Tyler, for the year Ending January Session 1835,
See Session January 1834, then in my hands four thousand Six hundred thirty
Eight Dollars and Twenty five cents $4638 25
Interest on the above for one year Two Hundred

WASHINGTON COUNTY, TENNESSEE

```
Seventy Eight Dollars & Twenty nine cents        $278 29
                              Total             $4916 54
Paid out Since Settlement                         217 44
                                                $4699 10
```

To J. Bricker Sheriff for Tax Eleven Dollars 49½/100	11 49¼
" Doct A. Mitchel for Phebe four Dollars 18¾/100	4 18¾
" Interest on the above Since paid	70
" Robt J. West fifty Six Dollars 45/100	56 45
" S Greer Clerk	2 62½
" Jones & Johnson forty three Dollars 69/100	43 69
" John Keys & Co thirty nine Dollars 11½/100	39 11½
" Wm Roberts	25 00
" Wilton Atkinson	20 50
" J. G. Eason four Dollars 43¾/100	4 43¾
" Four days	4 00

(p-231)   E. L. MATHIS Guardian for the MISS TYLERS &C

```
                                Amt Brot up     $212 19¾
My on the above                                    5 25
On hand by Sd Guardian & Services rendered       $217 44
```
leaves in my hands four thousand Six hundred ninety nine Dollars & ten cents
         E. L. Mathis
         Guardian &c.

The within Settlement has passed and the Court has approved of the same.
         Joshua Bourn
         Chareman protem

E. M. CARTERS Estate

WASHINGTON COUNTY
STATE OF TENNESSEE An Inventory of the property of E. M. Carter, which Exhibits the whole amount that has come to the hands of her Guardian D. A. Deaderick, and which is herewith filed for the Inspection of the Court viz.

 This amount invested by her father James Aiken Deceast for her use in a mortgage upon a plantation, where on Mrs. Elisabeth Aiken, the mother of Said Eliza now lives invested on the 26th day of December 1827 $1000.00

 This Sum recd by D. A. Deaderick of A. W. Taylor, being in part of a claim due to said E. M. Carter from A. C. Parks, formerly of Carter County & Collected by said Taylor 266 47
of which Sum $243 15 is Invested in the above named mortgage, amount yet in Said Taylors hands for Collection, being the Balance of said claim on A. C. Pairks. Supposed to amount to $250. the amount and certainty of Collection Doubtfull 250 00
Balance due on a note of hand, payable in Iron from W. B. Carter to Jas Aiken, for the use of E. M. Aiken with Interest counted to 1st Feb 1835. Doubtful as to the Certainty of Collection 114 51

(p-232)   E. M. CARTERS Estate

Celia a female Slave aged about 24
      Supposed value $
 Has three children viz.
1 Elbert aged about 5 Supposed value $

2   William aged about 3 Supposed Value $
3   Not named   "   3 months   "   W

Jonesbo Feb 7th 1835   D. A. Deaderick
                                        Guardian &c.
Dr. The Estate of E. M. Carter
    In a/c with her Guardian D. A. Deaderick 1834. March 13. To cash paid
A. W. Taylor his fee for collecting $266 47 of A. C. Parks
5 pr ct $13 32
25. To cash paid Mrs. Elizabeth Aiken for the use of
E. M. Carter   10 00
" To cash Invested in the mortgage on the farm on which
Mrs. E. Aiken lives   243 15
                                                $266 47

1834   CONTRA Co.
March 13 by cash received of A. W. Taylor for collections from
A. C. Parks $266 47
                                                000 00

COUNTY OF WASHINGTON }   D. A. Deaderick
STATE OF TENNESSEE   }   Guardian &c.
This day personally appeared before me Levi Bowers, a justice of the peace
for Sd. County D. A. Deaderick & made oath that the above Inventory of the
property of the Estate of E. M. Carter and the annexed account are correct
as he believes.
Sworn to & Subscribed before   D. A. Deaderick
me this 7th day of Feby 1835   Guardian
Levi Bowers   of E. M. Carter
Justice of the peace

(p-233)   CLARA WALTERS Estate

We the undersigned appointed at the last Session of the Court of Pleas &C
for Washington County State of Tennessee at the April Term thereof 1835, A
Committee to Settle with George Walters & Joseph Million, administrators of
the Estate of Clara Walters Deceast & report to July Sessions 1835, do find
Said administrators charged as pr Inventory
                            this sum $173 20
as by notes due & cash on hand   517 00
                                              $690 20
We find Sd admr has pd out as pr receipts   13 70
                                              $676 50
Allowed made Administrator for Services at 5 pr cent   34 50
                            Balance due $642 00
Given under our hands & Seals this 13th day of June 1835.
                            Saml Greer   (Seal)
                            Justice of the peace
                            Jacob Hartsell (Seal)
                            Justice of the peace
                            Levi Bowers (Seal)
                            Justice of the peace

                    MANERVA TYLERS Estate

We the undersigners appointed by the Honorable Court as a Committee to Settle with John Bayless administrator of Malinda Tyler, Deceast, and find the

following vouchers, one note on the Said John Bayless to the amount of
$654 18½
And we allowed the Said Bayless for collection   32 33 1/3
Bal $622 85

April the 20th 1835.

Henry King }
John M. Crawford } Committee
Ebinzer Barkly }

(p-234)   E. L. MATHIS (Guardian of A NELSON

Annual Settlement of the accounts between myself as Guardian & ward Alexander Nelson for the year Ending July Session 1835. See Settlement July Session 1834. Total amount in good funds Four thousand three hundred Seventy
three Dollars & 25/100 $4373 25
of the above Sum there are five hundred twenty four   524 73
Dollars & 73/100 in Green County on George T. Gilles- $3848 52
pie, have received No Interest Since Last Settlement
Deducted two hundred & thirty Dollars 91/100 Interest   230 91
Received thirty four Dollars 75/100 on Sd Manevuis note   34 78
Add five hundred twenty four Dollars 73/100 Gillispie   4114 21
in Green County   524 73
  $4638 94
Total add $20 50 half Becky & Vilets hire   20 50
  $4659 44
Paid out Since Settlement (viz)   176 59
  $4482 84

Guardians a/c Exclusive of any Boarding Sixty }
Seven Dollars & thirty Seven cents } $67 37
Nathan Gammons a/c   2 68¾
Jones & Johnsons a/c   8 21
Crawford & Kinneys a/c   40 33
M. G. Kinneys a/c   24 89½
pd for Tombstones for Nancy To Thompson   25 00
  $168 19¼
five pr cent on the above is   8 40
  $176 59¼

On hands by Said Guardian as compensation for Services and Expenses as Such which last Sum deducted leaves in the hands of said Guardian of Good funds to the amount of four thousand four hundred Eighty two Dollars & Eighty four ¼ cents, Exclusive of the Debts on Embree, James Patterson Deceast & James Allen, the land that was mortgaged by Allen to Secure his Debt has been Sold and Bought in by the Guardian, but has not received any rents or Interest the land was Bought in at Something over Eighteen hundred Dollars

E. L. Mathis Guardian
of A. Nelson

(p-235)   P. IRVIN'S Estate

STATE OF TENNESSEE } July 21st day 1835.
WASHINGTON COUNTY } pursuant to an order by Court that Levi Bowers, Jacob Hartsell & Saml Conley, be appointed a Committee to Settle with Patrick Eliott, administrator of John Eliott Deceast who was administrator of Patrick Elliott Deceast, with will annexed, and report, we being a Committee appointed met in Jonesborough 22nd day of July 1835, find in the hands of the

proceeds of the Sale of the administrators hands of the Sales of personal property and the amount of the sale of a man of Coller by name of Monday
$702 78

Vouchers Produced

No.		
1	Greenways & Jones Receipt	$26 49
2	John E. Copon a/c & Receipt in full	27 00
3	Zachariah Allens Receipt	2 00
4	Nimrod Willetts Receipt Funeral Expenses	8 00
5	John Copons Receipt in full	5 50
6	James Harveys Receipt	2 21
7	Zachariah Allens Receipt crying Sale	2 00
8	John E. Copon Receipt	7 50
9	Greenway & Jones	17 87
10	Greenways Receipt	9 30
11	S. B. Cunningham & Nelsons Receipt	12 00
12		4 00
13	Patrick B. Elliotts Receipt	3 73½
14	Patrick B. Elliotts Receipt	10 00
15	Do Do Do	30 00
16	Do Do Do	15 00
17	Do Do Do	45 18
18	Do Do Do	150 00
19	Do Do Do	3 51 1/3
20	George Elliotts note, Interest, amount	73 50
21	Saml Greers Receipt	2 25
22	Do Do Do	1 62½
23	Do Do Do	1 00

Taken over $

(p-236)   Both amts up $ $702 78

No.		
24	Sheriffs Receipt 1834	1 29
25	Do Do 1832 & 1833	4 00
26	Do Do 1830 & 1831	4 00
27	To attendance a number of days to Settle the Business of Said Estate at	136 62½
28	Smiths note	73 69

Find vouchers produced to amount of $680 27
To the Estate the amount of $22 60
paid claims note collected amount of $7 50
We hereby certify from the above Document that is a true Statement of Settlement. Given under our hands and Seals this 22nd day of July 1835.

          Levi Bowers (Seal)
          Justice of the Peace
          Jacob Hartsell (Seal)
          Justice of the peace
          Saml Conley (Seal)
          Justice of the peace

JESSE PAYNES Estate
Jonesbo Feby 12th 1836

We the undersigned being appointed by Court at the January Session 1836. Co Commissioners to Settle with James McAlister and Jacob Whistler, Executors

WASHINGTON COUNTY, TENNESSEE

of the last will of Jesse Payne Deceast, having in Jonesborough on the 12th day of Febry. 1836, Called upon Said Executors, they produced vouchers & an Inventory by which it appears that Six Hundred Seventy two Dollars & Sixty cents, Good funds came into their hands of said Estate and which they are chargeable with $672 60
out of which Said Executors have pd as follows
(to wit)

(p-237)   JESSE PAYNES Estate

By Vouchers

No.	Names	Amount		No.	Amt Brot up	$
1	Emmert	$20	39	34	Clark & West	$18 33
2	Thos Williams	7	25	35	Joseph Payne	12 25
3	J. G. Eason	25	11½	36	Henry McCracken	1 00
4	C. Long	1	00	37	Robert Reed	7 50
5	John Green	6	87½	38	John E Copan	3 71
6	H. Payne	1	00	39	Mahly Payne a/c	2 00
7	E. Shannon	4	37½	40	Do note	30 00
8	Buchenton	3	71	41	Do "	15 00
9	Greenway & Jones	26	00	42	Do "	11 00
10	Dosser Conat		50	43	Do "	4 00
11	Jos Payne	1	00	44	Do a/c	21 09½
12	Jos Bottles	10	00	45	Do order to Yancy	$ 9 84
13	B. Brown	2	00	46	Do order for	2 06
14	Bricker Tax	7	57	47	Do in a/c with	9 34
15	M. Glaise		50	48	Do Maxwell & Yancy	6 12½
16	Jesse Payne	1	00	49	Do order	4 90
17	M. Stephenson	54	15	50	Do Jones & Johnson	36 71
18	S. B. Cunningham	4	25	51	Do W. Greenway	22 25¾
19	N. Tucker	3	64	52	Do J. Eason	22 24
21	Barkleys	15	10	53	Do. A. Ingle	5 25
22	S. B. Cunningham	21	71½	54	Do Richd Greenway	10 25
23	John Greenway	7	41	55	Adam Broyles (proven	2 00
24	Wm Payne	20	00	56	Nathan Barnes (Judgement	7 00
25	E. L. Mathis	108	70	57	William Greenway a/c	1 75
26	J. D. Guynn	16	49	58	Joseph Mann	23 12
27	J. M. Broyles	2	50	59	Yancy	81½
28	John Stout	3	50	60	Alexander Brabson	3 50
29	Jno Humphreys	2	52	61	Robert Bean	4 00
30	Jas Graham	8	66½	62	Alexander Mathis	5 94¾
31	Lawrence Emmert	15	00	63	Thomas Nelson	1 95½
32	D. D. Judgement	6	75	64	Saml Huffman	50
33	John Payne	5	06¼	65	Lewis Jordon	1 41½
	Taken up	$			Taken over	$

(p-238)   JESSE PAYNES Estate

No. 66 N. Barnes $1 00 No. 67 Lawrence Emmert $1 00 No. 68 Sarah McClary $1 00 No. 69 John Toll $1 46 No. 70 John Gray $13 00 No. 71 Mahay Payne $2 0 No. 72 Allen Stout $1 55¼ the vouchers on all amounting to Seven hundred forty two Dollars 50/100 $742 50
The amount that came into the Executors hands   672 60
over paid Sixty Nine Dollars & ninety cents $69 90

The Said Exrs. are also chargeable with cash notes in their hands (to wit)
One note on W. Willett due the 15th Sept 1834 $40 83

One on H. Clark due Sept 15th 1835 for	$53 00
Also on S. Maxwell due 13th Sept 1834 for	13 05
One J. Bottles Sept 13th 1835 for	61 40
One on H. McCracken due Sept 20th 1835	22 25
One on H. Clark due 14th Sept 1836 for	60 00
& one on S. McClary due 14th Sept 1836 for	51 00
	$301 53
Subtract what was over paid by &c.	69 90
	$231 63

We also find in the Executors a note on Wm McCoy for ten dollars which was returned Desperate on the Inventory which is not yet collected. Given under our hands the day and above written.

        E. L. Mathis |
        John Stephenson | Commissioners
        Saml Conley |

We the Committee are of opinion that
James McAlester be allowed $50 00 for
thir Services & Jacob Whistler be allowed $15 00 as Executors

(p-239)   JOHN ELLIOTT'S Estate

STATE OF TENNESSEE | August Session 1st day 1836, pursuant to an order of
WASHINGTON COUNTY | Court that Jacob Hartsell, Henderson Clark and Joseph
McLin, be appointed a committee to Settle with Patrick B. Elliott, administrator, of John Elliott Deceast, who was annexed and report, we being a committee appointed met in Jonesborough 1st day of August 1836 find in the hand
of the proceeds of the rents of Lands and collection of other money in the
administrators hands.

No.		
1	Elliott Right	$35 00
2	John Carigars Right	15 00
3	James Seviers receipt fees of office	62½
4	Nathan Shipley Receipt	2 00
5	James Seviers Receipt	62½
6	Dossers Receipt Tax	1 70
		$55 05
7	Balance on former Settlement	22 48
		77 53
8	Clarks Receipts	62½
		78 15½

Amount paid out for Traveling from home to attend
Settling the Estate of Patrick Elliott Deceast and oth-
er business from 1835, up to August 1st 1836. 62 00
We find/the hands of the Administrators hands after 16 15½
allowing him for all Services rendered up to this date
We find in the hands of the administrators hands Sixteen
Dollars & fifteen cents. Given under hands and Seals the
day and date above

        Jacob Hartsell (Seal)
        Hend. Clark (Seal) Committee
        Joseph McLin (Seal)

WASHINGTON COUNTY, TENNESSEE

MICHAEL BROWNS Estate

STATE OF TENNESSEE
WASHINGTON COUNTY } Persuant to an order of the County Court of Sd County at Decr Session 1836 appointed Joshua Green, Henderson Clark & E. L. Mathis, a Committee to Settle with Michael Hayle Executor of the Estate of Michael Brown Deceast having met at the house of Joshua Greens Esqr on the 17th day of December 1836

(p-240) MICHAEL BROWNS Estate

and Calling on Said Hayle Extr &c for the papers he produced three Inventorys as lists of sale returned to the County Court of rents & profits arising from the rent of the Plantation Beloning to the heirs of the Said Michael Brown Deceast, (to wit) for the year 1830 $15 06½ for the year 1831 $16 40

		$31 46½
for the years 1832 & 1833 $2 50		2 50
& for the year 1834 $5 00 & 1835 $13 95		18 95
Amounting in all to fifty two Dollars 91/100 cents		52 91½

& Said Executor Mr. Hayle produced the following Vouchers (to wit) No 1 Recd of Joseph Brown Guardian of Michael

	Brown	$70 00	
No. 2	Recd of Joseph Brown Guardian &c	30 00	
" 3	Wm Dosser Const Receipt	5 50	
" 4	Jacob Hayles Rct for making Sd Browns coffin	4 00	
" 5	a true Receipt for 1819, 20, 21 & 1823	4 44¼	
" 6	Do Do 1825, 26 & 1827	3 18¼	
" 7 & 8	Do Do 1829 & 1830	1 78¾	
" 9	Do Do 1832	56¼	
" 10	Do Do 1833, 34 & 1835	1 68¾	
" 11	Do Do 1836	52½	
" 12	Recd of the clerk of the County Court	1 00	
" 13	Do Do Do	1 12½	
" 14	Do Do Do	50	
" 15	E. L. Mathis & Joshua Greens Rect part of the Committee &c	2 00	$126 31¾
			73 40¾

The Court allows the Sd Executor forty Dollars for his Services as Executor up to this time   40 00
$113 40

From the above statement there is in favor of Said Executor one hundred & thirteen Dollars & forty cents
Given under our hands & Seals Returned at February Session 1837

E. L. Mathis (Seal)
Joshua Green (Seal)   Committee
Henderson Clark (Seal)

(p-241) HENRY SLIGARS Estate

Agreeable to an order of the County Court June Term 1836, to us directed to Settle with Wm Sligar Executor of Henry Sligar Deceast, we met in the Court house on the 6th day of June, and after calling on the Executors for his papers he produced to us legal vouchers for money paid and Services rendered.

No. 1	Clerks Receipt 1 50 No. 2 Isaac Hartsell $2 00	$ 3 50
" 3	Clerk one day of sale	50
" 4	John Kennedy for advice	10 00

No. 5	Clerks Receipt .62½ 6 Do .50 7 Do .62½	$1 75
" 8	Wm Sligar for Services	5 00
" 9	Jacob Brown, Jesse Clark, Saml G. Bayless Committee	3 00

And find them charged by Inventory of Sale Two hundred and Thirty and Twenty Six cents, Given under our hands this 6th Day July 1836, which leaves a Balance in the Executors hands of $220 41

                       Jacob Brown (Seal)
                       Saml G. Bayless (Seal) Committee
                       Jesse Clark (Seal)

EPHRAM MURRAYS Estate

We the undersigned being appointed to Settle with Joshua Boring and Samuel Drake, administrators of Ephraim Murray Deceast, met in the Town of Jonesborough, Washington County on the 18th of March 1837

And from the amount of Sales and Inventories we find Said Administrators chargeable with this Sum $2492 09
and from vouchers presented being Receipts from No. 1 to No. 40 Inclusive which we Examined we find Sd administrators have paid out this Sum
                                                             2025 64¾
                                                          $466 44¼

(p-242)   EPHRAIM MURRAYS Estate

It is suggested to us that said administrators have been unable to collect the amount of $13 00 of the vandue Sale money which we pass over and leave for Further Settlement-- We find the above Sum yet in the hands of the administrators to be disbursed. Given under our hands & Seals this 18th day of March 1837

                       Saml Greer (Seal)
                       Justice of the peace
                       Jacob Hartsell (Seal)
                          Justice of the peace
                     Henry King (Seal)
                          Justice of the peace

POLLY T

STATE OF TENNESSEE }
WASHINGTON COUNTY }   Pursuant to an order of the County Court at May Session 1837, appointing John Humphreys, Saml G. Bayless & E. L. Mathis a Committee to Settle with Wm Nelson Guardian of Polly T   the met in Jonesborough on the 5th day of June 1837, and called uppon Said Guardian & he produced a Certificate from the clerk of Said County Showing the amount in his hands as Guardian amounting to $282 72
& we find in the hands (at this date) three hundred Eighty one dollars & Seventeen cents   381 17
Said Guardian produces an account of 4 days Services attending on Said Business he charges one dollar pr day   4 00
Also the clerks Receipt for $1 12 & the Committee   377 17

WASHINGTON COUNTY, TENNESSEE

```
charges $3 00                                              $4 12
Which leaves in the Guardians hands as above              $373 05
```
(to wit) three hundred Seventy three Dollars & five cents
Given under our hands this 5th day of June 1837.

           E. L. Mathis
           John Humphreys | Committee
           Saml G. Bayless

(p-243)   E. L. MATHIS Guardian &c of A. NELSON

Annual Settlement between E. L. Mathis Guardian & Alex Nelson his ward for the year Ending August Session 1837. See Settlement August 1st 1836. Total

```
amount in this county in good funds                       $3967 34
add $238 04 Interest on the above for one year             238 04
add $30 00 half of Beckys & Vilets hire for one year        30 00
add $55 00 Philis & Wms hire for one year                   55 00
Total four thousand two hundred ninety Dollars 38/100    $4290 38
Disbursed by said Guardian & Compensation for Services     219 85
Since last Settlement                                    $4070 53
No. 1  Crawfords & Kinneys a/c              $70 00
Interest on Patersons note over charged      58 14
Guardians a/c for clothing & paying for
making clothing, Horse food for one year
&c Exclusive of any charge for Boarding      81 25
5 pr cent on the Same Disbursement           10 00
                                            $219 85
```

Which last Sum Deducted leaves in my hands four thousand Seventy Dollars & fifty three cents, Exclusive of the Debts on Gillispie, Embree & Allen, on which I have received no Interest Since last Settlement.

           E. L. Mathis
           Guardian &c.

EPHRAIM MURRAYS Estate

We the undersigned being appointed by order of the County Court to settle with Joshua Bourn and Saml Drake, administrators of the Estate of E. Murray Deceast, met on the 13th day of November 1837, and after Examination of the Inventories of Said Estate find that Said Administrators from a former Set-
```
tlement are chargeable with this Sum                      $466 48½
```
And from Inventories returned Since the Last Settlement we Said administra-
```
tors chargeable with this amount                           3376 98
              Taken over                                  $3843 42½
```

(p-244)   EPHRAIM MURRAYS Estate

The whole amount chargeable and from vouchers produced are by us Examined from No. 41 to No. 55 Inclusive We Said administrators have paid this Sum
```
                                                          $2433 03
```
And we allow the Said Administrators for Settling Said Estate as <u>theire</u>
```
compensation for their Services this sum                   350 00
              Amount of credits                           $2783 03
Ballance to be Disbursed                                   1060 39½
```
Out of the above Sum the administrators has failed to Collect a note Given at the Sale by Robt & Charles Bean for $13 00, Given under our hands &

SETTLEMENTS OF ESTATES, VOLUME 00, 1790-1841

Seals this 13th day of Novr. 1837

        Saml Greer (seal)
        Justice of the peace
        Jacob Hartsell (Seal)
        Justice of the peace
        Wm Bourn (Seal)
        Justice of the peace

JACOB GOODS Estate

STATE OF TENNESSEE }
WASHINGTON COUNTY } In pursuance to an order of Court at August Session 1837, appointing Robert Reed, Joshua Green & E. L. Mathis a committee to Settle with Jacob Whisler & Solomon Good administrators of the Estate of Jacob Good Deceast-- having met at the House of Said Jacob Whisler & called on him for the papers, he the said Whisler, administrator produced a <u>coppy</u> of the Inventory by which Said administrators are chargeable with the Sum of Eight hundred Seventy Six Dollars 98/100 $876 98

Said Administrators produces vouchers (to wit)

No. 1	A note to be paid to Nancy Good, Daughter of Elisabeths, Principal & Interest	100 90
No. 2	Leroy Campbell Receipt for coffin	10 00
3	Receipt of S. Greer clerk	75
	Taken up	$111 65

(p-245)   JACOB GOOD'S Estate

	Amt Brot up	$111 65
No. 4	Receipt of S. Greer	2 00
5	John Guynns Receipt crying the Sale	2 00
6	Samuel Greers Receipt	25
7	Easterly Receipt for funeral Services	3 00
8	John Goods Receipt and Judgment	38 00
	Heirs Receipts	
9	Catharine Millers Receipt	36 00
10	Daniel Goods Receipt	45 00
11	Jacob Goods Do	15 00
12	John Goods Do	10 00
13	Sollomon Goods Do	36 00
14	Elisabeth Do Do	9 00
15	Margarett Weaving Receipt	41 00
16	Bayers Receipt for funeral Expenses	3 62
		$352 52
For Services rendered by Administrators		45 00
Committee charged $1 00 Each		3 00
		$476 46

from the above statement we find in the hands of the administrators four hundred Seventy Six dollars and forty Six cents--

       E. L. Mathis }
   By order of Joshua Green } Committee
       Robert Reed }

CASSIMARE MAYS Estate

A Statement of Settlement made with D. & S. May, administrators of Cassimare

May Deceast, August 7th 1838. Administrators charged as pr Inventories
$1252 03
And from receipts and vouchers from No 1 to 14 Inclusive it appears the administrators have paid out this Sum $107 28

Taken over

(p-246) CASSIMARE MAYS Estate

           Amt Brot up $107 28 $1252 03
It is considered the Settlement of the Estate worth this
Sum which is allowed   75 00   182 28
Balance due by Administrators $1069 75

        Saml Greer
          Clerk

MARY EARNEST Property

August Session 1838. A list of the property which came into my hands Belonging to Mary Earnest, minor heir of Wesley Earnest, viz, a negro Boy named Leonard which slave hired out for one year at $50 00, one mare & colt, one bed & furniture, one Bureau, one falling leaf Table, one old Side Saddle, one Spinning wheel, a note on Wasley Earnest due April 1839, for $27 32½ to be discharged in cupboard furniture, & tw Buckets, all the above named property is kept for Said Mary use & to be returned to her when She comes of age which will be in 1841.

        E. L. Mathis
        Guardian of Mary Earnest

CHRISTOPHER TAYLOR'S Estate

A Statement of Settlement made with James Taylor admr of Christopher Taylor Deceast 29th August 1838. Said administrator Chargeable as pr Invoices with this Sum $489 32
Said Admr is allowed this Sum for his Services 34 44½
Said administrators has paid for fees of office
this Sum   4 87½ 39 32
Balance in hands of administrator $450 00
To be Disbursed

        Saml Greer
          Clerk

(p-247) JOHN RANGES Estate

We the undersigned being appointed a Committee to Settle with John Wright, Administrator & Abigal Range, administratrix of John Range Deceast, Do find by the amount of Inventories returned, Said administrator & Administratrix chargeable with in the whole amount of Goods & Solvent Debts, to this
Sum $2008 47
Out of which Sd Administrator & administratrix has paid
out as pr receipts & vouchers presented & Examined 303 85
To this Sum allowed the administrator & administratrix
on the above amount   100 40 $404 25

This amount returned which is probable can be collected | $1604 22
& converted to the use of the heirs in trade | 321 33
To this amount Desperate & Lost | 359 10
Interest Calculated up to this date

  Given under our hands and Seals this the 2nd day of February 1838.
          George Crouch (Seal)
          Justice of the peace
          Henry King (Seal)
          Justice of the peace
          Lawrence Bowers (Seal)
          Justice of the peace

E. L. MATHIS Guardian of M. G. & E. TYLARS

Annual Settlement of the accounts between my Self as Guardian & wards Minerva G & Elizabeth Tylars, for the year Ending Feby. Term 1838. See Settlement Feby. Term 1837, then in my hands Two thousand nine hundred Eighty two Dollars 26/100 $2982 26
       One third par
Interest for one year on the above   178 94
Total thirty one hundred Sixty one Dollars & twenty
Cents $3161 20

(p-248)   E. L. MATHIS Guardian of M. G. & ELISABETH TYLAR

        Amt Brot up $3161 20
Disbursed by Said Guardian & Compensation for Services 118 34
Since last Settlement with 2½ pr cent on the same $3042 86
Paid to John Keys 2 a/c ninety five Dollars 53/100 $95 53
John G. Eason a/c Sixteen Dollars 93/100   16 93
Two Days Services $1 50 pr day   3 00
                115 46
2½ per cent on the Said Disbursed   2 88
                $118 34

Which leaves in my hands three thousand forty two Dollars and Eighty Six cents, one third of it par
          E. L. Mathis
          Guardian &c.

JAMES W. YOUNGS Estate

Settlement made with Wm Young and James H. Gillespie, Executors of James W. Young, Deceast, From Inventories returned Executors chargeable with this Sum $1039 74
& from Vouchers produced from No. 1 to No. 31 Inclusive Said Administrators paid out this Sum $577 96
Said Said Executors allowed for their Services 50 00 $627 96
Leaving this Sum in hands of Executors $401 78
Notes not collected & returned Desperate, John Wooldridge $25 00, William E. Derrick $25 00, Saml Bayless $10 00, Peter Holt $16 00 Thos Greer $1 00 Preston Houston $2 91, Zach Allen $7 00 James Allen $100 00 Thos Price Deceast Estate $9 47, Margaret Price $2 00, Josiah Parker $1 50--
The above Settlement 17th December 1838.
         Saml Greer Clerk

WASHINGTON COUNTY, TENNESSEE

DANIEL BOWMANS Estate

Statement of Settlement made with Jacob Bowman & Saml Bowman Executors of Daniel Bowman Deceast, from Settlement made by

(p-249)   DANIEL BOWMANS Estate

Said Executors, there being no Inventory returned Said Executors are chargeable with this Sum $1470 50
I find from vouchers produced from No. 1 to No. 8 Inclusive Said Administrators have paid out this Sum   62 50
Said Executors allowed for collecting & Disbursing Said Estate this Sum   75 00 $137 50
This Sum in the hands of Executors $1333 00
     Made 7th September 1838

                     Saml Greer Clerk

THOMAS HUNTS Estate

Statement of Settlement made with Henson Hunt, administrator of Thomas Hunt, Deceast, made 2nd October 1838, with Inventories returned Sd admr is chargeable with this Sum $3228 06
And from receipts & vouchers produced Said administrator has paid out this Sum $954 83½
Said administrator allowed for his Services this Sum   163 40   1118 23½
Leaving this Ballance in the hands of the Administrator $2109 83½
Given under my hand at office in Jonesborough this 2nd October 1838

                     Saml Greer Clerk

MICHAEL INGLE Estate

Settlement made with Alexander Mathis, Executor of Michael Ingle Deceast, made 3rd January 1838 By Inventory returned Said Executor is chargeable with this Sum $128 68½
By vouchers produced for money Expended from No 1 to No 12, Inclusive Said

                     Taken over

(p-250)   MICHAEL INGLES Estate

                Amt Brot over $128 68½
Executors has paid this Sum $98 82¾
Said Executor allowed for his Services this Sum   20 00   118 82¾
Leaving this Ballance in hands of Executor   9 85¾

                     Saml Greer Clerk

PEGGY RUBLE Estate

Settlement with Jacob Hartsell, Guardian of Peggy Ruble made 14th Decr 1838. Said Guardian Recd for rents for the year 1836.
47 Bushels of corn at 2/ pr Bushel amounting to $15 66 2/3
For 1837 No rents, For 1838. 74 Bu at 40 cts   29 60

SETTLEMENTS OF ESTATES, VOLUME 00, 1790-1841

Recd Cash $8 50, Recd for rents 74 Doz oats $12 33 1/3 $20 83½
                                                                                                              66 10

Guardian has paid out as per Vouchers from No. 1 to No. 3
Inclusive $10 83
By one Days Hawling by Lisenby   3 00
By Hawling corn & finding hands one day   4 00
By Hawling oats & two hands   4 00
By Hawling two loads of corn to town   6 00
By Cupboard & Beadstids   4 00
By clerks receipt for Settlement & recording   2 75
By Services rendered by Guardian 14 days   14 00 $ 48 58
Leaves this Ballance in hands of Guardian $17 52

                             Saml Greer
                             Clerk C. Court W. County

                      MARY PAYNES Estate

James McAlester, Guardian for Mary Payne in a/c 1st May 1838. To Ballance
on hand this in Sundry notes now due $285 06
Contra Cr. by a/c pd Mahala Starnes, as pr Bill rendered   5 71
By amt pd Saml Greer for office fees   1 62
             Amt taken up $7 33

(p-251)   MARY PAYNES Estate No. 3

                   To & By amt Brot up $7 33 $285 06
By amt pd S. Starnes as per bill   4 00
"   Cash pd John Keys   10 00
"   Cash pd John Keys   5 00
"   Cash pd for Tax for the years 1836, 37 & 38   7 00
"   Cash pd Doct Cunningham   6 25
"   Cash J. G. Eason, as pr Bill rendered   29 45
"   Cash pd B. F. Sachet on Judgement   10 20
"   Cash pd N. B. Watkins for Schooling   2 00
"   Cash pd E. Armstrong for Schooling   2 50
                        Ballance on hand $
To Error on the above a/c Sachets Judgment $10 20
                              James McAlister
                                 Guardian
To rents & profits this year $75 00
By amt pd for repairs &c as pr Bill will show   73 09½
                         Bal due   1 90½
                        Errors Excepted

                MARY PAYNE'S Estate No. 4

Guardians a/c vs Ward 1st May 1838
To Judgment in favor of William Patton $4 00
Amt of Robert McLins a/c for Schooling   3 00
To cash pd Clerk for office fees   1 25
"   amt pd Henry McCracken for   13 00
"   Keys & Co. as pr Bill rendered   15 71
                                                            $

Guardian to ward, Mary Payne
By note and Bonds on hand $462 45
    Ballance on hand 1st May 1839.
                           James Alester

WASHINGTON COUNTY, TENNESSEE

Errors Excepted

(p-252) JAMES W. YOUNGS Estate

Supplementary Settlement made with William Young and James H. Gillispie, Executors of James W. Young Deceast, who was Executors of Joseph Young Deceast, From Inventory of Sale of negros. Said Executor is chargeable with
this sum $1854 00
Interest on notes Before collected   194 53
From a former Settlement made with the Executors $2048 53
of Joseph Young, it appears Said Executors has paid out
over and above their assets.
Then Received this Sum $440 22½
And has paid on a note Lifted Given to
R. Irwin dated 16th Oct. 1815 this sum   475 20
Note Lifted Given to Wilkens Young dated 14th June
1821. This Sum   275 42
Note Lifted Given to Wilkens Young dated
22nd July 1818. This Sum   532 67
Received on note Given to Chaney Bourn
dated 16th June 1821. This Sum   407 97
Executor allowed for $2131 30½
Disbursement $90 00
Clerks fee   4 25
John Parke Sale   1 50 $90 75 $2227 05½
This amount over paid by Executors   178 52½
The above Settlement made 17th Decr 1838.

                              Saml Greer Clerk
                              Washington County

E. L. MATHIS, Guardian of ALEXR NELSON

Annual Settlement between E. L. Mathis, Guardian of Alexr Nelson, his ward for the year Ending August Term 1838. See Settlement August Term 1837. Then in my hands in Washington County Four thousand & Seventy Dollars & fifty three cents $4070 53

(p-253)   E. L. MATHIS, GUARDIAN OF ALEXR NELSON

                       Amt Brot up $4070 53
Add Interest for one year on the above $244 23
Add Wms his Boys hire for one year   36 00
Vilets & Beckys for one half Becklys hire
for Six months before Sold   25 00
Add for Land Sale formily Belonging to Col.
Nelson $340 00
Add half what Becky was sold for   2850 00
Total four thousand nine hundred Sixty five Dollars 76/100 $4965 76
     Disbursement by Sd Guardian Since last Settlement
A. Crawfords & Kinneys a/c See receipt $341 08
B. Nancy M. Pattons a/c for Serving   6 25
C. Easons a/c   1 50
D. Guardians a/c for money advanced to E. Ward
clothing & Services rendered   116 55

```
F Jacob Naffs a/c                         $14 47
                                          469 83
5 pr cent on the above Sum Expended        23 49    $493 32
                                                   $4472 44
```

Which leaves in my hands in this county four thousand four hundred Seventy two Dollars & forty four cents, Exclusive of E. Embrees note on which I have received no Interest. All which is Submitted to the worshipful Court of Washington County--

       E. L. Mathis,
       Guardian &c.

JOHN SLAGLE Estate

Settlement made with Nathan Barnes & John Slagle, administrators of John Slagle Deceast, made 30th day of October 1839. Said administrators chargeable as pr Inventories returned this Sum $922 86
Said administrators has Disbursed of Said Estate as pr vouchers produced from No 1 to No 15 Inclusive this Sum   155 51 2/3

      Taken over

(p-254)   JOHN SLAGLES Estate

```
                 Amt Brot over    $155 51 2/3     $922 86
Said Administrators allowed for their Services
in Settling Said Estate This Sum       75 00      230 51 2/3
Ballance in hands of administrators               $692 24 1/3
                 Saml Greer
                 Clerk County Court
```

E. L. MATHIS, Guardian of A. NELSON

Settlement made E. L. Mathis, Guardian of Alexander Nelson made August Term 1839.

```
Find in hands of Guardian in this County         $4472 44
Add Interest for one year                          268 32
Allens Land Sold to D. Allen                      1200 00
Interest on Same up to this date                    48 00
Hire Boys Wm & Jeremiah                             70 00
½ Hire Girl Vilett                                  17 50
                                                 $6076 26
Allowed Guardian for Services    $18 62
Disbursed by Said Guardian        372 55           391 17
                  5 pr cent on Same              $5685 09
Ballance in hands of Guardian being in current Bank notes
                            E. L. Mathis
                            Guardian &c.
```

JACOB HARTSELL GUARDIAN OF WM DULANEYS Heirs

Settlement of the Estate of William Dulaney, made with Jacob Hartsell, Guardian 3rd January 1839.

1st years Rent	$5 15
5 years Rent after paying for Improvements	1 13
Recd of Lands Sold to Daniel Huffine took notes 28th December 1838.	150 00
Taken up	$156 38

(p-255) **JACOB HARTSELL Guardian &c.**

Amt Brot. up		$156 38
rents for 1837. Note on Mrs. Dulaney 2nd Jany 1838		19 41
Amt. Chargeable		$175 69
Said Guardian Presents vouchers for money Disbursed from No 1 To No. 7 Inclusive amounting to this Sum	$18 66	
By Services allowed Said Guardian	16 00	34 66
Leaving this Ballance in hands of Guardian		141 03

           Saml Greer
           Clerk

E. L. MATHIS, GUARDIAN OF ELISABETH TYLAR

Annual Settlement of accounts between myself as Guardian and Elisabeth Taylor, for the year Ending Feby. Session 1839. See Settlement Feby. 1838. Then in my hands her part one third (par) fifteen hundred Twenty one Dollars 43/100 $1521 43

Interest on the above for one year, ninety one dollars 28/100   91 28
                              $1612 71

Disbursed by Said Guardian & compensation for Services rendered since last Settlement & 2½ pr cent on the money pd out   142 80
                       $1469 91

No		
1	Doct W. W. Bovells medical a/c with Interest since pd	$56 93
2	A. E. Jacksons a/c with Interest since pd	11 35
3	J. T. Broyles & Brothers a/c including Since paid	8 01
4	John G. Easons Dect a/c Including Interest Since paid	8 42
5	Elisabeth Receipt for	10 00
6	Crawfords & Kinneys a/c	54 99
	Two days Services	3 00
	pd clerk of the Court for 3 Settlements 1837, 1838 & 1839	3 75
		$146 45
	Two and half pr cent on the above	3 65
	Which leaves in my hands	$142 80
	fourteen hundred Sixty nine Dollars & ninety one cents $1469 91 1/3 par	

               E. L. Mathis
               Guardian &c.

(p-256)   JACOB KLEPPER, Guardian of the Heirs of JOHN KLEPPER

Settlement of the account of Jacob Klepper, Guardian of the heirs of John

Klepper and his children.

1838. June 12th Recd of Executor of Joseph Klepper Deceast	$86 45	
November 23rd also	25 00	
Also in Mississippi money	2 00	
1839 March 1st also	34 54	
	$147 99	

Said Guardian has Expended in Traveling	$122 25	
And produced Receipts for cash Disbursed from No 1 to No 6 Inclusive amounting to	14 50	
Paid to G. W. Millhorn in right of his wife Elisabeth as pr Receipts No 1, 2 & 3	870 51¾	
Paid Clerk for fees of Settlement	2 75	$1010 01¾

Guardian allowed one pr cent pr annum as his fee for   137 89
Trouble, Risk &c. $
Guardian chargeable with Interest on this amount on
the next annual Settlement from 1st Feby 1839 to date
of Settlement.
    Settlement made 1st Feby 1839.
                                Saml Greer
                                    Clerk

JOHN A BOWMAN, Guardian of SAML. KROUSE

Annual Settlement of John A Bowman, Guardian of Saml. Krouse made 6th May 1840 amount of cash Recd 6th May 1839.	$136 81	
Interest up to this date	8 20	
	$145 01	
By cash paid for Schooling	$1 12	
By cash paid clerk	50	
By cash paid clerk	2 75	4 37
Ballance on hand		$140 64

                                Saml Greer clerk
                                County Court

THOMAS A BAYLESS Estate

Settlement made with Wm Bayless, administrator of Thomas Bayless, Deceast,
administrators chargeable as pr Inventories returned this Sum
                                                $960 38¼
Administrators produces Vouchers from No 1 to No 22 Inclusive for this
amount $269 01
Administrators allowed for Services   25 00   294 01
                        Ballance due $666 37¼
Settlement made 23rd Sept. 1839
                                Saml Greer
                                    Clerk

CHRISTIAN GROVES Estate

Settlement made with James Brown & Wilson Atkinson Executors of Christian
Grove, Deceast, made 22nd day of August 1839. as pr Inventories Sd Executors
chargeable with this Sum $199 51¾

Said Executors produced vouchers from No 1 to No 17, Inclusive amounting to this Sum $168 27½
Said Executors allowed for their Trouble in Settling of Said Estate this Sum   20 00 $188 27½
    Bal due in hands of Executors   11 24¼
           Saml Greer Clerk
       County Court Washington County

WM BORRANS Estate

Settlement made with Thomas Fulkirson, administrator of Wm Barren, Dect. made 6th May 1839. Said andr. charged as pr Inventories with this Sum $158 43¼
Said Adr produced vouchers from No 1 to No 8 Inclusive amounting to this Sum $33 88½
Said administrator allowed for his Trouble & Expence this Sum   8 25   41 13½
                              $171 30¼

          Saml Greer, clerk

(p-257)   ## WILLIAM JACKSONS Estate

Settlement with George & Peter Jackson, Executors of William Jackson Deceast, made 3rd June 1839. Said Executor as pr Inventories chargeable with this Sum $746 81¼
vouchers produced from No 1 to 7 Inclusive $22 89½
         Coffin   5 00
                $27 89½
Labour & Expence in Gethering Hawling & Shucking corn   28 50
To Services as Executors in manageing Estate   50 00   106 39½
       Ballance in hands of Executors   640 45¾
           Saml Greer Clerk
           County Court

EPHRAIM MURRAYS Estate

Settlement made with Joshua Bourn, and Samuel Drake administrators of Ephraim Murray Deceast, on the 11th Novr. 1839. Administrators chargeable with the following amount as pr Inventories amount of notes on hand at Death of Intestate $560 00
Amount of rents for 1835   44 59
Amount of rents & negros Hire for 1836   261 47
The Sale of negros & Rents for 1837   3775 00
The hire of negros a few days   7 62
             Amt charged $6310 27
And from vouchers produced from No 1 to 69. Inclusive it appears Said administrator has Disbursed for Debts, charges, & to Legatees this Sum
        $6261 83
This Sum allowed administrators for their Services   350 00 $6611 83
Leaving this Sum over paid by administrators $301 46
           Saml Greer
           Clerk County Court

(p-258)   PETER RUBLE Estate

Statement of Settlement made with Henry Ruble, administrator of Peter Ruble
Deceast, By Inventories of Sale Said administrator chargeable with this
Sum $196 44
Note on Embree & Williams for   190000
Interest on Same up from Sept. 1836 to March 1839   28 50
Note on Administrator   38 00
                                                                 $449 44
Said administrator has pd out as Vouchers this Sum   15 50
                                                                 $434 44
Said Administrator allowed for his Trouble   35.
Settlement made 15th April 1839 $399 44
                              Saml Greer
                              Clerk County Court

                           ROBERT BEARDS Estate

Settlement made with James Beard & Daniel Deakins, Executors of Robert Beard
Deceast, made December 14th 1839. It appears from Settlement made with Ad-
ministrators (per set) the Ballance on of the first Sale was this Sum
                                                                 $648 84
And from Inventories of Sale of negros this Sum was
Received by the Executor $4013 00
It appears there was a Horse Sold which is not in the
Inventory for this Sum   58 00
And a cow for this Sum   11 25
Note on Joseph Beard principal & Interest   58 00
Note on Saml G. Chester   28 00
                                                                $4817 09

From Vouchers produced Said Executors has paid out
this Sum $949 20
To this Sum paid former Committee   3 00
this Sum allowed Executors for their
Services   200 00
this Sum allowed clerk for his Services
in making Settlement & altering record
and recording   5 00 $1157 20
                                                                $3659 89

(p-259)   ROBERT BEARDS Estate

                              Amt Brot. over $3659 89
Interest calculated on the above for one year and
a half amounting to this Sum   329 37
                                                                $3989 26
To this Sum left in the will to Martha Beard & ⎱
James Beard, being ½ kitchen & cupboard furniture & ⎰
Brass kettle & Smith Tools   48 25
                                                                $3941 01

Deduct from the above Sum $150. in which but five of the
Heirs are Interested   150 00
                                                                $3791 01
                              Saml Greer Clerk
                              County Court of Washington County

WASHINGTON COUNTY, TENNESSEE

JAMES BARNS Estate

Settlement made with John Hoss, administrator of James Barns, Deceast, made 7th May 1839. Administrator charged as pr Inventory of Sale this amount
$1221 06

Inventory of the Sale of Thomas Stevens Land and other cash Received
430 96
$1836 70

Administrator produced vouchers from No 1 to No 68 Inclusive to this amount $1680 53¾
Said administrator allowed for his Trouble &
Expense this Sum   91 80 $1772 33¾
Bal on hands $63 36¼
Saml Greer
Clerk

(p-260)   JANE ALLISONS Estate

Settlement made with R. A. Thompson Executor of Jane Allison Deceast, made 28th January 1840. Executor has Recd from Duncans & Blairs notes
$184 20

Note on Hiram Hampton		13 45
Note on James Tadlock Principal	$82 50	
Interest accrued up to 11th January 1840	14 33	96 83
Five notes on James Duncan & Hiram Hampton, Principal	$439 00	
Interest on Same up to 1st March 1840	52 68	491 68
1 note on Joseph Archer due 1st March 1841	$53 00	
Interest thereon from 31st May 1837 to 1st March 1840	8 74	61 74
1 note on Joseph Archer due 1st March 1842	$92 00	
Interest thereon from 1st March 1837 To 1st March 1840	16 56	108 56
		$956 66

Executor has paid out to Polly Ann Conley and his own wife Legatees, this Sum Specially left to them by Testator
184 20
$772 46

Executor has paid out for Debts, Funeral Expenses &c as pr Vouchers from No 1 to No 8 Inclusive this Sum
$69 87
Executor allowed for his Services this
Sum   45 00 $114 87
Being the neat Sum to be Disbursed $657 59
Saml Greer
Clerk

JACOB KLEPPER Guardian of the Heirs of JOHN KLEPPER

Settlement made with Jacob Klepper, Guardian of the Heirs of John Klepper

Deceast, and his own children--
Ballance due by Guardian on Former Settlement being Interest & Principal up
to 1st Feby 1839 $13651 10½
Interest on Said Sum up to 1st Feby 1840   819 06½
            Amt Taken uver $14470 16¾

(p-261)   JACOB KLEPPER Guardian &c.

                  Amt Brot over $14470 16¾

Recd of Thomas Wilson Executor this additional Sum on which Interest is to
Commence from this date 1st Feby 1840   2976 15
                                                      $17446 31¾

Guardian paid out cash for Traveling Expenses &
postage this Sum $75 00
Paid to G. W. Millhorn in right of his
wife Elisabeth this Sum   175 06¾
paid clerks fee for this Settlement 2 75
Guardian allowed 1 pr cent pr annum for
his Trouble Risk &c amounting to this
Sum   174 46 $427 27
Interest Chargeable on this amount untill next $17019 04¼
annual Settlement
     This Settlement made 1st Feby 1840
                              Saml Greer Clerk

            J. H. GILLISPIE Guardian of E. E. YOUNG

Settlement made with James H. Gillispie, Guardian of Elisabeth E. Young,
minor child of James W. Young Deceast, made 5th March 1840.
The hire of Reubin four years at $80 00 pr annum $320 00
The hire of Same Boy for two years at $90 00 pr annum   180 00
Elisabeth part of rents of Farms after paying repars
Each year for 4 years.   61 52
                                                       $561 52
Guardian allowed 1 Dollars pr weeks for Boarding Elisa-
beth Young 5 years and 5 months $277 50
By amt. Expended for Clothing Saddle &c.   132 81
To this amt pd for Tax, Schooling & loss of time of
negro man when he had his foot cut   33 32
By clerks fee for Settlement & recording Same   2 75 $446 38
Interest on the above amt. for 2½ years the Equated time   115 15
                                                                    16 38
                                                                  $131 50
              Saml Greer clerk of the County Court

(p-262)   JAMES MCALESTER Guardian of MARY PAYNE

James McAlester Guardian of Mary Payne, Dr to Notes on Hand amounting to
                                                    $475 25½
    Contra
By amount pd Adam Broyles as pr Bill rendered $15 04
" Tax paid Sheriff for 1839   3 60   18 64
Ballance on hand in notes of hand $456 61½

WASHINGTON COUNTY, TENNESSEE

May 1st 1840
James McAllester Guardian
for Mary Payne

WILLIAM JACKSONS Estate

Supplementary Settlement with George & Peter Jackson Executors of Wm Jackson Deceast, made 5th May 1840. To amount of Inventories for hire of negros for 1838. $120 00
Said Executors allowed as pr receipts for Taxes & Fees
of Clerk from No 1 to No 5 Inclusive this Sum $7 70
Said Executors allowed for his Trouble & Expense
in hireing Said negros & collecting money this Sum 10 00 $17 70
    This Sum in hands of Executors $102 30

Saml Greer Clerk
County Court W. County

S. PRICE Guardian of E. E. YOUNG &c.

Settlement made with S. Price Guardian of Elisabeth E. Young & Thomas Young minor heirs of James W. Young Deceast, made 4th June 1840. Said Guardian chargeable with this Sum as Guardian of E. E. Young, Guardians receipt
    $131 50

Paid out for ward $51 63
Cash paid Clerk   3 25   54 88
    Ballance in hands of Guardian $76 62

Saml Greer Clerk
of the County Court of Washington County

(p-263)   JACOB ELLIS Estate

Settlement made with William Ellis, Executor of the Estate of Jacob Ellis, Deceast, on the 25th March 1840.
From Inventories returned Executor charged with this
amount $293 82¼

Said Executor has paid out as pr receipts and vouchers
produced foram No 1 To No 42 Inclusive this Sum $1349 22
This Sum allowed Executor for his Trouble &
Expenses   50 00
     $1399 22
    Amt charged   293 82¼
This Sum paid out over assets received $1105 39¾

Saml Greer Clerk
of the County Court W. County

J. H. GILLESPIE Guardian of THOMAS E. YOUNG

Settlement made with James H. Gillespie, Guardian of Thos E. Young minor heir of James W. Young Deceast, made 5th March 1840. The rent of Plantation being his Share after paying repares each year for 4 years $61 52
Hire of negro woman & Boy for 4 years and 4 months at
$40 00 pr annum   173 33

☨ (See Errata for correction)

$234 85

Guardian allowed 1 Dollar pr week for Boarding 4 years
& 5 months $221 00
Amt. Expended for clothing & making cloths   51 22¾
Amt. Expended for Schooling & Tax of Land   20 75
Clerks fee for Settlement & recording
Same   2 75 $295 72¾
Guardian has overpaid which has been recd
this Sum $60 87¾

      Saml Greer Clerk
      County Court

(p-264)   JOHN A BOWMAN GUARDIAN &C.

Settlement made with John A. Bowman Guardian of Samuel Krouse made 6th May 1841.

To this amount due by former Settlement $140 64
Amt. Interest accrued this year up to 6th May 1841 8 43
              $149 07
By this Sum for fees of Settlement   2 75
    Ballance on hand   146 32

      Saml Greer Clerk
      of the County Court W. County

       JACOB KEIBLER Estate

Settlement made with Jacob Keibler administrator of Jacob Keibler Deceast, with the will annexed made 14th July 1841.
I find Said administrator chargeable as pr Inventories
not Including a note on Moses Ingersoll which is not
collected or <u>collectible</u> this Sum $3065 28¾

And Said administrator Produces Vouchers from No 1 to
8 Inclusive amounting to this Sum $70 70
Said administrator allowed for his Services
in collecting & paying out this sum 153 25 223 95
    Bal due the Estate $2841 33¾
from <u>assetts</u> which leave amt. to the hands of administrator, A Suit Pending for part of the Estate & the crier of the Sale and the attornies fees not Included in the credits.

      Saml Greer Clerk
      County Court W. County

(p-265)   JOHN ROCKS Estate

Settlement made with William Combs, Executor of John Rock Deceast, made 8th January 1841. Said Executor charged as pr Inventory with this Sum $49 58
Said Executor has paid out as pr vouchers
To Jesse Headrick this Sum $4 00
" James Arterburn   1 95
" Danl Kinny   1 50
" Lawson Gifford   75
" William Kincheloe   6 00

To J. Arterburn for Crying Sale	$1 00	
" Robert G. Hale clerking Sale	1 00	
" Clerk for costs	4 00	
" John Keys & Co	12 77	
" Fees for Settlement & recording	2 75	
This Sum allowed Executor for his Services	10 00	$45 72
Ballance on hand		$ 3 86

Saml Greer Clerk
County Court W. County

E. L. MATHIS Guardian of SAMPSON GANN

Oct. Session 1841. In obediance to the Statute in Such cases made & provided I make to your worships the following report of all the money, which has come/to my hands by Virtue my appointment as Guardian of Sampson Gann, heir at law of Nathan Gann Deceast Oct. 4th 1841. Then Received of G. W. Tilford, Six Hundred Dollars, in current Bank notes from G. W. Tilford, administrator of Nathan Gann Deceast, and I have given a bond to Said administrator to Indemnify him against any wrong calculation, or any Suit or Suits that may be Brought against him.

E. L. Mathis
Guardian &c.

(p-266)   J. KLEPPER GUARDIAN OF J. KLEPPER

Settlement made with Jacob Klepper Guardian of the Heirs of Joseph Klepper and his own children made 1st day of February 1840. $17019 04¾
Interest on Said amount up to this date   1021 14
This additional amount received from Executor   5413 35
                                                                         $23453 53¾

Deduct amount paid wards as pr Vouchers produced (to wit)
To G. W. Milhorn this Sum	$253 72¼	
" Charles Range & wife	1431 75	
" G. W. Milhorn	64 70	
" David Klepper	1435 27	
" Richard Carr	1440 28	
" Expenses in Travilling to Winchester Abington & for Postage &c.	51 16	
" This Sum allowed Guardian for time Trouble & risk in collecting & disbursing 1 pr cent	234 53½	$4911 42¼
		$18542 11½
Clerks fee for Settlement & recording		2 75
Nett amount in hands of Guardian		$18539 36½

Saml Greer clerk
County Court
Washington County

(p-267)   J. KLEPPER Guardian of J. KLEPPER Heirs.

J. Klepper Guardian of J. Klepper Heirs Settlement made with Jacob Klepper Guardian of his own children and the heirs of John Klepper Deceast, made 1st February 1842. Guardian charged as pr Settlement 1st February 1841, with this Sum $18539 36½

```
Interest on this up to this date              $1112 37½
Guardian charged with this amt recd this year    4300 00
                                               $23951 74

Guardian has disbursed and is Entitled to credit as
follows
Paid Daniel Campbell as pr Rect         $1442 89½
 "   David Klepper                        189 62½
 "   Richard Carr                         189 62½
 "   G. W. Milhorn                        189 62½
 "   Charles Range                        189 62½
 "   Daniel Campbell                      189 62½
 "   David Klepper                         58 82½
 "   Richard Carr                          58 82½
 "   Daniel Campbell                       58 82½
 "   Charles Range                         58 82½
 "   G. W. Milhorn                         58 82½
For Expenses in Travelling
postage &c.                                80 62½
Guardian allowed for Services &c.         239 51
Clerks fee for Settlement &c.               2 75
              Disbursements &c.         $3008 03
              Whole amount               23951 74
              Amt on hand                20943 71

                    Saml Greer
                         Clerk
```

(p-268)   ROBERT BEANS Estate

STATE OF TENNESSEE }
WASHINGTON COUNTY   } We the undersigned being apointed to Settle with
Clark Hunter administrator of Robert Bean Deceast, have met and from Examination of the papers do find Said administrator chargeable with this Sum.
                                                            $101 71

And we find that Said administrator has paid out as pr
receipts from No 1 to No 7 Inclusive this Sum $129 12½
And we find that the Intestate Executed his
note to the administrator for Twenty Dollars the
Principal and Interest at this time amounts to   21 50
And said Administrator Produces an account against
the Intestate for this amount   8 31
                                                $158 93½
We are of opinion Said administrator be allowed for his Services
this Sum $14 00
Given under our hands & Seals this 28th day of
November 1836.
                    Saml Greer
                    Joseph McLin

        JAMES McALESTER Guardian of MISS MARY PAYNE

Report of James McAlester Guardian of Mary Payne 2nd May 1836.
Do To one note of hand on Joseph Bottles $67 07
 " " one Do on Henry McCracken $22 69 1 Do on G. W.

Willett for $43 90 1 Do on Samuel Maxwell for
$14 22½ $80 81½
Do To one Do on Henderson Clark   23 55
                                                                              $171 43½

Contra by Allowance made by Court to Executor to
    To James McAlester $50 00
    To Jacob Wheatler   15 00
    By Robt Reeds a/c & Judgement   7 50   72 50
Leaving a Ballance on hand as above $98 93
                                                James McAlester
                                                   of Mary Payne

(p-269)   HENRY SLIGAR Estate

Agreeable to an order of the County Court of Washington County June Term 1836, to us Directed to Settle with Wm Sligar Executor of Henry Sligar Deceast, we met in the Court House and called on the Executor for his papers, he produced legal vouchers for money paid and Services rendered as follows.

No.			
1	Clerk for Recording will	$1 50	
2	Isaac Hartsell for crying the Sale	2 00	
3	Samuel Davidson clerk at Sale	50	
4	John Kennedy for advice	10 00	
5	Clerks fee in office	62½	
6	Do Do	50	
7	Do Do	62½	
8	Wm Sligar for Services	5 00	
9	Jesse Clark, Jacob Brown & Saml G. Bayless committee to make Settlement	3 00	
		$23 75	

And find the Executor charged by Inventory Two Hundred and
thirty for Dollars & twenty Six cents   234 26
Which leaves in the Executors hands $210 51
Given under our hands this 6th day of June 1836.
                                Saml G. Bayless (Seal)
                                Jacob Brown   (Seal) Committee
                                Jesse Clarke   (Seal)

E. L. MATHIS Guardian of the MISS TYLARS &C.

A annual Settlement of the accounts between myself as Guardian & wards (viz) Phebe, Minerva & Elisabeth Tylar, for the year Ending January Session 1836. See Settlement January Session 1835, then in my hands four thousand Six hundred ninety nine Dollars and ten cents $4699 10
Interest on the above for one year   281 94
Total four thousand nine hundred Eighty one Dollars $4981 04
04/100

(p-270)   E. L. MATHES Guardian &c.

                                                 Amt Brot up $4981 04
Disbursed by Said Guardian & Services rendered Since
last Settlement (viz)
No 1   N. Gammon (Treasurer) receipt fifty four
            Dollars & Eighty Seven cents & one half $54 87½

" 2	Greenway & Lockets account	$55 67½	
" 3, 4 & 5	(Phebes) Gibbs account	104 13	
" 6	Wm G. Rockholts account	26 72	
" 7	N. Gammon (Treasurer) Receipt	16 75	
" 8	Eason as (Treasurer) Receipt	15 60	
" 9	S. Maxwells a/c & Receipt	65 98	
" 10	J. Broyles a/c one Dollar	1 00	
" 11	Greenway & Locket	62 87	
Guardians a/c two days $1 00 pr day		2 00	
		$405 64	
Two & one half pr cent on the above		10 14	$415 75
Which leaves in my hands four thousand five hundred			$4565 29
Sixty five Dollars & Twenty nine cents.			

E. L. Mathis
Guardian

E. L. MATHIS Guardian of A. NELSONS Estate

Annual Settlement of the accounts between E. L. Mathes Guardian & Alexander Nelson, his ward for the year Ending August Session 1836. See July Session 1835. Total amount of Good funds four thousand four hundred Eighty two Dollars and Eighty four cents $4482 84¼
Subtract $525 75 on G. T. Gillispie of which Sum I   525 75
have received no Interest Since last Settlement $3957 09¼
Add $237 92 Interest on the last Sum   237 92
Add $30 00 half of Becky & Vilets hire for one year   30 00
                                                        $4225 01¼

(p-271)   E. L. MATHIS GUARDIAN OF A. NELSONS Estate

                                Amt Brot over $4225 01¼
Disbursed by Sd Guardian & Services rendered (257 67
Since last Settlement ($3967 34¼
    No 1   To Benj F. Locket $8 75
    " 2   " Joseph Mann   12 90
    " 3   " Crawfords & Kinneys Store
                a/c   148 05
Guardians account for Services rendered (
& articles advanced (75 75
Exclusive of any Boarding $244 45
5 pr cent on this Sum $244 45 is   12 22
which leaves in my hands three thous- $257 67
and nine hundred Sixty Seven Dollars &
thirty four ¼ cents. Exclusive of Embree,
Gillispie, Allen & Patterson.

E. L. Mathis
Guardian of Alex Nelson

ADAM WATTENBARGERS Estate

STATE OF TENNESSEE (
WASHINGTON COUNTY (We the under Signed being appointed by the County Court of Washington County at their October Term 1836 to Settle with

WASHINGTON COUNTY, TENNESSEE

Christian Zetty Senr & Frederick Fenceler Executors of the Estate of Adam Wattenbarger Deceast, having met this 29th day of October, 1836, at the house of Isaac McPherson Esqrs & then & there Called on the Said Executors for vouchers & they Submitted the following (viz)

No				
1	Jacob Wattenbargers receipt dated	Oct 15th 1836	$22 00
2	Adam Wattenbargers " "	Oct 14 1836	10 00
3	Solomon Wattenbargers " "	Oct 7 1836	22 00
4	F. F. Wattenbargers " "	Oct 7 1836	10 00
5	George Wattenbargers " "	Oct 7 1836	22 00
6	Solomon Wattenbargers " "	Oct 7 1836	1 00
7	Samuel Wattenbarger " "	Oct 7 1836	22 00
9	Adam Wattenbarger " "	Sept 28 1836	12 00
8	Saml Greer Junr Cider " "	Oct 3 1836	50
10	Adam Wattenbarger " "	Sept 28 1836	12 00

(p-272) ADAM WATTENBARGER Estate

No			
11	F. F. Wattenbargers Receipt Sept 28 1836	$12 00
12	William Wattenbarger " Oct 1, 1835	10 00
13	Michael Wattenbarger " Aug 20, 1834	10 00
14	Jesse Brown " Ap 25 1833	13 00
15	Adam Wattenbarger " Aug. 3, 1835	20 00
16	Shff Bricker Tax Receipt for the years 1831 & 1833	3 61½
17	Saml McKeehans Receipt Jany 22nd 1836	12 00
18	Jacob Wattenbargers " Aug. 12 1834	3 00
19	Adam Wattenbarger " Aug. 12, 1834	3 00
20	Saml Greers " " " "	62½
21	F. F. Wattenbarger " Jany 22, 1836	12 00
22	Michael Wattenbarger " Feb. 11, 1833	13 00
23	Solomon Wattenbarger " Do 11, 1833	13 00
24	William Wattenbarger " Do 11, 1833	13 00
25	Solomon Wattenbarger " June 23, 1836	12 00
26	F. F. Wattenbarger " Feb. 18, 1832	12 00
27	Samuel Wattenbarger " June 23, 1836	1 00
28	George Wattenbarger " Der. 25, 1833	26 00
29	George Wattenbarger " Do 25, 1833	15 00
30	Do Do " June 5, 1834	3 00
31	Do Do " Do 5, 1834	56 00
32	Solomon Wattenbarger " Do 5, 1834	3 00
33	F. F. Wattenbarger " Do 5, 1834	3 00
34	Shff Bricker Tax for 1834 & 1835	3 60
35	Samuel Wattenbarger Receipt Jan. 23, 1836	15 00
36	F. F. Wattenbarger " July 25, 1835	20 00
37	Saml Wattenbarger " Jan. 23, 1836	12 00
38	Adam Wattenbarger " June 8, 1835	13 00
39	Jacob Wattenbarger " June 8, 1833	13 00
40	George Wattenbarger " July 20, 1835	20 00
41	Do Do " June 28, 1836	12 00
42	Sarah Wattenbarger " Aug. 3, 1835	20 00
43	F. F. Wattenbarger " Feb. 18, 1832	60 00
44	Solomon Wattenbarger Recpt July 20th 1835	20 00
45	F. F. Wattenbarger " May 23, 1833	13 00
46	Sarah Wattenbarger	13 00
47	F. F. Wattenbarger " Sept. 15, 1832	13 00
48	Sarah Wattenbarger " June 5, 1834	3 00
49	Shff Bricker for Tax " 1832	1 00
50	Jacob Wattenbarger " Aug. 11, 1835	20 00

"	51	Shff Bricker Tax	" 1833	$ 1 81¼
"	52	Jacob Wattenbarger	" June 23, 1836	12 00
"	53	Michael Wattenbarger	" Nov. 4, 1835	20 00
"	54	Saml Wattenbarger	" June 25, 1836	56 00
"	55	John McGhee	" Aug. 28, 1835	1 00
"	56	Isaac McPherson	" " " "	1 00
"	57	Saml Wattenbarger	" Jan. 23, 1836	15 00
"	58	Jesse Brown	" Sept 11, 1835	10 00
"	59	D. Shff. Barkley	" Sept. 28, 1836	38 61
"	60	Michael Wattenbarger	" June 28, 1836	12 00
				$841 86¼

After examining the aforesaid vouchers we find the above Estimate to be the amount of funds paid out by Said Executors. Given under our hands this 29th day of October 1836.

      Saml Conley
      Isaac McPherson Commissioners
      Robert Reed

JOHN TIPTON Estate

In Compliance with an order of the County Court October Session, we the undersigned being appointed a Committee to Settle with David Sellers, Administrator of John Tipton Deceast, have proceeded to the Settlement, and find him David chargeable with the following Sums, the amount of the

(p-273)   JOHN TIPTONS Estate

Sale as Returned in the Inventory	$142 36¾
Recd of Saml Hunt, Redemption Money	54 52
Recd of Larry Snapp, for the hire of Bob a Slave	40 00
Recd of James H. Jones, for a Camp	7 00
Recd of Darling Jones	75
Recd of Moor Land	25
	$244 88¾

And we find his credit, to be paid to Samuel Tipton on a note
marked No. 1 $91 98

No 2	Thomas Kings Receipt	29 25	
" 3	Costs paid at Sundry Times	17 25	
" 4	James Seviers Receipt	12 00	
" 5 & 6	W. R. Dulany 2 Receipts	7 00	
" 7	John Ryland Do	5 00	
" 8	James V. Anderson Do	5 00	
" 9	Saml Greer Do	87½	
" 10	James Melvin Do	1 25	
" 11	Emmerson for Printing Do	1 50	
" 12	John Parker Do	2 00	
" 13	Abraham Sellers Do	2 00	$165 10½
We find him Indebted to the Estate the Sum of			79 78¼
No 14	And also a Recpt from Saml Hunt		27 88
		Ballance due	$51 90

In witness whereof we have hereunto Set our hands and Seals this 16th day of January 1836.

      Joshua Boring (Seal)
      John Hoss (Seal)

                                            Richard Carr (Seal)
We have made him his allowance for his Trouble the Sum of $25 00
                              John Hoss
                              Richard Carr
                              Joshua Boring

(p-274)   ROBERT MCCALLS Estate

Supplemental Settlement of the Estate of Robert McCall, Deceast, with Jemima McCall widow & Executrix of Said Deceast, by Joseph McLin & W. K. Blair, Commissioners this 4th July 1836. To Ballance on former Settlement returned to January Term 1836, as appears from clerks Book $303 87½
    July 2nd 1836
By amt pd Doct S. B. Cunningham $30 33½
 " S. J. W. Luckeys Receipt   2 50
 " Cash pd Thomas Haws on Mortgage   538 00
                                          $570 83½

We the Commissioners find that the Estate of Robert McCall Deceast, is Indebted to the administratrix the Sum of Two hundred Sixty Six Dollars ninety Six cents on the foregoing a/c July 4th 1836.
                              W. K. Blair
                              Joseph McLin Commissioners

           A. L. BARNES Guardian of JAMES BARNES heirs

May 30th day 1836. Washington County East Tennessee
An Inventory of notes and amounts
1 note on Galloway Campbell & Henry King $7 50
1 note on Elijah Shipley & John Ryland   16 00
1 note on John Nead & Michael Miller   13 00
1 note on Joseph Wolf & John Sayler   5 00
1 note on Vinate Fines Joseph Wolf   7 75
1 note on Harden Hopper & John Nead   21 65
1 note on Ransom Matlock & Elijah Shipley   6 25
1 note on Solomon Garber & John Nead   5 50
1 note on Thomas Stevens & John Stevens   4 00
1 note on William Ford & G. W. Mallonee   8 00
1 note on George W. Mallonee & John Mallonee   14 00

(p-275)   A L BARNES Guardian of JAMES BARNES Heirs

1 note on John Ryland & Elijah Shipley   5 75
1 note on Thomas F. Stevens & John Stevens   5 00
1 note on Michael Miller & John Nead   7 75
1 note on John Stevens & Henry King   20 85
1 note on Noah Daniels & John Carauthers   7 50
1 note on David Stevens & John Stevens   6 50
1 note on John Carauthers & Noah Daniels   7 75
1 note on John Ingle & John Stevens   4 00
1 note on John E. Copan & John Hoss   6 25
1 note on Robert G. West & Wm G. Lowry   5 75
    A. L. Barnes note   20 50
                                  Amount $206 45

DANIEL YEAGAR'S Estate

STATE OF TENNESSEE }
WASHINGTON COUNTY } In pursuance of an order of the County Court of Washington County October Session 1837. E. L. Mathis, John Humphreys, and Johua Green, appointed as a Committee to Settle with the Executors of Daniel Yeagar Deceast, accordingly the Said Committee met at the house of the Said Deceast, on the 8theOct. 1837 & called upon the Executors (to wit) Solomon N. Yeagar & Joseph J. Yeagar, for the papers they produced a copy of the Inventory which was a list of personal property which property was Sold on the 5th Inst. Which Sales amounted to foure hundred one Dollars 84¾/100 which Sum the Said Executors are chargeable with, they also produced vouchers (to wit)

No	Description	Amount
1	Peter Emmert & Co account Including a note on Susannah Yeager for $12. & J. F. Broyles	$60 43
2	James McLins Account	30 37
3	John & W. K. Blairs account	4 20
4	James F. Broyles Brothers	23 65
5	John C. Shields account	4 00
	Taken over	$

(p-276) DANIEL YEAGERS Estate

No.	Description	Amount
6	William Pattons account	$11 47
7	James Allens account	93
8	Alexander W. Brabsons	13 50
9	George W. Nelsons account	18 85
10	Mathew Stephenson for an order	5 25
11	Alexander Mathes a/c for cording	88
		$173 53

The amount of the Sale money the Interest discounted
now amounts to four hundred fourteen Dollars & Eighty
four cents & ¾ $414 84¾
The amount of the vouchers   173 53
Subtracted leaves in the hands of the   241 31¾
Executors this amount
Also we find in their hands Eight hundred
& forty Six D.   846 00
After the Interest for one year is Dis- $1087 31¾
counted.
The price of three Slaves Sold (to wit) Nancy, Stephen, & Melinda Ann, which makes at this date ten hundred Eighty Seven Dollars & thirty one ¾ cents.
No 12 Thomas Browns Rct. for Crying Sale $ 3 00
Three Dollars to the Commissioners   3 00
The Committee are of opinion that the Executors are En-   50 00
titled to $50. as a reasonable compensation in Settling   56 00
the business of Said Estate which last Sum Deducted leaves
in the hands of Said Executors ten hundred thirty one Dollars
& thirty one cents $1031 31
No. 13 Greer Clerk C. C. Rct & Luckys Rct & for   5 25
recording this Settlement Deducted $1026 06
Given under our hands this 9th day of Oct. 1837
                                E. L. Mathis
We the undersigned all heirs of the   Joshua Green   Committee
Estate of Daniel Yeager Dct beleiving John Humphreys
the above Settlement to be correct are willing for it to go reccord & that it shall be final. Given under our hands this 9th day of Oct. 1837. E. J.

WASHINGTON COUNTY, TENNESSEE

Yeager, Mary Yeager, Jacob K. Russell, C. F. Yeager, G. W. Nelson

(p-277)   ADAM PAINTERS Estate

STATE OF TENNESSEE |
WASHINGTON COUNTY | Oct. 24th 1837. In pursuance of an order of the County Court of Washington held at Jonesborough on the 1st Monday of June 1837. We Henderson Clark, William Gilleland, and Thomas McAdams, being appointed at the Term aforesaid as a Committee to Settle with Elisabeth Painter administratrix of the Estate of Adam Painter Deceast, have this day met and called on Mrs. Painter, She admitted the following amount of assets in her hands (viz) amount of property Sold at vendue $78 33½
Also one note on Samuel Painter   500 00
She afterwards produced the following vouchers (to wit) $578 33½

No			
1	John Carrs Receipt	$2	00
2	Gammon & Stuarts Receipt	42	79
3	Saml Greer Do	3	75
4	Joseph Manns Do	14	85
5	Joseph H. Bells Do	4	00
6	Her a/c part against the Estate	5	00
7	William Gilleland Receipt	1	00
8	Henderson Clark Do	1	00
9	Thomas McAdams Do	1	00
10	B. H. Bells Do	1	00
11	J. Wests Do cost in Suit with Stuart	2	00
12	Do Do Do J. D. Clark	1	00
13	Joel D. Clarks Receipt	4	20
14	Jesse Painters Do	43	00
15	Samuel Painter Do	43	00
16	Phillip Painter Do	43	00
17	David Painter Do	43	00
18	Aaron Painter Do	17	00
19	Adam Painter Do	43	000
20	Aaron Painter Do	43	00
21	William Painter Do	83	00
22	Samuel Painter Do	33	30
	Amt. Taken over	$434	89

(p-278)   ADAM PAINTERS Estate

                Amts. Brot over $434 89 $578 33½
                                                   434 89
                                                   143 44½
The a/c against the Estate $11 00
The part allowed the administratrix out of the Estate by the
Deceast   43 00
Her dower as layed off to her 20 00
the amount below   61 00 $ 135 00

The Ballance of the Estate is left in the hands of Samuel Painter, out of which he is to pay Eighteen Dollars to Polly Bowman wife of Aaron Bowman, it being the Ballance of the amount allowed her out of the Estate, She having received Twenty five Dollars. By hands of Jesse Painter, in a Saddle. Also forty three Dollars to Sally Gann wife of John Gann as her part of the Estate to be paid in treade Eaqual to corn at two Shillings pr. Bushel between this and the year 1844, the remainder to Sattisfyed some cost due from the Estate to Joseph West, John McGee & Thomas McAdams, leaving the Estate even, witness our hands this   day of   1837.

                William Gilleland
                Thomas McAdams   Committee
                Henderson Clark

ROBERT MOORES Estate

STATE OF TENNESSEE } 29th July 1836
WASHINGTON COUNTY } Persuant & in the obedience to an order of the Court of Pleas &c of Washington County at July Session thereof, we the Subscribers having been appointed to settle with John M. Crawford Executor, of the last will & Testament of Robert Moore Deceast, have this day met at the Court House, and made Said Settlement So far as the Same could be done, we find that Said Crawford as Executor of Said Robert Moore, Deceast, has paid (p-279) over to Sarah Moore, Sister & Devisee of Said Robert Moore Deceast, on the 26th April 1834, the following property (to wit) five head of Grown horses, three two year old colts, one Spring Colt, five milch cows, two steers, two years old, three yearlings, three Spring calves, Seven head of Sheep, Twenty head of hogs, one fore horse waggon, & Gears, three bar Shears plows, two Shovel plows, two mattocks, three hoes, three chopping axes, one crow bar, one Hansaw, Some Mill picks, one Clock, & Corner Cupboard, & Sixty Bushels of corn, nineteen Bushels of wheat, one hundred pounds of Bacon, one man's Saddle, Some bar Iron, for which property as aforesaid the Said Sarah Moore, Executed her receipt to Said John M Crawford, which is herewith filed maked (A)--

We further find Said Crawford chargeable with	$35 00
Dollars in Bank notes possessed by Sd Robert Moore, at his death.	
The Said Crawford is chargeable with fifty Dollars.	50 00
So much on an obligation Executed by Robert McDowel to Robert Moore, William Moore, & Sarah Moore, dated the 14th Decr 1833 & payable 14th Decr 1834.	
To amount of Edward Millions obligation for	6 00
To amount of David Mitchells obligation for	1 50
To amount of Hiram Gass note	5 93
To amount of Christian Longs obligation the Ballance is	12 85
" Amt of Book a/c against Christian Long	3 43
" amt of George Cochrans account	20 25
" Amt of a/c against Samuel Stephens	9 12½
" Amt of Rufus Scruggs note	15 00
" Amt of note on Thomas Stuart for	18 00
	$177 08½

         John M. Crawford Cr.

By amt pd Saml Stephens his proven a/c	$8 37½
" Cash paid John G. Eason	4 37½
" amt of Christian Longs proven a/c	44 17½
" amt of Doct. John Yancy a/c for medicine	10 00
" Clerk of County Court for fees	10 00
Amts Taken over $	

(p-280) Amts. Brot over $	177 08½
" Cash pd Doct. Cunningham the amt of R. Moores note	7 75
" paid Jacob B. E. account	3 19

WASHINGTON COUNTY, TENNESSEE

" George Cohrans Do	$25 00		
" Jeremiah Boyds a/c for R. Moores coffin	12 00		
" Sheriff of Washington Rect for Taxes	8 73		
" Clerk of County Court for fees	50		
" Do Do Do	1 50		
" A/cts of Dr. James King proven a/c	14 00		
" Sarah Moores Receipt for	19 00		
" J. Ryland Sheriff of Washington, Taxes for 1834	5 85		
Taxes for 1835	5 85¾		
" Cash pd Doct John N. Doaks Bill of attention	2 50		
" paid John Kennedy for advice as attorney	5 00		
" this amount allowed for Settling Estate	30 00	$217 80¾	
Bal in favor of adr.		40 ??¼	

The Vouchers on which the above Settlement is Herewith Exhibited 29th July 1836.

                        John Kennedy
                        John Bayless
                        Saml Greer

DAN D. ANDREW Estate

STATE OF TENNESSEE } July 1st 1837
WASHINGTON COUNTY } In pursuance of an order of the County Court held at Jonesborough, on the first Monday of June appointing us (viz) John Humphreys William Gilleland, & Thomas McAdams a Committee to Settle with Nancy Andrew, administratrix of the Estate of Dan D. Andrew Deceast, We have this day met & having called on Mrs. Andrew for the papers, and after a fair Examination find the following to be the result amt of Sale of property $113 36½
Amt. collected of Miles Scruggs   32 00
                      Taken up $145 36½

(p-281)   DAN D. ANDREWS Estate

                    Amt. Brot. up $145 36½

The following vouchers were produced

No. 1	William Tylers receipt	$124 98
" 2	Thos Gibbs receipt pr Wm Tyler	18 00
" 3	Her a/c against the Estate	5 00
" 4	John Humphreys receipt	1 00
" 5	William Gillelands Do	1 00
" 6	Thomas McAdams Do	1 00
" 7	Saml Greers clerks Do	2 37½
" 8	John McGees Do	1 00

                    John Humphreys   }
                    William Gilleland   } Committee
                    Thomas McAdams

ROBERT BEARDS Estate

We the undersigned appointed Committee by Court at September Session 1837, to Settle with Daniel Deakins and James Beard administrators of Robert Beard

Deceast, met at Jonesborough, on the 5th Sept. 1837 & from the Inventories we find Said administrators charged on Former Settlement with this Sum $648 84½
And the amount of Sale of negros   4013 00
Making this amount $4661 84½
for accounts paid Expenses &c Said Administrators produced vouchers from No 10 to No 36 Inclusive amounting to this Sum $504 20½
From the will of Robt. Beard Deceast, It appears there is a Special Legacy to Six Daughters Seventy Dollars Each making this Sum   420 00
& to five Sons five Dollars Each making this Sum   25 00 $949 20½
To this Sum paid Committee $3 00 $3712 64
" this allowed administrators   200 00   203 00
$3509 64

(p-282) The Ballance to be divided among the heirs Equally, Given under our hands & Seals this 5th Sept. 1837.

Saml Greer (Seal)
Justice of the peace
Jacob Hartsell (Seal)
Justice of the peace
Jesse Clark (Seal)
Justice of the peace

THOMAS HAMMONS Estate

STATE OF TENNESSEE
WASHINGTON COUNTY   Pursuant to an order of Court of Sd. County at April Session 1837, appointing the undersigned a Committee to Settle with John Hammons & Jacob Hammons Executor of the Estate of Thomas Hammons Deceast, having met at the late residence of the Deceast, the papers being produced by Said Executors by the Inventory a list of the Sale of property, We find them chargeable with the Sum of $202 22
We Consider the Said Executors are intitled to a credit to the amount the following vouchers calls for (viz)

No. 1 Due Bill on E. L. Mathis Receipted $4 87½
" 2 Saml Greer (Clerk of the C Court) receipt 1 53
" 3 Due Bill to D. Barkly pd to J. & M. Stephenson   99 28
" 4 Note to M & J. Stephenson Receipted   76 03
" 5 M & J. Stephenson proven account   1 92
" 6 Note to Stephen Brown Receipted   10 00
" 7 W. Willetts (Count) Do   16 75
" 8 J. F. Deadricks Do   9 70
" 9 William Reeds Do   17 92
" 10 John E. Copans (Doctor) Do   18 75
" 11 M & J. Stephenson, note of hand receipted   64 59
" 12 Note to M. & J. Stephenson Receipted for   16 68
" 13 Saml H. Stevens a/c Receipted for   34 54 $369 56½
Taken up

(p-283)   THOMAS HAMMONS Estate

Making in all three hundred Sixty nine Dollars 56½/100 $369 56½

```
John Brickers receipt for Cost                          $  5 00
       Amount of vouchers                               $374 56½
       amount of sales                                   203 22
       To amount over paid                              $172 34½
```
From the above Statement we find that the above named Executors have paid out $172 34½ more than what came into their hands by the Sale which they made, Given under our hands this 1st day of May 1837.

          Saml Conley   ⎱
          Robert Read   Committee
          E. L. Mathis   ⎰

REBECCA IRVINS Estate

STATE OF TENNESSEE
WASHINGTON COUNTY   We the undersigners being appointed commissioners to Settle with Joseph L. Burts, Executor of the last will & Testament of Rebecca Irvin Deceast, have this day called upon the Sd Burts, for the Inventory being produced. We find him charged with principal & Interest up to the date & rect. given in April 22nd 1835 by Thomas White Husband & Guardian of Jane White & children to the amount of Thirteen hundred Seventeen Dollars 98/100 $1317 98

And from Said papers We find that Said Executor has **payed** over to the Said Guardian all the assets (Exclusive of Ten Dollars, reserved for compensation which came his hands as pr Receipts will Show, Given under our hands this 2nd day of October 1837.

          Saml Conley   ⎱
          Joseph McLin   Commissioners
          E. L. Mathes   ⎰

(p-284)   JAMES McALESTER Guardian of MARY PAYNE

```
May 1st 1837. James McAlester Guardian of Mary Payne in a/c Dr. To Bal-
lance of cash on hand                                        $80 00
To cash received of Saml McCracken on a note                  12 00
"  cash recd of William Payne for Hire of negro               51 00
                                                            $143 00

By cash pd to B. F. Lockett on Judgment        $10 20
"  Cash pd John G. Eason as pr a/c rendered     25 00
"  cash pd Doct Doak by Henderson Clark          8 00
"  cash pd Edward Armstrong for Schooling        2 95
"  cash Jacob Whistler for Serving as Executor  15 00
        Allowance made by Court                $61 95
        Ballance on hand this day                          $81 04
Notes due
One note on Henderson Clark for   $60 00
One note on Joseph Payne           15 31
One note on John G. Eason          40 00
"      "   Ballance on Henderson Clark  4 79
One note on Henry McCracken        22 69
One note on G. W. Willett          40 98
                                 $183 77
```
                    Jas McAlester
                    Guardian for
                    Mary Payne

SETTLEMENTS OF ESTATES, VOLUME 00, 1790-1841

ROBERT BEANS Estate

We the undersigned appointed by order of the County Court to Settle with Clark Hunter Administrator of Robert Bean Deceast, report as follows,
Amt. as pr Inventory Filed at June Term 1837-- $46 07½

Said administrator to be credited as pr Vouchers
    1 clerks fee   1 87½
            Bal. Due the Estate $42 20½

(p-285)   ROBERT BEANS Estate

The Committee thought the administrator Entitled to the aditional compensation of $6 00
By former Settlement Ballance over paid   71 22½
Witness our hands & Seals this 1st day of July 1837   77 22½
                                        Saml Greer (Seal)
                                        Justice of the peace
                                        W. K. Blair J. P. (Seal)
                                        Joseph McLin J. P. (Seal)

WILLIAM SMITHS Estate

Pursuant to an order of the County Court at Novr Session 1836, appointing William Gilleland, Thomas McAdams, and E. L. Mathes a Committee to Settle with Michael Copp, Executor of Wm Smith Deceast, met on the 26th of Novr. 1836 at the house of Wm Wilsons, after calling on Said Michael Copp, for the papers he produced the Inventory as amount of Sales amounting to $83 00 Which sum he is chargeable with.
he also produced vouchers (To wit)

No.					Description	Amount
1	S. Greer clerk County Court Receipt					$1 12½
" 2	" Do	"	"	"	Do	2 00
" 3	Brickers receipt for Tax					3 37
" 4	Smiths note to Michael Copp					26 00
" 5	John Copps account					20 00
" 6	Wm Wilsons Receipt					1 00
" 7	John Ganns Probit to his Expences for taking care of Sd Smith while Sick & for funeral Expences					27 75
	Commissioners receipt one dollar Each					3 00
						13 00
						$97 24½

From the above amount as statement it appears   14 24½
that the Executor has paid out the amount of

(p-286)   WILLIAM SMITHS Estate

one dollar twenty four ½ cents more than what assets came into his hands besides compensation for his Services for which the Court allows thirteen Dollars which makes in all paid out of Said Estate as Executors own funds & Services rendered fourteen Dollars & twenty four ½ cents, Given under our hands & Seals this 3rd day of April 1837.
                                        E. L. Mathis
                                        Wm Gilleland   Committee
                                        Thos McAdams

WASHINGTON COUNTY, TENNESSEE

EDWARD WEST Guardian of ARCHD DOAK

May the 6th 1837. pursuant to an order of the County Court for Washington County & State of Tennessee began & held on the first Monday of May 1837, ap-pointing John Humphreys and Samuel G. Bayless and William Gilleland, as a Committee to Settle with Edward West Junr. Guardian of Archibald A. Doak, one of the heirs of John Doak Deceast we have this day met pursuant to Said order & calling on Edward West Guardian &c he produced to us the following vouchers (to wit)

No		Amount
1	Joseph Manns Receipt for	$6 00
2	John G. Eason Do	3 00
3	Harvey Scroggs Do	1 50
4	James McLing Do	64 00
5	John McMackin & Margaret Bricker Do	3 00
6	Joseph Manns Do	3 53
7	John Doaks Do	24 00
8	Joseph Manns Do	27 07½
9	John Brickers Do for Tax	49½
10	" Do Do " "	1 35
11	John W. Doaks Do	10 00
12	John & W. K. Blairs Do	45 00
13	Jane Doaks Do	50 28
	Amt Taken up	$

(p-287)   EDWARD WEST Guardian &c.
                Amt Brot up $

No		Amount
14	Joshua Hartsell Receipt	.50
15	John Brickers Do	50
16	" Do Do for Tax	50.
17	" Do Do " "	2 00
18	Edward Wests proven account	155 35½
19	Jno Humphreys & Saml G. Bayless Receipt	2 00
20	William Gilleland Do	1 00

Amounting to four hundred & Six Dollars Eight & one ¼ cents. $406 08¼

And we find Edward West Junr Guardian &c for A. A. Doak charged with three hundred ninety Seven Dollars and thirty Seven and fourth cents, which leaves a <u>Ballance</u> due Edward West Junr of Six Dollars & Seventy one cents, Given under our hands & Seals this Sixth day of May 1837.

        John Humphreys (Seal)
        William Gilleland (Seal)   Committee
        Saml G. Bayless (Seal)

GEORGHE CROUCH Guardian of SOLOMON KROUSES Heirs

We the undersigned being appointed a Committee to Settle with George Crouch Guardian of the heirs of Solomon Krouse Deceast, met on the 26th August 1837 and from the amount of the Settlement made with the administrator of Said Estate there appears to have passed into the hands of Said Guardian on the 15th Oct. 1835, This Sum $691 51½

It appears to our Satisfaction that Guardian George Crouch is entitled to a credit out of the above Sum for one hundred Dollars, being the amount of receipt Given by Michael Krouse the Father of the Said Solomon Krouse Deceast, to Said Solomon Krouse in his life time in Consideration of a Tract of land which the said Michael Intended to convey to the Said

(p-288)   GEORGHE CROUCH Guardian Sd. KROUSE'S Heirs

Amt Brot. over $691 51½

Solomon, but which was not done in his life time and Likewise a credit for an aditional Sum of one hundred and Six Dollars actually paid by Said Guardian to Said Michael to Secure the title to the Said Tract of Land which two Sums as above Specified was paid out of the above Sum charged to the Guardian in the aforesaid Settlement with the administrator of the Said Estate amounting in all to two hundred & Six Dollars Sd Guardian Presented to us the Deed to the heirs of Solomon Krouse Deceast, Executed by Said Michael Krouse on the 12th day of Oct. 1834 & registered in the registers office of Washington County 22nd January 1835, all which appears of record. Say this Sum of $206 00

Guardian chargeable with this amount $485 51½

Add to the above the compound Interest on the amount from 15th Oct. 1835 To 3rd Sept 1837, being this Sum   56 57½

We find Said Guardian has received for rents and Profits of Plantation up to this time   162 00

Sum Total chargeable to Guardian $704 00

Said Guardian presented receipts for Schooling repairs &c from No 1 to 12 Inclusive amounting to this Sum $48 28

for this Sum paid Committee   3 00

By this Sum allowed Guardian for his Services   10 00

By this Sum being 5 pr cent for disbursing the Sum of $51 28   2 56½ $63 84¾

Leaving this Sum in Guardians hands $640 24¼

Given under our hands & Seals this 26th Augt. 1837.

         Saml Greer (Seal)
         Justice of the peace
         Jesse Clark Seal
         Justice of the peace
         E. L. Mathes (Seal)
         Justice of the peace

The within Settlement was Brought before the Court & approved of and at Sept Term 1837.
     Saml Condly
     Chareman P. T.

(p-289)   A. L. BARNES Guardian of J. BARNES Deceast

The Inventory for the Sale in the year 1837, and the date of notes 2nd day of February, the credit of nine months,

No			Amount
1	note	A. L. Barnes amount is	$40 84
2	"	Vine & Fine Do	10 25
3	"	David Sellars Do	42 50
4	"	Reuben Lacy Do	10 00
5	"	Albert King Do	5 27
6	"	John Colback Do	10 25
7	"	Michael Miller Do	6 69
8		Billy F King Do	12 40
		Amt. of Notes	$138 20

GEORGE CROUCH Guardian of the heirs of SOL KROUSE

Settlement with George Crouch Guardian of Solomon Krouse heirs, made 6th May 1839.

To amount of Last Settlement made 26th August 1837	$640 24¼
" this amt. being the compound Interest for one year and Eight months	65 55
" the rent of Farm for 1838	42 00
" amount of Debt recovered off B. Shipley	14 00
	$761 79¼

By a voucher Produced from No 1 to No 6 Inclusive $38 14
" this Sum being 1 pr cent on the ammount for Trouble
and risk &c.   7 61   45 75
                    Ballance due wards $716 04¼

This Sum deducted being handed over to John A. Bowman Guardian of Saml
Krouse   143 20¾
Ballance due the rest of the heirs $572 84

Saml Greer clerk

(p-290)   JACOB HUNTERS Estate

Settlement made with John & Clark Hunter administrators of Jacob Hunter Deceast made 29th May 1840. Said Administrators chargeable as follows, as pr

Inventory ammount of Sale of Personal property		$760 58½
Ammount of sale of negros		1109 72½
Ammount recd on notes Collected		55 00
Amt of Gifts previous to the death of Testator	$3363 67	
Deduct this Sum allowed off D. C. Hunters account upon refference	201 00	$3162 67
		$5087 98

Said administrators has paid Ann
Hunter in her life time as pr receipts No 17 this Sum $198 15
John Hunter one of the administrators account against Said Estate
made with Intestate in his life
time   97 34
Clark Hunter one of the administrators
account against Said Estate made with
Intestate in his life Time   119 59
Said Administrators produced receipts & vouchers from No 1 to
17 Inclusive To this amount   137 17½ $552 15¼
                Amt to be divided $4535 72¼

Said administrators having yet to collect and from Jesse
B. aHunter this Sum $518 55
With Interest thereon from 12th May 1838

Saml Greer Clerk
County Court W. County

(p-291) A. L. BARNES Guardian of all the Heirs of J. BARNES Deceast.

The amount of the third Inventory note James F. Floid	$14 25
" A. L. Barnes	23 25
" John & Jabes Murray	14 25

"	B, McFall	$14 25
"	A. L. Barnes	13 75
"	William Massengill	29 00
"	Vine & Fine	10 87½
		$119 37½

These notes was due the 13th of Decr 1838

A. L. BARNES Guardian &c.

The fourth Inventory for the year 1839.
    A. L. Barnes $25 00
Note Frances F. Williams   75 00
the amt of the fourth Inventory is $100 00
These notes was due the 4th of February 1839.
A. L. Barnes Guardian of all the heirs of James Barnes Deceast

---

NANCY BAYLESS Widow of JESSE BAYLESS Deceast

We the undersigned freeholders of Washington County after being duly Sworn have proceeded to Set apart to Nancy Bayless, widow of Jesse Bayless, Deceast, So much of the crop and provision on hand as will be Sufficient in our opinion to Support her and her family one year after the Death of her Said Husband, we set apart to her for Said Support & purpose the following articles (to wit) Two cows Pide & white, Fifty Bushels Irish potatoes, Two Hundred Bushels of corn, all the Garden Saved. Five fat hogs that is in the pen, all the flax and wool on hand, Six Bushels (p-292) wheat, all the husks and tops, one Tub of Sowercraut, one Hundred and Twenty five pounds Salt, and all the chickens on hand, and the dried fruit that is on hand, also thirty pounds of coffee, and Twenty pounds of Sugar, All the above articles for the Benefit of Said widow. So Say we all this December 21st day 1840

                        Joseph Longmires (Seal)
                        Enoch Jobe   (Seal) Commissioners
                        Wm Longmires (Seal)

LEANN McGEE widow of WM McGee Deceast

STATE OF TENNESSEE   Sept 12th 1840
WASHINGTON COUNTY   We the undersigned being appointed a Committee by the County Court of Said County to Lay off and Set apart to Leann McGee (And family) widow and relies of William McGee Deceast, one years allowance from and after the Death of her Said Husband, and after being duly Sworn as the Directs. We proceeded to lay off Said allowance as follows (to wit) Four choice Hogs out, and Two Shoats in the pen, and the Bacon on hand, one milk cow, & three head of young cattle, corn in the crib Supposed to be Twenty Bushels, also fifty Dollars to be taken out of the Estate to purchase corn in addition to what is on hand, and Twenty Dollars to purchase flour, Ten Dollars for coffee and Sugar, three Dollars for Salt, all the flax, cotton & wool on hand thread & linen, five Dollars to purchase Leather as Shoes &c.

                        E. L. Mathes
                        John Bricker   Committee

John Humphreys

(p-293)   SAML KIBLER Guardin of the Heirs of M. Ingersoll

Settlement of Saml Kibler, Guardian of Caroline and Prudence M. Ingersoll made 12th November 1840

One note due 22 May 1840 for this Sum	$100 00
One Do " 27th July 1840 for this Sum	112 09½
One Do " 31 Augt. 1840 for this Sum	110 32
Amt. with which Guardian is chargeable up to the dates	$322 41½
Cr. by Clerks fees	3 25
Ballance in hands of Guardian	$319 16½

      Saml Greer clerk
      of County Court

LEONARD COLYER Guardian of the minor heirs of J. SLAGLE

Settlement with Leonard Colyer Guardian of his own children who were minor heirs of John Slagle Deceast, made 23rd Novr 1840. The whole amount now

in my hands being a note on Saml Early for this Sum		$79 00
Interest on Same up to 15th Instant		12 64
		$ 91 64
By amt of costs paid, clerk of County Court	$3 00	
" cost of the Settlement	2 75	5 75
" Ballance in hands of Guardian on the 15th Novr. 1840		$85 89

      Saml Greer Clerk
      of County Court

JACOB ROBINSONS Estate

Settlement with William Robinson, Executor of Jacob Robinson Jur Deceast, made 15th Oct. 1840. Said Executor is Bound by the will to let Felix Robinson have nine Dollars & Catharine Hilton, have nine Dollars, and the Ballance to be divided Between three Sisters, Mary, Sarah & Elisabeth Robinson, Said Executor produced the Receipts of

(p-294)   JACOB ROBINSONS Estate

Sarah Robinson for this Sum	$160 00
of Elisabeth Robinson for this Sum	160 00
and the rct. of Jonathan Wixler & Mary his wife for this Sum	160 00
No receipts produced for Felix a/c $9 00	
No receipts produced for Catharine Heltons Share of $9 00	

      Saml Greer Clerk
      County Court

JACOB KIBLERS Estate

Settlement made with Jacob Kibler administrator of Jacob Kibler Deceast, with the will annexed, Said Administrator chargeable with the Sum as pr Inventory of Sale of personal Estate $1406 29
To cash on hand as pr Inventory 360 62½
$1766 91½

Said Executor has paid out as pr Receipts & vouchers this amt to wit) for coffin & shroud $13 00
To Doct. Brabson 10 00
" Bricker for Taxes 2 40
" Clerks fees Including this Settlement 6 00   31 46
The Ballance in the hands of Administrator $1735 51½
on the above Items, In this Settlement the amount of notes due the Estate on hands at the Death of Testator not Included, Settlement made 28th November 1840.

        Saml Greer Clerk of the
        County Court, Washington County

E. L. MATHES Guardian of A. NELSON &c.

Annual Settlement Between E. L. Mathes, Guardian and his ward Alexander Nelson, for the year Ending Augt. Term 1840. See Settlement August 1839. There is in hands of Guardian Exclusive of Embrees & Gillispies debts

(p-295)   E. L. MATHES Guardian &c.

This Sum $5703 71
Add Interest on the above 342 22
Add Wm & Jerrys Hire 73 00
$6118 93

  Disbursed by Said Guardians
West & Crouches account $48 72
<u>Scholling</u> & Boarding at Embree & Henry College 46 00
John Payne for Schooling 2 00
To 50 Bushels oats 12 50
Recd A. A. Mathes Schooling 2 50
Joseph Manns account 1 12
5 per cent on $372 55 Disbursed last year which was not allowed 18 60
5 per cent on Disbursements for this year on $112 84 5 64 $137 08
$5981 85
Additional vouchers paid to Charles Lovett for work done on
Lott in Greenville $26 42
Commission on Same 1 32   27 76
     In hands of Guardian $5954 11
    Saml Greer clerk
    County Court Washington County
    Tennessee

A. L. BARNS Guardian of JAMES BARNES Heirs

A Settlement made with A. L. Barnes Guardian of the minor heirs of James Barnes, Deceast, made 30th May 1840. Amount of Inventory returned dated 30th May 1840. Notes due Twelve months after date $206 45
Ammount of Interest thereon compounded up to this date
being three years   39 41
                     Amt Taken over $245 86

(p-296)   A. L. BARNES Guardian of JAMES BARNES, Heir's

                     Amt Brot. over $245 86
Amt of Inventory returned for 1837. date of notes 2nd
Feby 1837. due nine months after date   138 20
Amt. of Interest thereon compounded for 2 Y & 7 months   22 49
Amt. of Inventory for 1838. Notes due 13th December 1838   119 37½
Interest thereon compounded up to date being 1 year & 5 months   10 12
Amt of Inventory 1839. Notes due 4th Feby 1839.   100 00
Interest thereon up to this date being 1 year & 3 months   7 50
Amt of Sales for 1840   47 226
                                                  $690 80½

Said Guardin produced receipts & vouchers from No 1 to
No 8 Inclusive amounting to this Sum $34 02
Paid for coffin for Ann Elisa   5 00
Paid Doctor Bill   8 87½
Paid for Crying Sale   2 00   49 89½
                                                  $640 91
Said Guardian allowed for his trouble up to this date   15 00
               Ballance in hands of Guardian $625 91
                        Saml Greer Clerk
                        County Court

WILLIAM JACKSONS Estate

Settlement with George Jackson, Executor of William Jackson Deceast, made 11th December 1840. To amount of Inventory for hire of negros for the year 1839. $165 00
Said Executor has paid out for Taxes on negros and fees
for copy in the Suit Given against this Sum   5 20
for Inventory of Hire & Settlement to clerk   2 75
                                  $7 95
                    Amt Taken up $157 05

(p-297)   WILLIAM JACKSONS Estate

                     Amt Brot. up $157 05
Leaving this Sum to be paid out heirs - - -
Said Executor allowed for his Services in hiring out &
collecting money this Sum   10 00
Neat Ballance in hands of Executor $147 05

WILLIAM GREENWAYS Estate

Settlement made with Joshua Green and William Greenway administrators of William Greenway Deceast, During the contest about the will made 25th February 1840.

Said Administrators chargeable as pr Inventory returned dated
June 3rd 1839. $23 12½
Also " " Nov.
26th 1839 17 00
$40 12½

Said administrators has paid out this Sum for fees of office
as pr Recpt. March No 1 $2 25
Administrators allowed for Trouble & Expences 24 00
pd for this Settlement & recording same 2 75   29 00
Ballance in hands of Administrators $11 12½

        Saml Greer Clerk

ARCHABALD GLASCOCK Estate

Settlement made with William McCall, Administrator of Archabald Glascock Deceast, made the 1st June 1841.
Said administrator chargeable as per amt of Sale and cash
received $5889 61
To amt. as pr Inventory of notes due the Intestate in his
life time as pr returns of Inventory & Interest received
thereon   1610 39
John Hartmans note not but down in Inventory   19 21
   Whole amount of Estate $7519 21

(p-298)   ARCHABALD GLASCOCK Estate

        Amt Brot over $7519 21
I find said Administrator has paid out as pr receipts and vouchers produced
from No 1 to No 50 Inclusive this Sum $310 67
To this amount allowed administrator   75 95
" this amt pd Clerk for Settlement & record 2 75   689 37
Ballance in hands of administrator $6829 84

        Saml Greer Clerk

E. L. MATHES Guardian of A. Nelson &c.

Annul Settlement of E. L. Mathes Guardian of Alexander Nelson for the year Ending August Term 1841. See Settlement of 1840. There is in hands of Guardian as pr last years return Exclusive of Embrees & Gillispies Debts
this Sum $5954 11
Interest on the Same for one year   357 24
Wms Hire 7 months   35 00
George's Hire 5 months   16 66
One half Vilets Hire 18 months   26 25
Embrees Debt added   1171 23
George T. Gillespies Added   864 97
  $8425 46

```
5 pr cent on the above              $421 27
paid J. F. Broyles & Brothers a/c    154 34
 "   Shff Bricker for Tax for 7 years back  14 22
 "   Shff Willett for  " 2 years       9 00
 "   clerk for two Settlements         3 00      $601 83
Ballance in hands of Guardian                    $7823 63
```

      Saml Greer Clerk
      County Court
      Washington County Tennessee

(p-299)   **PETER CLICK'S Estate**

STATE OF TENNESSEE)
WASHINGTON COUNTY) Settlement made with David Click administrator of Peter Click Deceast, On the 11th 1841 Administrator charged as per Inventory of Sale with this Sum $185 56
Jacob Clicks note   11 00
   No Interest Included $196 56
Said Administrator produced receipts and vouchers from
No 1 to No 17 Inclusive amounting to this Sum $67 36
This amount allowed administrator for his Services 20 00   87 36
Ballance in hands of Administrator $108 19
to be divided among the heirs.

      Saml Greer
      Clerk Washington County

      END

INDEXES

WASHINGTON COUNTY

SETTLEMENTS OF ESTATES VOL. -OO-
1790 - 1841

ORIGINAL INDEX

Note: Page numbers in this index refer to those of the original volume from which this copy was made. These numbers are inserted within parentheses throughout the text, as (p 124)

A.

Samuel Adams, 126
Frederick Andes, 176
Acres Jacob, 227
Allison, Jane, 260
Andrew, Dan D. 280

B.

Roberts, Blanchard, 43
Edmund Beane, 46
Henry Bowers, 52
John Bayles, 91
Cyrus Broyles, 93
Elizabeth Brown, 95
John Barkley, 98
Daniel Bayles, 113
Samuel Bitner, 115
Jacob Brown (waggon maker) 116
Samuel Brison, 128
Michael Brown, 140
Jesse Billingsly, 149
Thomas Brown, 158
Wm Bayles, Guardian, 160
Thos Brown, 165
Jonathan Bacon, 168
Elias Bowman, 170
Peter Burgner, 180
Wm Bayles (Guard Tyler), 199
Barnes, Walker, 208
Bayles, Reuben, 213
Bricker, John Guar, 217
Brown, Thos, 223
Beard, Thos, 224
Bayles, Reese Guar, 226
Brown, Micahel, 239
Bowman, Danl, 248
Bowman, Jno A. Guar, 256
Bayles, Thos, 256
Barron, Wm. 256
Beard, Robert 281, 258
Barnes, Jas, 259
Bowman, Jno A., 264

Bean, Robt., 268, 284
Barns, A. L. Guar, 274, 289, 291, 295
Bayles, Nancy, 291

C.

Archabald Carmicle, 19
Andrew Carson, 63
John Cowen, 65
William Colyar, 69
George Clouse, 125
John Crouch, 133
Samuel Culbertson, 136
John Coffman, 139
Jacob Clawson, 164
Joseph Crouch, 184
William Carson, Jr. 197
Carter, E. M., 231
Crouch, George 287, 289
Colyer, Leonard, 298
Click, Peter, 299

D.

Jeremiah Dungans, 36
Wm Dulaney, 155
Doak, John W., 210

E.

Kellion Ernheart, 45
William Ellis, 49
Elihu Embree, 77
John Embree, 118
Peter Epperson, 150
Elliott, John, 239
Earnest, Mary, 246
Ellis, Jacob, 263

F.

Josiah Franklin, 18
Thomas Ford, 24
Josiah Franklin, 42

Hannah Ford, 43
Martin Feazell, 44
John Ford, 44
Hannah Ford (Alias) Harrison, 51
James Farmer, 59
Josiah Franklin, 72
Mary Fawbush, 90
Martin Feazell, 99
Josiah Franklin, 112
Martin Feazell, 130
George Fraker, 131
Barney Ford, 145
Josiah Franklin, 156
Wm Fletcher, 166

G.

John Grimsley, 70
Jacob Gyre, Senr., 122
James Grayham, 126
Jacob Gyre, 161
John Guyre, 194
Christian Graves, 256
Goods, Jacob, 244
Gillespie, J. H., 263, 261
Greenway, Wm., 297
Glasscock, Archd., 297

H.

Samuel Hair, 16,
John Hammer, 31
Philip Huffhine, 48
John Hunt, 53
John Hunt, 58
Meshek Hale, 66
Nicholas Hale, 67
John Hunt, 71
Matilda & Eliza Hair, 81
Dewey Hunt, 82
Sarah Hunt and others, 90
Uriah Hunt Sen., 101
Jacob Hoss, Junr., 129
Hunt, Thos, 249
Hartsell, Jacob, 254
Hammons, Thos., 282
Hunter, Jacob, 290

J.

David Job, 8
Susannah Johnson, 95
Abigail Jobe, 97
Irvins Patrick, 235
Ingle, Michael, 249
Jackson, Wm., 296, 262, 257,
  Irvin, Rebecca, 283

K.

John Klepper, 188
Conrod Kyker, 186
Krouse, Sol, 228
Klepper, Jacob, 260, 256, 266, 267
Keebler, Jacob, 264, 294
Keebler, Saml Guar, 292

L.

John Little, 62
John Laws, 112
George Little, 148
David Lemmon, 191
Saml B. Love, 201

M & Mc.

Samuel McQueen, 7
John Mauck, 10
Ann Miller, 12
John Mercer, 17
Hugh McAdams, 25
Alexander Moore, 26
John McGinness, 27
William Miller, 41
John McNeal, 46
John Miller, 60
Hannah E. McCardell, 81
David Mitchell, 89
Joseph Mercer, 114
Henry Martin, 119
Edward Million Senr., 130
John McClure, 140
Rachel Mercer, 189
Robt McLin, 194
Mathes, E. L. Guar., 209
Melvin, John, 211
Mathes, E. L. Guar., 212
Mathes, E. L., 225, 230, 215, 216
McCall, Robt. S., 227
McClary, Seth, 229
Mathes, E. L., 234, 243, 247, 252
Murray, Ephraim, 243, 241
Mays, Cas., 245
Mathes, E. L., 254, 255, 265, 269
Murray, Ephr., 257
McAlester, Jas., 262, 267, 284
Mathes, E. L. 270, 294, 298
McCall, Robt., 274
Moore, Robert, 278
McGee, Leon, 292

N.

John North, 6

SETTLEMENTS OF ESTATES, VOLUME 00, 1790-1841

Alexander M. Nelson, 152
Wm Nelson, 163
A. M. Nelson, 171
Wm Nelson guardin P. Tyler, 193
Nelson, Wm. Guar, 242

O.

Ephraim Overhulser, 175

P.

Peter Parkeson, 1
Mordica Price, 4
Henry Powel, 13
James Parker, 56
Henry Parker, 56
Henry Powel, 75
Philips Parks, 138
Thos C. Patton, 177
Thos. Price, 198
Payne, Jesse, 236
Payne, Mary, 250
Price, L Guar, 262
Painter, Adam, 277

R.

Lewis Rennoe, 3
Richard Roberts, 29
James Roberts, 55
Amanda Jane Russell, 81
Isaac Ruble, 147
Richard Roberts, 156
William Russell, 189
Range, John, 247, 218
Ruble, Peggy's, 250
Ruble, Peter, 258
Rocks, John, 265
Robinson, Jacob, 293

S.

John Swonger, 33
Alexander Stuart, 134
Alexander Stuart, 142
Abraham Smith, 174
Sligar, Henry, 269, 241
Slagle, John, 253
Smith, William, 285

T.

Alexander Trotter, 3
William Tyler, 22
William Tyler, 23
Abraham Tipton, 34

William Tyler, 47
William Tyler, 49
William Tyler, 54
William Tyler, 71
Samuel Templin, 79
William Tyler, Jr., 91
William Tyler heirs (daughters) 92
William Tyler heirs 100
William Tyler (Polly) 117
William Tyler, 144
Joseph Tucker, 146
M. Tyler, 181
Tyler, Wm., 204
Telford, Thos, 205
Tyler, Manerva, 233
Taylor, Chris 246
Tipton, John, 272

W.

William Ward, 11
William Wood, 12
Adam Wattenbarger, 51
Adam Wattenbarger, 83
Michael Woods, 96
Henry Winkle, 116
Mary Wright, 148
John Williams, 157
Adam Wattenbarger, 167
Walter's, Clara, 233
Wattenbarger Adam, 271
West, Edward, 286

Y.

Catharine Young, 68
William Young, 73
Thomas Young, 124
John Young, 139
Joseph Young, 200
Young, Jas. 221
Young, Jas W., 252, 248
Yeager, Danl, 275

273, (names)

End.

ERRATA FOR INDEX

Left out:

Jobe, (Job), Enoch, 292
Job, John, 98
Jobe, (Job), Joshua, 97
Job, Phebee, 9
Job, Samuel, 208

R.

Rodgers, R., 56
Ruble, Peter, 258

W.

Walters, George, 7, 61, 233

End.

SETTLEMENTS OF ESTATES, VOLUME 00, 1790-1841

WASHINGTON COUNTY

SETTLEMENTS OF ESTATES VOL. -00-
1790 - 1841

NEW INDEX

Note: Page numbers in this index refer to those of the original volume from which this copy was made. These numbers are inserted within parentheses throughout the text, as (p 124)

A.

Abington, 266
Able, Ezekiel, 2
Acres, Jacob, 227, 228
Acton, James, 159, 162, 213
Adams, John, 3, 11, 133
Adams, Samuel, 126, 127
Aiken, E. M., 231
Aiken, (Aikin], James, 11, 33, 74, 117, 124, 231
Aikin, John, 85
Aiken, John A., 97, 114
Aiken, Elisabeth, 231, 232
Aiken, George & James, 124
Aiken, Mathew, 24, 25, 29, 56, 60, 129, 133, 151
Alester, James, 251, (McAlester)
Alford, Ryley, 104
Allen, 254, 271
Allen, D., 254,
Allen, Gillispie & Emuree, 243
Allen, Isaac, 195
Allen, James, 153, 209, 212, 234, 248, 276
Allen, James & Embree, E. 212
Allen, Zachariah, 235, 248
Allison, David, 1
Allison, Jane, 81, 260
Allison, Robert, 150
Allison, William, 157
Anderson, 161
Anderson, James V, 20, 158, 162, 168, 193, 273
Anderson, Joseph, 4
Anderson, Lwois, (Louis], 1, 162
Anderson, Robert, 117, 124
Andes, Frederick, 176, 177
Andes (Andis), John, 113, 176
Andrew (Andrews), Dan D., 22, 23, 47, 54, 181, 280, 281
Andrew, Nancy, 54, 280
Anthony, Abraham, 6

Atkinson, 212
Atkinson, Hurtle W., 75
Atkinson, Mary, 75
Atkinson, Wilton, 230, 256
Archer, Joseph, 260
Armsreng (?), E., 251
Armstrong, Edward, 284
Arrington, Thomas, 35
Arterburn, (Arturburn), James, 169, 265
Austin, Benjamin, 28, 56

B.

Bacon, Charles, 20, 25, 52, 128, 169
Bacon, James, 169, 170
Bacon, John, 45, 56, 169
Bacon, Jonathan, 25, 103, 150, 168, 170
Bacon, Thomas, 129
Bacon, Joseph & Thomas, 219
Bail, John, 5
Bail, Joseph, 164
Bailes, Isaac, 15
Bails, Daniel, 14
Baker, 1
Baker, Francis, 2
Baker, Susanna, 99
Balches, Saml, 11
Bales, Joseph, 191
Ball, 5
Ball, Samuel, 44
Ball, Thomas, 14, 127
Baltimore, 150
Barcrofft, Jonathan, 13, 20
Barger, George, 64
Barger, Wiland, 63
Bark, Robert, 65
Barkley, 237, 272
Barkley (Barkly), Daniel, 153, 159, 160 161, 163, 166, 170, 172, 175, 187, 191, 201, 202, 204, 282.
Barkley, Ebenezer, 228, 233
Barkly, Glasscock, & Link, 191
Barnes, A. L., 274, 275, 289, 291, 295,

296
Barnes, Elisa Ann, 296
Barnes, J., 289, 291
Barnes, James, 33, 259, 274, 275, 291, 295
Barnes, Joseph, 136
Barnes, Nathan, 229, 230, 237, 238, 253
Barnes, Thomas, 208
Barnes, Thomas, 77
Barnes, Walker, 208
Barnhert, Abraham, 140
Barron, Jacob, 208
Barron, Thomas, 149
Barran, (Barron), Wm., 256
Bary, Braxton, 219
Bass, 2
Basket, John, 149
Basket, Richard, 151
Bayer, ? 245
Bayles, 100
Bayles, (Bayless) Daniel, 113, 114, 117, 226, 227
Bayles, Daniel L., 213, 214, 215
Bayles, George, 75
Bayles, Hezekiah, 91, 131, 132, 135, 142, 146, 153, 172, 179, 180, 184, 192, 193
Bayles, Jessee, 113, 291, (Bayless)
Bayles, Joanna, 75
Bayles(Bayless) John, 91, 181, 204, 233, 280
Bayles, John D., 113
Bayles (Bayless) Joseph, 266
Bayles, M. M., 181
Bayles (Bayless) Nancy, 291
Bayles (Bayless) Rebecca, (?) 213
Bayles (Bayless) Reese, 91, 102, 226, 227
Bayles, (Bayless), Richard, 113, 213
Bayles (Bayless) Reubin, 47, 213, 213, 214, 215, 216
Bayles, Reuben, D., 113
Bayles (Bayless), Samuel, 15, 27, 56, 162, 248
Bayles, Samuel (Senr)., 18
Bayles, Samuel D., 113
Bayles (Bayless) Samuel G., 159, 165, 224, 241, 242, 269, 286, 287
Bayless, Saml G., & Humphreys, Jno., 287
Bayless, Thomas A., 256
Bayles, Vilet, 23
Bayles, (Bayless) William, 13, 15, 16, 19, 22, 23, 27, 28, 39, 47, 48, 49, 50, 51, 54, 55, 71, 72, 79, 80, 92, 95, 96, 97, 98, 100, 101, 116, 123, 124, 125, 131, 139, 144, 145, 149, 160, 181, 199, 204, 256.
Bayles, William Jr., 22, 27
Bayless, Young, 226
Beard, James, 224, 225, 258, 259, 281
Beard, Martha, 225, 259
Beard, Robert, 224, 258, 259, 281
Beard, Thomas, 58, 224, 225, 258
Beaver, 113
Bean, Baxter, 52, 202
(Beane)
Bean, Charles & Robt., 244
Bean, Edmond, 46, 49, 151
(Beane)
Beane, Mark, 103
Bean, Robert, 237, 268, 284, 285
Bean, Robt & Charles, 244
Bedford County, 142
Bell, B. H., 277
Bell, John, 124
Bell, Joseph, 218
Bell, Joseph H., 277
Berkley, 146
Berkley (Berkly), Daniel, 54, 55, 63, 64, 69, 78, 82, 91, 129, 131, 132, 135, 144, 145, 146, 147, 148.
Berkley, D & Ebenezer, 84
Berkley, Daniel & E. B., 119
Berkley, Ebenezer, 119
Berkley, John, 98, 146
Berry, John, 119
Bickley, Daniel (?) 64
Biddle, John, 112
Billings, Jessee, 149
Billingsley, Jacob, 149
Billingsley, Jessee, 149
Bitner, (Mrs)., 115
Bitner, Margaret, 115
Bitner, Samuel, 115
Blackburn, Benjamin, 96
Blackburn, Joshua, 93
Blackburn, Samuel, 26, 58, 96
Blair, 59, 61, 71
Blair, Brice, 4, 122, 123
Blair, & Duncan, 260
Blair, John, 16, 17, 22, 39, 40, 46, 47, 86, 88, 119, 162, 202, 204
Blair, John & W. K., 275, 286
Blair, Samuel, 20, 41
Blair, Thomas, 15
Blair, Wm., 117, 124, 125, 139
Blair, W. K., 274, 285
Blakely, John, 20
Blakely, Leady, 20

Blakely, Thomas, 15, 20
Blanchard, Robert L., 43
Blount County, 26
Blyth, 3
Blyth, Saml 9,
Bogart, Samuel, 31, 32, 133
Booth, Joseph, 196
Boren, Absolom, 4
Boren(Bourn) (Boring) Chaney, 4, 5, 33, 200, 252
Boren (Bourn) (Boring), Joshua, 68, 129, 134, 198, 201, 221, 223, 231, 241, 243, 257, 273
Boren, Vincent, 62
Bourn (Boren), Wm., 244
Bottles, Henry, 114
Bottles, Joseph, 237, 238, 268
Bottles, William, 114, 166
Bovell, William, W., 211, 255
Bowers, 52
Bowers, Henry, 52
Bowers, John, 52
Bowers, Lawrence, 247
Bowers, Leonard, 1
Bowers, Levi, 166, 189, 209, 211, 229, 232, 233, 236
Bowers, Nancy, 52
Bowers, Valentine, 218
Bowser, John, 208
Bowman, 52, 188
Bowman, Aaron, 278
Bowman, Daniel, 31, 52, 53, 65, 248, 249
Bowman, Elias, 14, 170
Bowman, Jac., 52
Bowman, Jacob, 248
Bowman, John, 66
Bowman, John A., 256, 264, 289
Bowman, Joseph, 37, 59, 60, 61, 62, 68, 129
Bowman, Peter, 124
Bowman, Polly, 278
Bowman, Saml., 248
Bowman, Saml D., 171
Bowman (Boman) S. D., 171
Boyd, J., 212
Boyd, Jeremiah, 280
Brabson (Dr) 294
Brabson, Alexander, 237
Brabson, Alexander W., 276
Brabson, Ephram, 98
Brabson & Miller, 64
Brabson, Thomas, 14, 17, 42, 63, 119, 152, 172
Bragg, Davis, 20
Briant, 123

Bricher, Jno., 106
Bricker, 208, 212, 237, 272, 285, 294, 298
Bricker, J., 230
Bricker, John, 23, 29, 44, 69, 84, 87, 99, 100, 108, 112, 130, 134, 158, 168, 169, 171, 192, 195, 214, 217, 218, 283, 286, 287, 292
Bricker, Margaret, 286
Bricker, William, 23, 181
Brison, Samuel, 103, 128
Britten, John, 146
Britten, (Brittin, Britton), Joseph, 6, 7, 116, 117, 124, 125, 137, 139
Brook, Horner, 66
Brown, 146
Brown, Col, 139
Brown, Aaron, 132
Brown, Abraham, 18, 27, 131
Brown, Abraham, Junr., 131
Brown, Abraham, Senr., 131
Brown, B., 237
Brown, Bend., 166
Brown, Bird, 156, 196
Brown, Caldwell, 35
Brown, Conrod, 18, 28
Brown, Elizabeth, 95, 146
Brown, Elijah, 45, 50, 55, 155
Brown, Elijah, 45, 50, 55, 155
Brown, Gabriel, 196
Brown, George, 116, 141
Brown, Isaac N., 28
Brown, Jacob, 6, 7, 16, 18, 27, 30, 35, 36, 42, 44, 45, 46, 47, 48, 54, 55, 57, 71, 72, 79, 80, 95, 99, 100, 101, 113, 114, 116, 130, 131, 132, 138, 148, 149, 153, 156, 159, 163, 165, 172, 176, 177, 194, 197, 204, 212, 215, 223, 224, 241, 269.
Brown, Jacob (Col), 72, 112
Brown, James, 150, 256
Brown, Jessee, 131, 167, 168, 272
Brown, John, 4, 70, 122, 127, 150
Brown, John C., 136
Brown, Joseph, 10, 11, 39, 96, 117, 122 124, 127, 140, 150, 240
Brown, Mary, 40, 128, 133
Brown, Michael, 10, 118, 140, 141, 239, 240
Brown & Patton, 130
Brown, Samuel, 56
Brown, Solomon, 56
Brown, Stephen, 282
Brown, Thomas, 23, 25, 60, 63, 89, 118, 128, 135, 157, 158, 162, 165, 171, 194, 223, 224, 275
Brown, Thos. J., 89

WASHINGTON COUNTY, TENNESSEE

Brown, William, 27, 96, 166, 192, 202
Browning, Charles, 85, 87
Broyles, 205, 206
Broyles, A., 172
Broyles, Adam., 93, 94, 99, 152, 237, 262
Broyles, Cornelius, 207
Broyles, Cyrus, 93, 94
Broyles, Daniel, 94
Broyles, Eve, 180
Broyles, J., 270
Broyles, Jacob, 180, 183
Broyles, James, 143, 152, 172, 183
Broyles, J. F., 275, 298
Broyles, James F., 140, 141, 143, 157
Broyles, James F. & Brothers, 275
Broyles, J. M., 237
Broyles, James T., 93
Broyles, J. T. & Brothers, 255
Broyles, Jas Jr., 180
Broyles, Jas Sr., 180
Broyles, Thomas D., 93
Broyles, Tobias, 94
Brummit, Andrew, 182
Buchenton ?, 237
Bulbur, (Mrs), 1
Burgner, Eve, 180
Burgner, (Burghner), Henry, 140, 143, 180
Burgner, Peter, 180, 182, 183, 184
Burk, Robert, 52
Burns, Mary, 118
Burres, John, 34
Burris, Adam, 35
Burts, Joseph L., 283
Bustard, Claudias, 96
Butler (Buttler) Sussannah, 219, 220
Butler (Buttler) Zachariah, 219, 220
Byerly, Samuel, 157
Byler, Abraham, 4

C.

Cable, Peter, 149
Cade, Russ, 150, 151
Cahile, Elisha, 25, 128
Caldwell, Andrew, 1
Campbell, Abraham, 151
Campbell, Alexander, 131
Campbell, Careck, 15
Campbell, Daniel, 267

Campbell, Enos, 158
Campbell, James, 214
Campbell, Jeremiah, 12
Campbell, & King, Henry, & Galloway, 274
Campbell, L., 170
Campbell, Wm., 76
Campbell, Leeroy, 84, 244
Campbell, Zac, 1, 2
Carden, David, 202
Carder, John, 70
Carder, Samuel, 70
Carmicle, Archibald, 15, 19, 20, 21
Carmicle, Daniel, 19
Carmicle, Isbell, 13
Carmicel, James, 13
(Carmicle)
Carmicle, Jane, 20
Carmicle, John, 19
Carmicle, (Carmichael), William, 153, 172
Carney, John, 12
Carr, John, 277
Carr, Richard, 58, 62, 65, 68, 71, 74, 134, 155, 166, 189, 199, 211, 266, 267, 273
Carriger, Godfrey, 2, 122
Carriger (Carigar) John, 239
Carriger, Michael, 2
Carrol, Luke, 14, 98
Carson, 64
Carson, Absolom, 64
Carson, Andrew, 41, 63, 64
Carson, Lemuel, 64
Carson, Margaret, 197
Carson, Moses, 41, 64
Carson, Moses W., 64
Carson, William, 197, 198
Carter, Alfred M., 133, 213
Carter County, 38, 40, 213, 231
Carter, E. M., 231, 232,
Carter, Eml., 1
Carter, John, 123
Carter, Landon, 2
Carter, George W., 35
Carter Taylor & Carter, 35
Carter, Wm., 39, 40, 213
Carter, Wm. B., 28, 202
Carter, W. B., 231
Caruthers, James 163, 218
(Carothers)
Caruthers(Carsuthers) John, 275
Caruthers (Carrethers, Careathers), Jonathan, 24, 33, 35, 37, 62, 139, 202
Caruthers, Samuel, 63
Cashedy, John, 124
Cashedy, Robert, 113

SETTLEMENTS OF ESTATES, VOLUME 00, 1790-1841

Caskill, Elisha, 108
Chapman, Benjamin, 133
Charleton (Charlten) John, 41, 194
Charleton (Charlton) Pointer, 14, 41.
Charleton, Rebecca, 64
Cheraw, 229
Chester, 161
Chester & Blair, 71
Chester (Doctor), 29
Chester, John, 27, 126, 127, 149, 150, 164, 200
Chester, John P., 159, 162, 181
Chester, Samuel G., 27, 85, 106, 131, 152, 172, 258
Chester, William, 189
Chester, William P., 13, 16, 31, 47, 52, 64, 72, 72, 82, 84, 85, 86, 89, 94, 96, 112, 114, 115, 127, 130, 135, 136, 140, 141, 142, 144, 151, 154, 158, 159, 161, 162, 163, 164, 165, 170, 175, 181, 187, 196, 199, 213.
Childers, William P., 149
Church, Robert, 20
Clack, John, 78
Clark, 239
Clark, Barnes, 96
Clark, Henderson, 99, 238, 239, 240, 268, 277, 278, 284
Clark, J. D., 277
Clark, Jesse, 184, 241, 269, 282, 288
Clark, Joel D., 277
Clark, John, 96, 78, 146
Clark & West, 237
Clawson, Jacob, 164
Clawson, Samuel, 164
Clem & Hunt, 188
Click, David, 195, 299
Click, Jacob, 299
Click, Peter, 299
Clifton, A. C., 77
Clinger, Daniel, 45
Clouse, Adam, 125
Clouse, Elizabeth, 125
Clouse, George, 125
Cloyd, John, 178
Cock, Wm., 122, 123
Cocke, 123
Coffman, John, 139
Cohrans, George, 279, 280
Colback, John, 289
Cole, John, 192
College, Embree & Henry, 295

Collet, Isaac, 136
Collom, Jno. 30
Collom, (Collem) Jonathan, 10, 17, 18, 23, 44, 49, 96, 115, 116, 126, 127, 130
Collom (Collum) Jonathan, H., 173
Collom, Wm., 107
Colyar, Alexander, 23, 69
(Colyer)
Colyar, John, 69
Colyer, Leonard, 293
Colyer (Colyar), William, 5, 19, 46, 69, 90, 98, 123, 138, 140, 148, 151, 152, 172, 175, 192, 193, 214, 215, 226
Colyeer, Wm., 161, 162, 163, 165
Combs, William, 265
Commin, Daniel, 89
Condly, Saml, 288
Conley, Polly Ann., 260
Conley, Saml., 227, 228, 235, 236, 238, 272, 283
Cook, Joseph, 14
Cooper, Ellenor, 39
Cooper, James, 136
Cooper (Coper) Joel, 9
Cooper, Joseph, 60
Copan (Copon), John E., 235, 237, 275
Copan, John E. (Dr)., 282
Copp, Jacob, 141
Copp, John, 285
Copp, Michael, 285
Copp, Mechalir, 46
Cosson, John E., 203, 235, 275, 282
Cotton, Cullen, 15
County Bedford, 142
County Blount, 26
County, Carter, 38, 40, 213, 231,
County, Cook, 143
County, Green, 26, 45, 146, 188, 209, 212, 234
County, Madison, 26
County, Scott, 162
County, Washington, 31, 36, 43, 44, 63, 66, 86, 126, 128, 136, 185, 197, 277, 280, 291
County, White, 202
Cowan, James, 86
Cowan (Cowen), John, 65
Cowan, Michale, 18
Cox (Mrs)., 80
Cox, Danl (?), 19
Cox & Harris, 77
Cox, Isaac D., 34
Cox, Priscella, 79
Cox, Slum, 19

Crawford, John, 60
Crawford, John M., 160
Crawford, John M., 157, 158, 168, 175, 197, 198, 233, 278, 279
Crawford & Gammon, 201, 202
Crawford & Kinney, 234, 243, 253, 255, 271
Crawford, Samuel, 52, 55, 155, 203
Crawford, Saml & Co., 201, 202
Crawford, William, 14, 70
Cromwell, John, 50, 54
Crookshanks, Wm., 86
Crouch, George, 53, 90, 247, 287, 288, 289
Crouch, John, 133, 134
Crouch, Joseph, 9, 22, 23, 24, 29, 69, 122, 123, 184, 185, 186
Crouch, Joseph Jr., 133
Crouch, Polly, 133, 134
Crouch & West, 295
Crouse, Michael, 86, 113
Crusoe, John, 29
Culbertson, Andrew, 136
Culbertson, James, 136
Culbertson, Jane, 136, 137
Culbertson (Cutbertson), Joseph, 136
Culbertson, Josiah, 136
Culbertson, Samuel, 136, 137
Cunningham, (Dr)., 251, 280
Cunningham & Kenney, 163, 169
Cunningham, Martha, 87
Cunningham & Nelson, 235
Cunningham, Samuel B., 87, 89, 130, 132, 191, 212, 235, 237, 274
Cunningham, Wm M., 173
Custer, William P., 1

D.

Damron (Damran), John, 162, 210
Dandridge, 54
Daniels, Noah, 275
Davault (Devault), Frederick, 31, 83, 84, 101, 168
Davidson, Samuel, 269
Davis, Charles, 48, 148, 166
Davis, Jemima, 9
Davis, John, 73, 157
Davis, Joseph, 9
Davis, N., 4
Davis, Nathan, 1, 2, 31, 35
Davis, Saml., 14

Deaderick, 212, 216
Deaderick, D. A., 64, 231, 232
Deaderick, Dad, 48
Deaderick, David, 14, 25, 28, 44, 46, 63, 69, 77, 85, 129, 140, 196
Deaderick, & Co., David, 96
Deadrick, J. F., 282
Deaderick & Kinney, 209
Deaderick & Son, M., 50, 108
Deakins, D., 131
Deakins(Deacons), Daniel, 131, 166, 224, 225, 258, 281
Deakins, James, 79, 105, 119
Deakins, Milly, 113
Deakins(Deacons), Richard, 225
Dean, Mary, 11
Dearoys, Wm., 149
Deatheridge, Bird, 151
Deckard, John, 219
Deeds, Philip, 129
Delaney (Dr)., 77
Delaney (Dulaney), Mrs, 182, 225
Delaney (Dulaney), Elkanah R., 129
Delaney, James, 155, 182
Delaney, Rebeccah, 155, 182
Delaney (Dulaney), William, 155, 254
Delaney (Dulaney)., W. R., 273
Denham, Philip, 9
Denton, Joseph, .4, 150
Depew, James, 52
Depwe, Jas., & Jno., 190
Depew, Isaac, 15, 118
Derrick, William E., 248
Doak, 152
Doak (Dr)., 284
Doak, A. A., 287
Doak, Alexander, 217, 218
Doak, Archibald A., 211, 286
Doak, D., 181
Doak, Jane, 210, 217, 286
Doak, Jane A., 211
Doak, John, 30, 286
Doak, J. N., 144
Doak, John N., 211, 280
Doak, John W., 210, 286
Doak, S. H., 144
Doak, Saml W., 180
Doak, Samuel (Rev)., 96
Doane, John, 13, 25, 29, 64, 87, 119
Dockins, 201
Dogan, John, 70
Dosser, 225, 237, 239
Dosser, William, 56, 83, 85, 89, 113, 132, 134, 146, 155, 159, 166, 196, 240
Douglass, John, 208
Douglass, Samuel, 108

Drake, Ephraim, 152, 172
Drake, Samuel, 241, 243, 257
Duffield, 11
Duncan, Andrew, 20, 128
Duncan, Benjamin, 34
Duncan, & Blair, 260
Duncan, James, 103, 104, 105, 260
Duncan, John, 60
Duncan, Joseph, 14, 15, 18, 19, 20, 108, 109, 110, 128, 197
Duncan, Samuel, 63, 64
Dungan, 38
Dungan (Mrs)., 39
Dungan (Dangan], Mary, 37, 38, 39, 40
Dungan, Jeremiah, 36, 37, 38, 39, 40
Dunworth, Charles, W., 65
Dunworth, Thomas, 219
Dozan, John, 70

E.

E. ?, Jacob B. 280
Eaden, James, 2
Earles (Early), Richard, 7
Earley, Thomas, 48
Early, John, 48
Early, Samuel, 48, 196, 293
Earnest, Henry, 141
Earnest, Henry & Co., 17
Earnest, Mary, 245
Earnest, Peter, 96
Earnest, Wesley, 246
Eason, 82, 253, 270
Eason & Co., 212
Eason, J., 237
Eason, John, 82
Eason, John G., 17, 31, 32, 44, 66, 69, 107, 113, 114, 119, 128, 132, 169, 176, 188, 189, 191, 194, 195, 197, 203, 218, 220, 230, 237, 248, 251, 255, 279, 284, 286.
Eason, John G. & Co., 173
Easterly, 245
Edgemon, Esther, 77
Edmonson, N., (Col), 203.
Ewards (Edwards), Abel, 137
Elliot, 239
Elliott, George, 235
Elliott (Eliott), John, 235, 239
Elliott, Minerva, 235
Elliott (Eliott), Patrick, 235, 239

Ellis, Jacob, 24, 31, 32, 33, 46, 49, 52, 53, 58, 59, 65, 71, 129, 189, 208, 211, 221, 263
Ellis, William, 46, 49, 263
Embree, 105, 106, 203, 234, 271, 298
Embree, Allen & Gillispie, 243
Embree, E., 212, 253
Embree, E. & Allen, James, 212
Embree, E. & E., 77, 119, 149, 153, 173
Embree, Elihu, 77, 78
Embree, Elijah, 77, 78, 82, 89, 102, 108, 109, 153, 173
Embree & Gillispie, 294, 298
Embree & Henry College, 295
Embree, John, 118
Embree, Mary, 118
Embree & Williams, 258
Emmert, 237
Emmert, Lawrence, 237, 238
Emmert, Peter, 219
Emmert, Peter & Co., 275
Emmerson, 273
English, James, 150
English, Nathan, 70
Epperson, John, 102
Epperson, Martha, 151
Epperson, Peter, 150, 151
Epperson, Wm., 151
Ensor, Thomas P., 97
Ernhart, Killion, 45
Ernheart, Killion, 45
Erwn (Erwin), Alen, 169
Erwin (Erivn), Alen, 169
Erwin, Alexr., 169
Erwin, Sarah, 169
Erwin, Wm., 201
Erwin, Wm S., 224
Estes, John B., 77

F.

Fain, John M., 201
Falls, James, 140
Farmer, James, 59
Farnsworth, Jeremiah, 157
Faubush, Polly, 87
Fawbush, Mary, 90
Fawbush, Robert, 51, 86
Feazel, Martin, 44, 99, 130 (Feazell)
Feazel (Fesel), Mary, 143
Fellows, Abraham, 10
Felts, William, 27
Fenceler, 83
Fenceler (Finuler), Frederick, 51, 83, 84, 85, 86, 87, 88, 89, 90, 167, 271.

Fench, (Atto)., 71
Ferguson, J., 1
Ferguson, John, 194
Finch, 207
Finch (Finck) Aaron (Aron), 65, 68, 113, 131, 162, 191, 205, 206
Finch, Thomas, 45, 56
Finck, (Atto), 100
Finck (Finch), Aron (Aaron), 65, 68, 113, 131, 162, 191, 205, 206
Finck, Thomas, 56
Findley, Daniel, 29, 96
Fine, Vinate (Vinet), 274, 289, 291
Fink, Wm M., 17
Finuler, (Fenceler), Frederick, 51, 83, 84, 85, 86, 87, 88, 89, 90, 167, 271
Fitzgerrald, 208
Fitsgarrel, James, 149
Fletcher, Wm., 166
Flin, Arthur, 151
Floid, James F., 291
Floyd, Isaac, 11
Fondwill, Lewis, 153
Ford, Barney, 145
Ford, Hannah, 48, 51
Ford, Horatio Junr. 24
Ford, Isbell, 24
Ford, John, 44, 45
Ford, Mary, 11, 145
Ford, Thomas, 24, 150
Ford, William, 274
Fox, Adam, 65
Fraker, Adam., 15
Fraker, Eleanor (Ellenor), 131, 178
Fraker, George, 131, 132
Fraker, John, 132
Fraker, Michael, 132
Frame, Archabald, 13, 19
Frances, John, Jr., 35
Franklin, Josiah, 18, 19, 42, 72, 112, 156
Fry, John, 66
Fulkirson, Thomas, 256
Fuller, James, 45
Fulmer, John, 218

G.

Galloway, Campbell & King, Henry 274
Gammon, 82, 208, 212
Gammon & Crawford, 55, 66, 201, 202
Gammon, N., 270
Gammon, Nathan, 234
Gammon, & Son, 203
Gammon & Stuart, 277
Ganes, Ephraim, 218
Gann, Adam, 10, 20, 46
Gann, Jacob, 96
Gann, John, 278, 285
Gann, Nathan, 265
Gann, Sally, 278
Gann, Sampson, 265
Garber, Solomon, 274
Gardner, Peter, 25, 128
Garland, Gutridge, 136
Garner, Brice, M., 9
Garret, William, 143
Gates, John, 149
Gibbs, (Phebe), 270
Gibbs, Thos., 281
Gibson (Dr)., 77
Gibson, J. 39
Gibson, Jeremiah D., 37, 38, 39, 40
Gibson, Orpha, 39
Gibson, Spencer E., 17, 128
Gibson, Thomas, 37, 38
Gifford, John, 150
Gifford, Lawson, 265
Gillaland, Robert, 124
Gillaland, (Gilleland, Gilleyland), William, 71, 72, 94, 96, 112, 141, 143, 144, 154, 173, 174, 176, 179, 180, 181, 183, 184, 186, 193, 226, 227, 277, 278, 280, 281, 285, 286, 287.
Gillispie, 271
Gillispie, Allen, 41
Gillispie & Embree, 294, 298
Gillispie, Embree & Allen, 243
Gillispie, George, 117, 122, 124
Gillispie (Gillespie), George, T., 26, 153, 173, 209, 212, 234, 235, 270, 298
Gillispie (Gillespie), James, 152, 172, 221
Gillispie (Gillespie), James H., 248, 252, 261, 263
Gillispie (Gillespie) & Patterson, 209
Gillispie, Thomas, 26, 96, 122, 153
Gillum, Jeremiah, 65
Glaise, M., 237
Glass, Hiram, 83, 201, 279
Glass, Jessee, 63
Glass, Joseph, 15
Glass, Wm., 41
Glasscock, (Glascock), Archabald, 25, 43, 70, 128, 150, 161, 191, 297, 298

SETTLEMENTS OF ESTATES, VOLUME 00, 1790-1841

Glasscock & Isaac Horton, 190
Glasscock, Link & Barkly, 191
Godbey, Joseph, 73
Good & Co., 209
Good, Daniel, 245
Good, Elisabeth, 244, 245
Good, Jacob, 244, 245
Good, John, 245
Good, Margaret, 245
Good, Nancy, 244
Good, Solomon, 244, 245
Gordan, James, 4
Gott, John, 43, 46, 49, 63, 65, 66, 67, 78, 207, 208
Gott, Lott, 150
Gott, William, 213
Grage, Nathan, 149
Graham, Jas., 237
Grahl, Augustus, 85
Gran, Rebecca, 189
Grant, David, 35
Graves, Christian, 256
Gray, James, 17, 86, 96, 200
Gray, John, 17, 102, 143, 238
Gray, R., 77
Gray, Thomas, 122
Grayham, James, 126, 237
Grayham, Ellenor, 126
Grayham, Saml M., 112
Grayham, Wm., 35
Green, Arnold, 17
Green, Ira, 26, 96
Green, John, 196
Green, Joshua, 46, 239, 240, 244, 245, 275, 276, 297.
Green County, 26, 146, 209, 212, 234, 237
Greenville, 76, 154, 212, 295
Greenway, 235
Greenway, John, 237
Greenway, John & Co., 22
Greenway & Jones, 113, 147, 173, 195, 209, 212, 235, 237
Greenway & Lockett, 220
Greenway, Richard, 152, 172, 237
Greenway, William, 237, 297
Grimsley, John, 70, 197
Grimsley, Magdaline, 70
Greer, 146, 276
Greer, Andrew, 1
Greer, Andw. Senr., 1
Greer, Joseph, 1, 3
Greer & Kennedy, 44
Greer, Samuel, 21, 31, 42, 43, 50, 55, 56, 61, 63, 78, 83, 85, 86, 108, 109, 112, 117, 135, 142, 147, 149, 157
161, 165, 169, 170, 178, 185, 187, 189, 196, 198, 201, 202, 227, 229, 230, 233, 235, 242, 244, 245, 246, 248, 249, 250, 252, 254, 255, 256, 257, 258, 259, 260, 261, 262, 263, 264, 265, 266, 267, 268, 272, 273, 277, 280, 281, 282, 285, 288, 289, 290, 293, 294, 295, 296, 297, 298, 299.
Greer, Saml, Junr., 271
Greer, Thos., 248
Greer, Thos. D., 225
Guinn, 28
Guinn & Harris, 29
Guinn (Guynn), James, 153, 201, 202
Guinn, (Guynn), John, 245
Guinn, John D., 83, 157, 167, 191
Guinn (Guynn), J. D., 237
Gyre (Guyer), Henry, 48, 123, 152, 162, 172
Gyre, J., 122, 123, 162
Gyre, J. & Henry, 122
Gyre, Jacob, 122, 123, 161, 163
Gyre, Jacob Jr., 123
Gyre, (Guyer), John, 194, 195, 196, 197
Gyre (Gyer), Jonas, 162, 195, 196

H.

Hadden, J. N., 202
Hair (Hare), Samuel, 16
Hair, Eliza Jane, 81
Hair (Hare), Isaac, 81, 190
Hair (Hare), Isaac & Jacob, 190
Hair, Jacob, 219
Hair, Matilda, 81
Hale, George, 149, 190
Hale (Hayle), 240
Hale, Isabella, 25, 128
Hale, Joseph, 150
Hale, Masheck, 66
Hale, Nicholas, 67
Hale, Richard, 67
Hale, Robt. G., 265
Hale, Walter, 77
Hale, Wat., 107
Hale, Zachariah, 66
Halfacre, 219
Hall, Wm., 70
Hamelton, 11
Hamilton, Joseph, 124
Hammer, Isaac, 31, 61, 129
Hammer, Jacob, 31
Hammer, John, 31, 32, 61
Hammer, Joseph, 31
Hammer, Jonathan, 31, 35
Hammer, Margaret, 31

Hammons, Jacob, 282
Hammons, John, 282
Hammons, Thomas, 282, 283
Hampton, Hiram, 260
Hampton, Jessee, 27
Hannah, Grace, 207
Hannah, J., 206, 207
Hannah, H., 207
~~Hannah, J., 207~~
Harmon, Adam, 96, 141
Harrell, Milly, 113
Harris, 28
Harris, Benja., 56
Harris, George, 18
Harris, George C., 18, 28
Harris & Quinn, 29
Harris, H., 201
Harris, John C., 48, 56, 127, 147, 178
Harrison, Hannah, 51
Harold, Amason, 70
Harrold, Mattock, 15
Hartman, Henry, 13, 108
Hartman, John, 128, 169, 191, (Hartmant) 297
Hartman, Joseph, 15
Hartsell, Charles, 166, 195
Hartsell, E. Tetris, 77
Hartsell, Hannah, 196
Hartsell, (Hartsel), Jacob, 48, 57, 74, 90, 113, 114, 147, 155, 161, 162, 163, 166, 176, 177, 182, 198, 199, 201, 211, 223, 224, 229, 233, 235, 236, 239, 242, 244, 250, 254, 255, 282
Hartsell, (Hartsel), Isaac, 159, 166, 195, 213, 214, 241, 269
Hartsell, Joshua, 287
Harvey, Alexander, 155
Harvey, James, 27, 38, 113, 235
Harvey, John, 182
Hathorn, Noah, 124
Hawn, Adam, 136
Hawn, George, 122
Hawn, Sabastian, 122
Haws, Conrad, 105
Haws, John, 150, 151
Haws, Thomas, 150, 274
Headerick, Jacob, 2
Headerick, Joseph, 2
Headerick (Headrick), Jesse, 265
Helms, John, 13
Helton, Catharine, 294
Henderson, George, 70
Henderson, William, 202

Hendley, George, 29, 30, 156
Hendley, Isaac, 29, 214, 215
Hendley, Joshua, 44
Herdred, Solomon, 8
Hendrix, Solomon, 9
Hendrey, (Hendry), Abraham, 9, 37
Henley (Henly), George, 166, 184
Henry, Spencer, 28
Hensley, George, 178
Herrold, John, 136
Hicks, Abraham, 161
Hicks, John H., 48
Hicks, Wm., 103
Hill, Jane, 136, 137
Hilton, Catharine, 293
Hinkel, 212
Hinkle, G., 28
Hinkle, Joseph, 85, 87, 90
Hise, John, 202
Hodgease, Jarred, 122
Hogart, William, 134
Holsbee (Holibee), John, 45, 56
Holland, Martin, 150
Hollet, 1
Holms, James, 64
Holms, Saml., 88
Holt, Daniel B., 172
Holt, David R., 153
Holt, Peter, 248
Hope, Nancy, 157
Hope, William, 128
Hopper, Harden, 274
Hornberger, Jacob, 48
Horton, Daniel, 70
Horton, Isaac & Glosscock, 190
Hoskins, John, 1
Hoss, Abraham, 129
Hoss, Henry, 43, 46, 49, 52, 53, 58, 59, 60, 61, 63, 66, 68, 74, 78, 100
Hoss, Jacob, 11, 116, 145
Hoss, Jacob, Jr., 129
Hoss, John, 35, 36, 39, 68, 188, 259, 273, 275
Hoss, Mary, 129
Howel, Charles, 25, 119
Howel, E. S., 202
Howard (Mrs)., 209
Howard, J., 109
Howard, Jacob, 23, 28, 29, 65, 113, 179, 185
Howard, J. H., 173
Howard, John, 35
House, George, 24
House, M., 9
Houston, James & William, 218
Houston, John, 36, 37, 39, 40, 129
Houston, Preston, 248

Hoyle, 240
Hoyle, (Dr)., 173
Hoyle, Jacob, 141, 240
Hoyle, (Hoyl), Michael, 140, 141
  239
Huffhine, Philip, 48
Huffine, Daniel, 254
Huffman, Saml., 237
Hulse, 208
Humphreys, 1
Humphreys, George, 36, 37, 65,
Humphreys, Jacob, 182
Humphreys, Jehue, 8
Humphreys, Jessee, 8
Humphreys, John, 153, 173, 176,
  181, 184, 186, 193, 210
  211, 215, 218, 237, 242,
  275, 276, 280, 281, 286, 287,
  292
Humphrey, Jno & Bayless, Saml G.,
  287
Humphreys, M., 9
Humphreys, Moses, 8, 9, 24, 37
Humphreys, William L., 63
Hundley, John S., 27
Hunt, 113,
Hunt, Benjamin, 102, 103, 104
  106, 109
Hunt & Clem, 188
Hunt, Dicey, 82, 104, 107, 109
Hunt, Elizabeth, 53
Hunt, Henson, 133, 249
Hunt, Jessee, 82, 103, 104, 107,
  109, 113
Hunt, John, 53, 58, 71
Hunt, Lewis, 129
Hunt, Maria, 58, 90
Hunt, Peter, 103, 104, 108
Hunt, Sally, 58
Hunt, Samuel, 35, 39, 40, 44,
  45, 53, 61, 66, 70, 71
  90, 133, 134, 149, 201, 202,
  203, 273
Hunt, Sarah, 90, 106, 109
Hunt, Simon, 127
Hunt, Smith, 103, 104, 105, 106,
  107, 108, 109, 110, 111
Hunt, Smith & Thomas, 101
Hunt, Thomas, 25, 102, 104, 105,
  106, 107, 108, 109, 110,
  111, 249
Hunt, Uriah, 19, 25, 82, 101,
  102, 103, 104, 105, 106,
  107, 108, 109, 110, 111,
  150.
Hunt, Widow, 104
Hunt, Wm., 82, 103, 106, 108

Hunter, Ann, 12, 290
Hunter, Clark, 268, 284, 290
Hunter, David, 177
Hunter, David C., 195
Hunter, D. C., 290
Hunter, Dompsey, 2
Hunter, Jacob, 12, 33, 34, 45, 46, 48,
  57, 90, 122, 145, 176, 177, 182,
  290
Hunter, Jesse B., 290
Hunter, John, 122, 290
Hunter, John & Clark, 290
Hunter, Joseph, 48
Huskal, Frederick, F., 173
Hutchings, Charles, 136

I.

Iles, William, 17
Ingersoll, Caroline, 293
Ingersoll, M., 293
Ingersoll, Moses, 264
Ingersoll, Prudence M., 293
Ingle, 23
Ingle, A., 237
Ingle, Adam., 29
Ingle, John, 31, 114, 124, 275,
Ingle, Michael, 249, 250
Ireland, Thomas, 48
Irvins, P., 235
Irvin, Rebecca, 200, 283
Irwin, Alexand., 14
Irwin, James, 124
Irwin, R., 252
Irwin, William, 113
Isbell, James R., 73, 133

J.

Jackson, A. E., 255
Jackson, George, 150, 257, 262, 296
Jackson, Peter, 257, 262
Jacson, (Jackson), Samuel, 69
Jacksons School House, 217
Jackson, William, 43, 51, 150, 257,
  262, 296, 297
Jacob, B. E., ?, 280
Jacobs, Dufty, 127
James, R. C. J., 219
Jellico, 72
Jenkins, Hugh, 7
Jinkin, George, 102
Jislen, Jonathan, 70
Job, Abigail, 8, 9, 97, 98
Job, Abel, 9
Job, Abraham, 9, 33, 35, 97, 98, 133
Job (Jobe), David, 8, 9

✶ (See Errata for correction)

✶ Johnson, Robt., 195
Johnson & Jones, 230, 234, 237
Johnston, Benjamen, 15
Johnston & Embree, E. & E., 77
Johnston, James, 150
Johnston, James S., 22, 69, 119
Johnston, Susannah, 95
Jones, Aaron, 164
Jones, Crawford, 162
Jones, Darling, 33, 273
Jones, Elizabeth, 119, 121
Jones & Greenway, 147, 173, 195, 209, 212, 235, 237
Jones, Henry, 2, 219
Jones, James, 14
Jones, James H., 273
Jones, Jessee, 70
Jones, John, 119
Jones, John B., 121
Jones & Johnson, 230, 234, 237
Jonesboro, 40, 72, 77, 91, 165, 168, 171, 232, 236
Jonesborough, 77, 84, 126, 175, 194, 224, 235, 236, 239, 241, 242, 249, 277, 280, 281
Jordan, Lewis, 98, 152, 237
Jordan, L. Jr., 172
Jordan, Lewis, Sr., 172

K.

Keefhaver, Nicholas, 66
Keel, John, 6
Keen, Enoch, 25
Kelley, Kinchen, 31, 32, 59
Kelley, Richard, 37
Kelley, Wm., 129
Kellow, Wm., 208
Kelsey, Nathaniel, 54
Kelsey, William, 12
Kennedy, 11, 20, 60, 197, 198, 225,
Kennedy, John, 4, 9, 10, 20, 21, 23, 26, 28, 35, 39, 40, 44, 56, 62, 73, 85, 86, 123, 127, 129, 133, 151, 159, 169, 179, 180, 181, 201, 241, 269, 280
Kennedy, Samuel, 66, 165
Kennedy, Scott, 207
Kenner (Kener), Joseph, 31, 113
Kenney, & Cunningham, 169
Kenney, D., 110
Kenney, Daniel, 100
Kenney, Daniel (Dr)., 81
Kenny & Nelson, 203

Kepple, Jacob, 93
Kepper, John, 267
Kerl, L., 190
Kerlin, Joseph, 48
Kerts, John, 128
Kerwood, John, 41
Keys & Co., 251
Keys, Jeremiah, 164, 191
Keys, John, 248, 251
Keyes, John & Co., 239, 265
Kibler (Keibler), Jacob, 20, 151, 264, 294
Kibler, James, 15
Kibler, Saml., 293
Kiker, Conrad, 45
Kile, John, 6
Kincannon, A. A., 219
Kincheloe, George, 150
Kincheloe, William, 265
King, Albert, 289
King, Billy F., 289
King, George G., 220
King, George & William, 218, 220
King, Henry (Hy)., 12, 16, 24, 31, 32, 33, 34, 36, 37, 39, 40, 47, 62, 65, 95, 96, 97, 98, 125, 129, 138, 139, 145, 221, 223, 224, 225, 233, 242, 247, 275
King, Henry, Galloway, Campbell, 274
King, James (Dr)., 280
King, Robt., 184, 185
King, Thomas, 34, 218, 273
King, William, 4, 220
Kinney & Crawford, 243, 253, 255, 271
Kinney & Cunningham, 163
Kinney, Danl., 190, 265
Kinney & Deaderick, 209
Kinney, M. G., 225, 226, 234
Kitsmiller, Martin, 149, 218
Kitsmiller, David, 219
Klepper, 113
Klepper, David, 266, 267
Klepper, J., 266, 267
Klepper, Jacob, 188, 256, 260, 261, 266, 267
Klepper, John, 188, 189, 256, 260
Klepper, Joseph, 256, 266
Knox, Samuel, 126
Knoxville, 144, 160, 174, 184, 185, 216, 217, 228
Korts, John, 13
Kotz, John, 119
Krouse, Daniel, 228
Krouse (Krous), Michael, 52, 287, 288,
Krouse, Samuel, 256, 264, 289
Krouse, Solomon, 228, 229, 287, 288, 289

SETTLEMENTS OF ESTATES, VOLUME 00, 1790-1841

Krouse, Susannah, 228, 229
Kurts, John, 41
Kyker, Conrad, 186, 187
Kyle, Absolem, 19, 20

L.

Lacky (Lackey), Thomas, 4, 19, 202
Lacy, Reuben, 289
Land, Moor, 273
Lane, Tidence, 133
Lane, Samuel, 133
Laws, John, 112
Leesburgh, 83, 101, 167, 190
Lemmons, David, 191, 193
Leslie (Lislee, Lesley), Jonathan, 30, 33, 36, 149,
Lightner, Christian, 167
Lincoln, Isaac, 11
Lindsey, Wm., 35
Lineberger (Linebarger), Nicholes 45, 195
Link, Glasscock & Barkly, 191
Link, John, 22, 24, 41, 42, 64, 76, 84, 86, 89, 91, 94, 111, 112, 115, 120, 121, 132, 141, 143, 144, 154, 157, 158, 159, 165, 168, 170, 173, 174, 175, 179, 180, 183, 184, 191, 192, 193, 207, 210, 211, 216, 217, 218
Link, Jno., 160
Linn, Ceasor, 30
Linster, E., 176
Little, George, 62, 148, 220
Little, John, 11, 62, 63
Locket, Benj F., 271 284
Lockett, B. F., 284
Locket & Greenway, 270
Long, C., 237
Long, Christian, 279
Long, Henry, 47
Long, James, 129
Long, Thomas, 47
Longmire, Elizabeth, 220, 221
Longmire, John, 219, 221
Longmire, Joseph, 100, 101, 113, 114, 292
Longmire, Wm., 292
Looney, Abraham, 152, 172
Love, John, 4, 36, 37, 38, 39, 40, 136, 203
Love, Polly S., 203
Love, Robert, 137, 203, 204
Love, Samuel, 204
Love, Samuel B., 33, 201, 202,
203, 204
Love, Thomas, 129
Lovell, Charles, M., 23
Lovett, Charles, 295
Lowry, Wm G., 275
Lusk, Margaret, 12
Lusk, Samuel, 33
Lusk, Robert, 2,
Luckey, S. J. W., 274
Luckey, 276
Lucky, L. J., 216
Lucky, L. J. W., 217
Lyle, Saml., 210

M.

Maclin, Joseph, 120
Maclin, Robert, 12, 13
Maclin, Saml., 84
Madison County, 26
Mallonee, G. W., 274
Malonee, George W., 274
Malonee, John, 59, 60, 63, 220, 274
Manes, Hugh, 220
Mann, Joseph, 237, 271, 277, 286, 295
March (Marsh), Henry Senr. 227
Marsh, Abell, 120, 121
Marsh, Ann, 120
Marsh, Henry, 14, 16, 75, 76
Marsh, Henry Sr., 75
Martin, Caleb, 120, 121
Martin, Clee, 120, 121
Martin, Edward L., 27
Martin, Elias, 120
Martin, Henry, 20, 119, 120, 121
Martin, Hugh, 25
Martin, John, 119, 120
Martin, Joseph, 14
Martin, Richard, 102, 103, 104
Martin, Richard B., 106, 107, 120, 121
Maryland, 79
Massey, Juball, 203
Massingail (Massengill), William, 20, 291
Mauk, John, 10
Matlock, Ransom, 274
Matlock, Sarah, 150
Matheny, Elijah, 14,
Matherly, Levi, 15
Mathes, A. A., 295
Mathes (Mathis), Alexander, 17, 99, 140 161, 237, 249, 276
Mathes (Mathis), Alexander C., 211
Mathes, Allen H., (Mathis), 86
Mathes (Mathis), Ebenezer, 210
Mathes (Mathis), Ebenezer L., 92, 152, 154, 204

Mathes (Mathis), E. L., 64, 91, 114, 171, 172, 176, 178, 184, 185, 186, 193, 194, 197, 204, 205, 209, 210, 212, 215, 217, 216, 218, 224, 225, 226, 230, 231, 234, 237, 238, 239, 240, 242, 243, 244, 245, 246, 247, 248, 252, 253, 254, 255, 265, 269, 270, 271, 275, 276, 282, 283, 285, 286, 288, 292, 294, 298
Mathes, James, 41
Mathes, W., 194
Maxwell, S., 238, 270
Maxwell, Samuel, 268
Maxwell, Saml., 48, 202
Maxwell & Yancy, 237
May, 162
May, Cassimare, 245, 246
May, D & S., 245
Mays, Adam, 214
Mays, John, 195
Melbourn, Joseph, 64
Melson, Wm., 161
Melvin, James, 211, 273
Melvin, John, 106, 211
Melvin, Joseph, 124
Melvin, Rachel, 155, 211
Mercer, Abner, 189
Mercer, Eliza, 18
Mercer, Ellenor, 115
Mercer, John, 17, 18
Mercer, Joseph, 114, 115
Mercers, Rachael, 189
Mercer, Thos., 189
Mercer, Thomas, W., 114, 115
Might, Geo., 185
Milhorn, Elisabeth (Millhorn), 256, 261
Millhorn (Milhorn), G. W., 256, 261, 266, 267
Millhorn, G. W., (Mrs)., 256
Miller, Abraham, 61
Miller, Ann, 12, 13
Miller, Catharine, 61, 245
Miller, Henry, 60, 61, 219
Miller, Isaac, 18
Miller, Jacob, 53, 61, 68, 119, 219
Miller, James, 96
Miller, John, 31, 41, 60, 62, 133
Miller, Joseph, 61, 68
Miller, Michael, 274, 275, 289
Miller, P. M., 26
Miller, Samuel, 48, 60, 61

Miller, Solomon, 61, 169
Miller, Thomas, 124
Miller, William, 5, 14, 16, 41, 42, 64, 96, 159
Million, 192
Million, Edward, 130, 279
Million, Jacob, 28
Million, John, 130, 179, 191, 192
Million, Joseph, 233
Million, Robert, 18, 130
Mills, Harr, 15
Millsap, James, 2
Mississippi, 26, 229, 256
Mitchell (Mitchel), 29, 49
Mitchell (Mitchel), A., 230
Mitchell, Adam., 113
Mitchell & Co., 29
Mitchell, D., 17
Mitchell, David, 46, 87, 89, 90, 279
Mitchell (Mitchel), David S., 202
Mitchell, John, 89, 131
Mitchell, Polly, 89
Mitchell, S. D., 21
Mitchell, Thomas, 41
Mitchell, Thos Senr., 167
Mitchell, William, 17, 22, 24, 29, 30, 41, 44, 96, 97, 115, 116, 126, 139, 140
Mitchell, William & Co., 29
Montgomery, William, 12
Moore (Mrs)., 26
Moore, A., 26
Moore, Alexander, 26
Moore, James, 4
Moore, R., 280
Moore, Rebecca, 96
Moore, Robert, 28, 278, 279
Moore, Sarah, 279, 280
Moore, William, 279
Moorisons, Jos., 11
Morgan, Gabriel, 70
Morrison, Robert, 41
Moyers, 4
Moyers, Frederick, 5
Mullens, Jesse, 197
Murr, John, 146
Murr, Patience, 146
Murray (Murrey), Christopher, 149
Murray (Murrey), Ephraim, 28, 241, 242, 243, 244, 257
Murray, Jabes, 291
Murray, John, 291
Murray, Roland P., 208
Muskengam, 20

Mc.

McAdams, Hugh, 14, 25, 128

McAdams, Isabella, 25, 127
McAdams, Robert, 29
McAdams, Thomas, 277, 278, 280, 281, 285, 286
MCAdams, William, 183, 184
McAlister, 18
McAlister (McAlester), James, 17, 51, 186, 236, 238, 250, 251, 262, 268, 284
McAlister, John, 13, 18, 19, 22, 25, 29, 33, 48, 52, 53, 74, 79, 122, 128, 129, 136,
McBee, Ganum C., 201
McBride, 166
McBride, Alexander, 73
McCall, Jamima, 227
McCall, Jemima, 274
McCall, Robert, 274
McCall, Robt S., 227
McCall, William, 297
McCampbell, Ann, 173
McCardel, Hannah E., 81
McClarey, Joseph, 33
McClary, Jessee, 229, 230
McClary, S., 238
McClary, Sarah, 230, 238
McClary, Seth, 229, 230
McClary, Wm., 229, 230
McCellen, Isaac B., 149
McClellan Greer & Co., 33
McClure, Ervin, 152
McClure, Ewing, 172
McClure, John, 140
McCorcle, Frances A (Doctor) 35
McCorcle, John, 77, 119
McCord, David, 153
McCorel, Daniel, 173
McCoy, William, 17, 22, 238
McCracken (McCraken), 35
McCracken, H., 238
McCracken, Henry, 28, 46, 237, 251, 268, 284
McCracken, John, 24, 28, 30, 53, 62, 127, 133
McCraken, Robert, 54
McCracken, Samuel, 133, 189, 284
McCracken (Saml) (Mrs)., 189
McCrall, Gabrial, 172
McCraw, Gabriel, 153
McCray, Charles, 7, 136
McCray, Daniel, 136, 137
McCray, Henry, 28, 56, 162
McCray, George, 153, 173
McCutchen, Wm., 122
McDennee, Micajah, 57
McDowel, Robert, 279
McEfee, John, 43, 52, 133

McFall, B., 291
McGee, 99
McGee (McGhee), John, 17, 100, 168, 177 272, 278, 281
McGee, Leann, 292
McGee, William, 29, 217, 292
McGiffeys, (Mrs), 185
McGinnis, Elizabeth, 27, 28
McGinnis, Jessee, 93
McGinnis, John, 27, 28
McGinnis, Joseph, 27
McGinnis, Thomas, 86, 88, 118
McGinnis, Thos (Mrs), 86
McGinty, Alexr., 1
McGlaughlin, Archl, 89
McInturff, Gasper, 136
McInturff, Isreal, 202
McInturff, J., 202
McInturff, John, 201
McIntush, D., 185
McKee, (Mr.), 77
McKee, A., 28, 48
McKee, Adam, 18, 23, 25, 133
McKee, Robert, 159, 185
McKee, W., 28, 48
McKee, Wm & Adam, 69
McKeean, Saml., 175
McKeehan, Saml., 272
McKehen, Saml., 84
McKenny, John A., 21, 173
McKie, Alexander, 140
McKin, Edward, 129
McKinney (McKinny), 162
McKinney, John, 122
McKinney, John A., 20, 26
McKinny & Taylor, 185
McKinsey, 151
McLin, Alexander 10
McLin, Clenah, 194
McLin, James, 209, 216, 275, 286
McLin, John, 194
McLin, Joseph, 84, 85, 86, 111, 143, 144, 146, 154, 158, 160, 164, 168, 171, 173, 174, 175, 176, 181, 194, 210, 239, 268, 274, 283, 285
McLin, Thomas, 194
McLin, R. D., 194
McLin, Robert, 12, 23, 194, 251
McMackin, John, 286
McMakin, Thomas, 95
McNabb, David, 133
McNeal, J., 46
McNeel (McNeal), John, 46, 141
McNees, 205, 206, 207,
McNees, G. A. G., 207
McNees, G. G., 205
McNees, Saml, 205, 207

McPherson, Isaac, 271, 272
McPheters, Wm., 87, 167, 168
McQuean, Hannah, 7
McQuean, Samuel, 7
McRenolds, Thomas, 136

N.

Naff, 216
Naff, Jacob, 253
Nashville, 214
Nead, John, 274, 275
Nelson, (Col), 253
Nelson (Doctor), 29
Nelson, A., 225, 226, 234, 243, 254, 270, 294, 298
Nelson, Alexander, 209, 212, 225, 234, 243, 252, 253, 254, 270, 271, 294, 298
Nelson, Alexander M., 25, 152, 153, 154
Nelson, A. M., 171, 172, 173, 174, 178, 185, 209
Nelson, Claburn, 161
Nelson & Cunningham, 235
Nelson, D., 202
Nelson D(Doctor), 28
Nelson, David, 66, 110, 111, 119, 132, 191
Nelson, David (Doctor), 53, 68, 77
Newman, Saml., 185
Nelson, George W., 276
Nelson, G. W., 276
Nelson, James, 14, 129
Nelson, John, 22, 23, 29, 30, 63, 69, 143, 152, 153, 154, 162, 168, 180
Nelson, John (Col), 225
Nelson, John (Senr), 152, 172
Nelson & Kenny, 203
Nelson, Mark W., 163
Nelson, Minerva G., 154, 173, 180
Nelson, Nathan, 14
Nelson, Nancy, 154, 174, 209
Nelson, Nancy ?, 234
Nelson, Sarah, 13
Nelson, Thomas, 140, 194, 237
Nelson, William, 3, 23, 29, 117, 148, 163, 184, 185, 186, 193, 242.
Norris, Philip T., 57
No. Carolina, 9
North, George, 6, 123
North, John, 6, 7
Norwood, John, 11, 129

O.

Odeneal, Bartholomew, 15
Odeneal, William, 66
Ore (Orre), Sample, 27, 178, 179
Ore, Wm., 126
Overall, Isaac, 215, 216
Overholser (Overhulser), Ephraim, 175
Overholser, Jacob, 17
Overholster, Saml., 84
Owens, Rachel, 29
Owens, Elias, 119

P.

Pactoles, 77
Painter, (Mrs), 277
Painter, Aaron, 277
Painter, Adam, 277, 278
Painter, David, 277
Painter, Elisabeth, 277
Painter, Jesse, 277, 278
Painter, Phillip, 277
Painter, Samuel, 277, 278
Painter, William, 277
Parke, John, 252,
Parker, 56
Parker, James, 27, 56, 57, 98, 130, 140
Parker, John, 73, 147, 220, 273
Parker, Josiah, 48, 248
Parker, Sarah, 56
Parkison, Peter, 1, 2, 3
Parks, Philip, 138, 162
Parks, A. C., 231, 232
Parson (Atto), 100
Parsons, P., 40
Parsons, Peter, 39, 53, 141
Paterson, 243
Patterson, 113, 271
Patterson & Gillespie, 209
Patterson, J., 212
Patterson, James, 13, 151, 153, 172, 209, 234
Patton & Brown, 130
Patton, John, 22, 24, 25, 28, 43, 45, 51, 55, 61, 85, 95, 100, 131, 132, 178
Patton, John P.?, 179
Patton, Joseph, 152, 172
Patton, Mary, 178
Patton, Nancy M., 253
Patton, Thomas, 149
Patton, Thomas C., 28, 30, 45, 47, 51, 54, 55, 71, 72, 99, 100, 101, 112, 115, 130, 131, 132, 140, 144, 148, 149, 160, 161, 177, 178
Patton, William, 17, 29, 44, 93, 96,

99, 140, 141, 180, 251, 276.
Payne, H., 237
Payne, Jessee, 9, 10, 17, 18,
    41, 86, 115, 116, 118, 123,
    126, 153, 172, 173, 236,
    237, 238
Payne, Jessee (Junr)., 18, 41
Payne, Jessee Sen., 17
Payne, John, 237, 295
Payne, Joseph, 237, 284
Payne, Mahay, 238
Payne, Mahly, 237
Payne, Martha, 146
Payne, Mary, 250, 251, 262, 268,
    284
Payne, Thomas, 19
Payne, & Wattenberger, 86
Payne, Wm., 237, 284
Pearce, James, 37, 38, 39
Pearce, William, 66
Pennsylvania, 123, 126, 127
Penny, James, 26
Peoples, Richard, 182
Peoples, Samuel W. H., 36
Peters, Christian, 2
Peters, John, 78
Phillips, Batey, 23
Phillips, Rial, 169
Pickens, Joseph, 136
Pitner, John, 4
Polly, James, 136
Polly, John, 137
Pool, Labon, B., 56
Powel, (Atto), 71
Powel, Henry, 13, 14, 15, 16,
    75, 76
Powel, Mary, 75
Powell, Joanna, 75
Prather, Thomas, 10
Preston, Robert, 113
Price, Dolphin, 36
Price, James, 36
Price, Margaret, 248
Price, Mordicai, 4, 5, 122
Price, S., 262
Price, Sion, 178, 179
Price, Thomas, 35, 198, 248
Pring, Nicholas, 18, 131
Pugh, David, 35
Pugh, David & Wm., 136
Pursell (Purcell, Pursel), George
    13, 25, 64, 84, 98, 146
Pursley, William, 3, 12, 13

Q.

Quillon, Charles, 161, 162, 163

R.

Rages, Jefferson, 220
Ralston, John, 14
Ramsey, Catharine, 140
Range, Abigail (Abigal), 218, 220, 221,
    247
Range, Charles, 266, 267
Range, Charles (Mrs), 266
Range, Jacob, 35, 149, 203, 220
Range, James, 32, 60
Range, Jefferson, 219, 220
Range, John, 36, 218, 219, 220, 221,
    247
Ranges, Sarah, 221
Ranges, Susannah, 220
Rangs, Jacob, 220
Reasoner, Nicholas, 61
Read, Robert, 283
Rector, Benjamin, 70, 82, 150
Rector, John, 15
Reed, James, 13
Reed (Read) Robert, 131, 237, 244, 245,
    268, 272, 282
Reeve, Mark & Son, 218
Reeves, Mark & Son, 219
Rennoe, Charles, 11, 38
Rennoe, Lewis, 3
Renone, John, 3
Ress, Edward, 64
Reynolds, Moses, 1
Rhea, John, 123, 136
Richards, David, 12
Rimal, John, 130
Rimel, Jacob, 180
Rinehart, John, 122
Roberts, Elbert, 156
Roberts, Eliza, 156
Roberts, James, 55
Roberts, Nacky, 156
Roberts, Nancy, 156
Roberts, Nicky, 156
Roberts, R., 29
Roberts, Richard, 29, 30, 156
Roberts, Sarah, 156
Roberts, Thomas C., 146
Roberts, Thomas Q., 55, 134
Roberts, Wm., 230
Robertson, John, 197
Robeson, David, 161
Robinson, David, 102, 105
Robinson, Elisabeth, 293, 294
Robinson, Felix, 293, 294
Robinson, Jacob, 293, 294
Robinson, Jacob, Jur., 293
Robinson, James, 35
Robinson, Mary, 293

✻ (See Errata for correction)

Robinson, Sarah, 293, 294
Robinson, William, 293
Rockholt, Wm G., 270
Rocks, John, 265
Rodes, Elisha, 5
Rodgers, John, 122
Rodgers, Reuben, 51
Rodgers, Thomas, 124
Rogcown, Rebecca, 202
Rogers, 161
Rogers, David, 155
Rogers, Rebin, 202
Rolston, John, 128
Ross, Oliver B., 45, 85, 103, 202
Ross, V. B., 202
Royston, Joshua, 20
Ruble, Henry, 258
Ruble, Henry E., 147
Ruble, Isaac, 147
Ruble, John, 124
Ruble, John G., 48, 147
Ruble, Peggy, 250
Rulands, John, 177
Rust, Micajah, 133
Russell, Amanda Jane, 81, 82
Russell, Benjamin, 81
Russell, David, 81, 134, 142
Russell, Jacob K., 276
Russell, James, 81, 82, 190, 191
Russell, Robert, 190, 191
Russell, Thomas, 27
Russell, William, 81, 189, 190
Ryan, John, 20
Ryland, 113
Ryland, (Majr)., 201
Ryland, J., 280
Ryland, John, 19, 55, 63, 64, 66, 70, 85, 87, 135, 155, 195, 196, 201, 202, 273, 274, 275
Rymal, Jacob, 183

S.

Sachet, B. F., 251 ?
Sailor, John, 129
Salts, Daniel, 81
Salts, Henry, 18
Salts, John, 131
Sanders, Reuben, 4
Sands, Benjamin, 15
Sands, Isaac, 190
Sayler, John, 274
Saylor, John (Sailor), 97, 129, 218, 220
Scott, David & Ab., 219
Scott, Thomas, 122
Scott, Wilson, 166, 196

Scroggs, Harvey, 286
Scruggs, Miles, 280
Scruggs, Rufus, 279
Seates, David, 182
Seehorn, John J., 157
Seehorn, William, 157
Sell, Adam, 61
Sellars (Sellers), Abraham, 273
Sellars (Sellers), David, 220, 272, 289
Sellars, Thomas, 118
Sergant, Frederick, 22
Sevier, James, 2, 4, 5, 6, 9, 10, 11,
    17, 20, 25, 29, 31, 37, 46, 54,
    56, 61, 73, 76, 83, 86, 89, 94,
    98, 100, 109, 115, 127, 128, 132,
    134, 135, 141, 143, 147, 152, 155,
    156, 157, 158, 159, 161, 163, 164
    168, 169, 171, 172, 179, 180, 183
    191, 192, 196, 197, 198, 211, 213,
    214, 220, 239, 273
Sevier, E. G., 86
Sevier, Elbert, 152
Sevier, Elbert F., 172
Sevier, J., 188
Sevier, John, 4, 153, 173
Sevier, Valentine, 124
Sevier, Vallentine, 117
Shanks, William, 15
Shannon, E., 237
Sheffield, George, 8, 9
Shell, Joseph, 219
Sherfey, John, 65, 164, 190
Sherfey, S. Q., 219
Shields, David, 93
Shields, John, 117, 124
Shields, John C., 275
Shields, Joseph, 169
Shields, Joseph & Nancy, 169
Shields, William, 13, 15, 41
Shipley, B., 289
Shipley, Benjamin, 58, 71, 103
Shipley, Elijah, 274, 275
Shipley, Nathan, 11, 22, 25, 26, 37, 38
    42, 44, 45, 46, 49, 51, 53, 55, 66
    71, 78, 79, 80, 125, 126, 127, 128
    134, 137, 144, 145, 149, 151, 153,
    159, 172, 204, 208, 224, 225, 239,
Simmerly, 2
Simmerman, Danl., 88
Simmerman, John, 60
Simpson, John, 48
Slagle, G., 202
Slagle, Henry, 133, 182
Slagle, J., 293
Slagle, John, 129, 253, 254, 293
Slemmons, William, 23, 158
Sligar, Henry, 241, 269

Sligar, Wm., 166, 241, 269
Sliger, W. C., 196
Slyger, Adam, 122
Slyger, Henry, 87
Slyger, John, 28
Slyger, Wm., 195
Smalling, Jonathan, 133
Smith, 236, 285
Smith, Abraham, 174, 175
Smith, Edward, 1, 2
Smith, Elijah (Elija), 35, 174, 175
Smith, George, 13, 39, 152, 173,
Smith, Isaac, 174, 175
Smith, Jacob, 1
Smith, Jessee (Jessie), 152, 172
Smith, John, 178
Smith, John T., 164, 171
Smith, Joseph, 54
Smith, Levi, 174, 175
Smith, Martha, 13, 174, 175,
Smith, M. J., 171,
Smith, Nathal, 15
Smith, Richard, 28
Smith, Turner, 4, 27
Smith, Seth, 171
Smith, William, 41, 285, 286
Smith, Wm. Jr. 86
Smith, Wm C., 195
Smith, Zebulon, 37, 38
Snapp, John, 26
Snapp, Joseph, 141
Snapp, Larry, 273
Snapp, Lawrence, 52
Snapp, P., 26
Sots, John, 119
Spradling, John, 167
Spurgin, Wm., 102
Squibb, Dicey, 82, 107, 109
Suter, Jonathan, 202
Swenney, Wm., 2
Swingle, George, 125
Swonger, John, 33, 34
Swonger, Joshua, 203
Stanfield, Samuel, 15
Starmer, Catharine, 179
Starnes, Jacob, 27
Starnes, Mahala., 250
Starnes, S., 251
Stephens, Samuel, 279
Stephenson, E. (Mrs), 77
Stephenson, John, 13, 14, 15, 16, 17, 18, 19, 25, 42, 64, 69, 70, 76, 87, 95, 99, 105, 110, 126, 127, 128, 132, 146, 160, 161, 164, 171, 194, 197, 208, 226, 227, 228, 238
Stephenson, J. & M., 70, 282
Stephenson, John & Mathew, 135
Stephenson, Johnson, 25
Stephenson, M., 64, 237
Stephenson, M. & Co., 64
Stephenson, M & J., 171, 282,
Stephenson, Mathew,(Matthew), 66, 87, 119, 128, 132, 146, 154, 164, 169, 194, 276
Sterns, Peter, 207
Stevens, David, 275
Stevens, John, 274, 275
Stevens, Saml H., 282
Stevens, Thomas, 39, 259, 274
Stevens, Thomas F., 275
Stockhouse, Wm., 220
Stormer, John, 86, 114
Stormer, Samuel, 86
Stout, Allen, 238
Stout, Daniel, 23, 93
Stout, John, 17, 23, 46, 94, 99, 237
Stover, Daniel, 11
Strain, John, 3, 12, 13, 15, 16, 41, 42 76, 95, 119, 134, 164, 171, 194, 197, 198
Strain, Robt., 226
Strain, R. W., 85
Stuart, 277
Stuart, (Mr)., 1
Stuart, Alexander, 13, 134, 142
Stuart, David, 13, 151
Stuart & Gammon, 277
Stuart, James, 1, 2, 3, 122, 136
Stuart, John, 135, 197
Stuart, Mary, 135
Stuart, Robert, 20, 149
Stuart, T., 202
Stuart, Thomas, 5, 118, 151, 279

T.

Tadlock, J., 123
Tadlock, James, 260
Tate, John, 1
Tate, Samuel, 1
Taylor, 14, 162, 188
Taylor, Alfred, 203
Taylor, Andrew, 37, 38, 213
Taylor, A. W., 231, 232,
Taylor, Charles, 2
Taylor, Christopher, 246
Taylor, Elisabeth, 255
Taylor, Henry, 177
Taylor, Isaac, 52, 133,
Taylor, Isaac (Doctor), 35
Taylor, Jacob, 146

WASHINGTON COUNTY, TENNESSEE

⚹ (See Errata for correction)

Taylor, James, (Col) 203
Taylor, James, 246
Taylor, James P., 35, 64, 85, 88, 93, 97, 109
Taylor, Leeroy, 25, 35
Taylor, Leroy, 194
Taylor, Levi, 25
Taylor⚹ McKinny, 185
Taylor, Nathl, 11
Taylor, Thomas, ~~202~~ 89, 202
Teamil, David, 57
Templin, (Mrs), 80
Templin, Priscilla, 79
Templin, Samuel, 79, 80, 166
Tennessee, 39, 76, 135, 142, 149, 178
Tadlock, John, 6, 19
Terry, Wm., 190
Thompson, 234
Thompson, D., 198
Thompson, Jesse, M., 77
Thompson, Joseph, 66
Thompson, J. M., 195
Thompson, R. A., 260
Thompson, R. A., (Mrs), 260
Thompson, Seth, 37, 38, 39
Thornton, R., 122
Thornton, Robert, 4,
Thrasher, Isaac, 13
Tiffin, Henry, 150
Tilford, Elizabeth, 205
Tilford, George W., 205
Tilford, G. W., 206, 207, 265
Tilford, Miran, 205
Tilford, Thomas, 205, 206, 207
Tipton, 2
Tipton (Col), 1
Tipton, A., 35, 36
Tipton, Abraham, 9, 34, 35, 36, 133
Tipton, Jacob, 1
Tipton, James J., 34, 36
Tipton, John, 35, 272, 273
Tipton, Jonathan, 9
Tipton, Samuel, 1, 9, 273
Tipton, Stephen, 8
Toll, John, 238
Trotter, Alexander, 3
Truit, William, 27
Tucker, Abraham, 146
Tucker, John, 146
Tucker, Joseph, 14, 146
Tucker, Jonathan, 4
Tucker, N., 237
Tucker, Reece, 146
Tylar, M. G., & E., 247, 248
Tylar, Minarva G., 247, 248

Tyler, 160
Tyler, Betsey, 49, 54, 71, 92, 100, 144, 160, 181, 199
Tyler (Tylar), Elizabeth (Elisabeth), 204, 216, 217, 230, 247, 248, 255, 269
Tyler, Malinda (Milinda), 49, 54, 71, 92, 100, 144, 160, 181, 199, 204, 216, 217, 230, 233, 234, 269
Tyler, Matilda, 71
Tyler (Tylar), Phebee (Phobe), 49, 54, 71, 92, 100, 144, 160, 181, 199, 204, 216, 217, 230, 269
Tyler, Polly, 117, 193, 242?
Tyler, William, 20, 22, 23, 24, 29, 47, 49, 50, 51, 54, 71, 72, 91, 92, 100, 117, 144, 145, 160, 176, 181, 204, 215, 216, 281

U.
   (none)

V.

Vance, David G., 27, 33, 56
Vance, D. G., 17, 19, 21, 117
Vance, W. K., 26, 202
Vance, William, 89
Vance, William K., 98, 153, 172
Vaner, Wm K., 152
Varner, Jacob, 30, 148
Vaught, Wm., 93
Virginia, 2, 3, 71, 215, 216

W.

Waddell, John, 143, 144
Waddle, John S., 211
Waddle, Jonathan, 180
Walker, John, 120, 121
Walker, Tracy (Treacy), 120, 121
Walker, William, 128, 197
Wallace & Co., 173
Walters, Clara, 233
Walters, John, 56
Ward, William, 11, 73, 124
Washington County, 31, 36, 43, 44, 63, 66, 86, 126, 128, 136, 185, 197, 277, 280, 291
Watkins, N. B., 251
Watson, Samuel, 56, 149
Wattenbarger, (Widow), 84
Wattenbarger (Wattenberger), A., 86, 87, 88 Adam
Wattenbarger/(Wattenberger), (Waterbarger), 51, 83, 84, 85, 86, 87, 88, 89, 167, 168, 271, 272

SETTLEMENTS OF ESTATES, VOLUME 00, 1790-1841

Wattenbarger (Wattenberger), Elizabeth, 87, 88
Wattenbarger, F. F., 271, 272
Wattenbarger, George, 271, 272
Wattenbarger, (Wattenberger), Jacob 87, 167, 271, 272
Waterbarger, Michael, 168, 272
Wattenbarger (Wattenberger, Waterbarger), Peter, 84, 86, 87, 167
Wattenbarger, Samuel, 271, 272
Wattenbarger, (Wattenberger), (Waterbarger), Sarah, 85, 167, 272
Wattenbarger, (Wattenberger, Waterbarger), Solomon, 85, 86, 87, 88, 168, 271, 272
Wattenbarger (Wattenberger, Waterbarger), William, 83, 167, 272
Wearer, Fd., 78
Welds, John A., 68
Wells, H., 203
West & Clark, 237
West & Crouch, 295
West, E., 99
West, Edward, 286, 287
West, Edward Junr., 286, 287
West, J., 277
West, Joseph, 278
West, Robert G., 275
West, Robt. J., 230
Wheatler, Jacob, 268
Wheeler, Elizabeth, 62
Wheeler, (Wheler), William, 27
Wheelock, John K., 151
Whistler (Whisler, Wheatler), Jacob, 86, 236, 238, 244, 268, 284
White County, 202
White, James, 31, 32, 60, 195, 213, 214, 215
White, Jane, 283
White, Richard, 70
White, Terry, 67, 70, 204
White, Thomas, 283
White, William, 220
Whitehead, M., 14
Whiteside, Jenken, 123
Whitson, Charles, 9
Wilcox, (Willcocks), James, 15
Wilcox, John, 218
Wilds, John, 120, 203,
Wilds, John A., 158
Wilds, John A. & Co., 84
Wiley, Abel, 119
Wiley, Jas W., 146
Wilkles, John, 46
Willcocks, James, 15
Willett, 298

Willett, G. W., 268, 284
Willett (Willet), Nimrod, 28, 235
Willet, Nimrod C., 134   W.
Willett, Willitt, Willet),/162, 238, 282
Williams, Abraham, 20, 54
Williams, Ann., 157
Williams, Archibald, 4, 8
Williams, Benjamin, 157
Williams & Embree, 258
Williams, Frances F., 291
Williams, George, 1, 38, 122, 202
Williams, Jama, 157
Williams, James, 157
Williams, Joel, 23
Williams, John, 140, 141, 157, 220
Williams, John L., 35
Williams, John S., 202
Williams, L., 188
Williams, Peggy, 157
Williams, Saml., 157
Williams, Thomas, 157, 237
Wilson, Crouch & Nelson, 71
Wilson (Willson), David, 41, 42, 63, 95, 111.
Wilson, Isaac, 140, 152, 172
Wilson, James, 126
Wilson, Robert, 152
Wilson, Robert C., 112, 172
Wilson, Thomas, 261
Wilson (Willson), William, 22, 24, 47, 89, 94, 99, 115, 126, 130, 140, 141, 143, 153, 162, 168, 172, 285
Winchester, 215, 216, 266
Winkle, Henry, 116
Winkle, John, 116
Witt, Burjes, 122
Wixler, Jonathan, 294
Wixler, Mary, 294
Wood, 71
Wood, Hannah, 12
Wood, John, 9
Wood, M., 205, 206
Wood, Michael, 96, 97
Wood, Michael Jr., 96
Wood, Mile, 205
Wood, Mils, 207
Wood, Saml, 7
Wood, William, 12
Woods, Michael, 96, 97
Woodstock, 215, 216
Wooldridge, John, 219, 248
Woolf, (Wolf), Joseph, 129, 274
Worley, H., 220
Worley, J., 219
Worley, John, 220
Wright, 142

Wright, J., 219
Wright, John, 133, 218, 221, 247
Wright, Mary, 148
Wright, Samuel, 36
Wyly, Jas W., 170

X.

Y.

Yancy, 237
Yancy, John, 279
Yancy & Maxwell, 237
Yeager, C. F., 276
Yeager, Daniel, 18, 275, 276
Yeager, E. J., 276
Yeagar, Joseph J., 275
Yeagar, Solomon N., 275
Yeager, Mary, 276
Yeager, Susannah, 275
Yearley, David, 10
Young, Catherine (Catharine), 68, 221, 222
Young, Charles, 200
Young, E. E., 261, 262
Young, Elisabeth, 261
Young, Elisabeth E., 261, 262
Young, Ervin, 222
Young, Esther, 33, 200
Young, James, 73, 218, 221, 222, 223
Young, James H., 202
Young, Jas M., 200
Young, James W., 31, 32, 33, 34, 36, 40, 45, 48, 51, 73, 74, 97, 98, 113, 126, 155, 198, 200, 203, 222, 223, 248, 252, 261, 262, 263
Young, John, 139
Young, Jonathan, 24, 33, 36
Young, Joseph, 8, 9, 11, 12, 33, 34, 35, 73, 117, 124, 137, 139, 148, 200, 201, 252
Young, J. W., 73
Young, Mary, 73, 117, 124
Young, Robert, 124
Young, Thomas, 117, 124, 125, 262
Young, Thomas E., 263
Young, Thomas, T., 113
Young, T. T., 188
Young, Wilkins, 200, 252
Young, William, 73, 74, 248, 252
Young, William H., 221

Z.

Zettey, Barbary, 146

Zetty, C., 87, 88
Zetty, Christian, 51, 84, 85, 86, 87, 88, 89, 90, 167, 168
Zetty, Christian, Jr., 88
Zetty, Christian, Senr., 85, 87, 271

End.

ERRATA

(Note 1. The page numbers for ERRATA refer to the pages of the original volume, and are to be found enclosed between parentheses through out the body of the manuscript.)

(Note 2. Where paragraphs or instruments covering half a page, or more, have been omitted, and additional page has been inserted immediately after the one in erros, as: page 102 is followed by 102a, which contains the omitted items. This correction is not to be confused with entries for ERRATA.
Shorter ommissions are to be found under ERRATA.)

(p-179) Left out: -- "Interest on the above sum until the sale notes came due $1 87".
(p-203) Left out: -- "Saml B. Love $29 40".
(p-226) Left out: -- "68 76 Leaving a Balance due Young Bayless of $11 99½ and to Joseph Bayless".
(p-264) Left out: -- "Returned".

www.ingramcontent.com/pod-product-compliance
Lightning Source LLC
Chambersburg PA
CBHW080431230426
43662CB00015B/2240